Our Billi.

Ian Clayton has been a freelance writer and broadcaster for twenty-five years. He has presented programmes on BBC TV, ITV Yorkshire and the Discovery Channel, and also regularly on radio. He has led workshops in prisons, hospitals, schools and art centres, and has worked in America, Russia and all over Europe, as well as throughout Britain. His previous book, *Bringing it all Back Home*, was published in 2007 – 'the perfect book for anybody who defined their life through music and the memories of their youth' (Joanne Harris).

Ian was born and still lives in West Yorkshire, with his partner, Heather, and son, Edward. He likes listening to jazz and blues, reading about folklore and music halls, and indulging in tap-room conversation and gentle subversion.

Our Billie

IAN CLAYTON

PENGUIN BOOKS

PENGUIN BOOKS

Published by the Penguin Group
Penguin Books Ltd, 80 Strand, London WC2R ORL, England
Penguin Group (USA) Inc., 375 Hudson Street, New York, New York 10014, USA
Penguin Group (Canada), 90 Eglinton Avenue East, Suite 700, Toronto, Ontario, Canada M4P 2Y3
(a division of Pearson Penguin Canada Inc.)
Penguin Ireland, 25 St Stephen's Green, Dublin 2, Ireland (a division of Penguin Books Ltd)
Penguin Group (Australia), 250 Camberwell Road, Camberwell, Victoria 3124, Australia
(a division of Pearson Australia Group Pty Ltd)
Penguin Books India Pvt Ltd, 11 Community Centre, Panchsheel Park, New Delhi – 110 017, India
Penguin Group (NZ), 67 Apollo Drive, Rosedale, North Shore 0632, New Zealand
(a division of Pearson New Zealand Ltd)
Penguin Books (South Africa) (Pty) Ltd, 24 Sturdee Avenue,
Rosebank, Johannesburg 2196, South Africa

Penguin Books Ltd, Registered Offices: 80 Strand, London WC2R ORL, England

www.penguin.com

First published in 2010
2

Copyright © Ian Clayton, 2010
The moral right of the author has been asserted

For further permissions see page 262

Set in 11/13 pt Monotype Bembo
Typeset by Rowland Phototypesetting Ltd, Bury St Edmunds, Suffolk
Printed in Great Britain by Clays Ltd, St Ives plc

A CIP catalogue record for this book is available from the British Library

ISBN: 978-0-141-04233-6

www.greenpenguin.co.uk

Penguin Books is committed to a sustainable future
for our business, our readers and our planet.
The book in your hands is made from paper
certified by the Forest Stewardship Council.

I dedicate this book to MAG (Mines Advisory Group),
a humanitarian organization clearing the remnants of conflict
for the benefit of communities worldwide.

www.maginternational.org

Contents

Foreword

Every day in my capacity as presenter of *Woman's Hour*, I sit opposite people who have a story to tell. Often the stories are sad, but, like doctors or lawyers, we journalists have to learn to distance ourselves from the heartbreak we confront, in order to save our own sanity. But just occasionally someone touches you so closely that you can't put them out of your mind. Ian was one of those.

He's a bluff, tough Yorkshireman – the kind I grew up with – but there was no denying the abject heartbreak that faced me that morning as he recounted the terrible events which led to the death of his lovely daughter, Billie, and there was no concealing the dreadful guilt he carried with him – the sense that he had somehow not protected her from danger as a father should.

The heartbreak jumps out from these pages, but there is hope in them too. Ian's writing celebrates his daughter's life, and he, Heather and Edward have somehow found a way to grieve for her, remember her and include her in their family without being maudlin and without allowing a tragic accident to destroy three more lives. Billie, I'm sure, would be proud.

Jenni Murray, October 2009

Introduction:
Why I wanted to write this book

We buried our Billie at noon on a blustery spring morning in May 2006. The first swallow to come back home flew over our heads as we lowered her wickerwork coffin into a hole that had been dug in the sandstone earth at North Featherstone cemetery. Some school teachers from St Wilfrid's High School lined up by the cemetery wall to pay their respects. St Wilfrid's was the school that Billie had been longing to go to because, she said, they had vegetarian options for school lunch and she could learn to speak Russian or Japanese there.

At ten o'clock in the evening of that day, our friend Gillian Moore phoned us from London to say that she had arrived home safely but that she'd lost her purse, or it had been stolen. She told me she thought Billie's funeral had been a wonderful celebration of her life and she said she was glad she had been brave enough to look at Billie lying in her open coffin, even though she'd been frightened by the idea. Before today, Gillian had last seen Billie eating an ice-cream on a wall near the Globe Theatre alongside her son Hamish and Billie's twin brother, Edward.

I cried when I told Gillian I missed Billie and I didn't know what I could do about the missing. She said, 'Ian, you'll do what you always do. You'll make a story about Billie and you'll help yourself in your grief by telling that story.' Gillian has always said that I live my life to tell stories about it. That's probably true but, then, most of my stories have been about living, learning, laughing. My stories are about good times and journeys, about exploration and adventure. Some have been about disappointment in my childhood and others about let-downs and frustrations in my home town since the 1984–5 miners' strike. I never thought I would tell stories about coping with the death of my lovely nine-year-old daughter. People will tell you it's against the natural order of things, that children are not supposed to die before their parents.

In the 1990s, I ran a writers' workshop at a centre in Castleford, helping people to write down their life stories. One time a little old fellow joined. He told us he had been a comic and singer in the working men's clubs. For the first three weeks he didn't say much and wrote even less. Then one day he cleared his throat and said, 'I have something to tell you all. I used to have a little lad. He got run over in the street outside our house and he died. It happened in 1955.' He started to cry, and some of the ladies in the group put their arms round him. I asked him if he wanted to write about it. He said, 'I don't think I can.' He never came back to the workshop and I never saw him again.

I talked on the phone for nearly an hour that night, reaching out to a dear friend two hundred miles away. I knew when I put the phone down that, yes, I would tell stories about my Billie and that those stories would be inspired by friendship, by a sense of humanity that came from Billie herself, by community and by a bloody-minded determination not to give in to the grief. I am not a religious man. I won't pray and hope things will get better. I'll rely on friends and family, and beyond that, I'll reach out to embrace the voices of my ancestors. And seeing as my ancestors were all hard-as-nails coal-miners, boxers, rugby-league players and members of working men's clubs, this story will be a tough one. I'll tough this out. Do what needs to be done for my partner, Heather, and my lad, Edward. I will not lie on my sofa and cry, though I could. I'll get on with life and seek more adventure. I owe that to those I love and have loved.

Our losing Billie is not just our loss: Billie is lost to the world. She would have been somebody, a musician, perhaps a poet, certainly a humanitarian; she would have flown. And in that lies a conflict. Within minutes of the lady doctor telling me in Hereford Hospital that Billie was clinically dead she became no longer just our Billie.

This book gets its title from something Edward said to me on the journey back from Hereford to Yorkshire. He thought we ought to bring Billie's body back in the car with us. I told him that the authorities wouldn't allow us to do that. I tried to explain to him that the hospital and the police were interested in Billie. He didn't want to understand that, and said, 'But she's our Billie!'

Our Billie became the subject of a post-mortem. Her death was investigated in some detail by the police, and the mortician at our local undertaker's wouldn't let us see her until she had completed some 'cosmetic' work. The funeral director wanted to close and secure her coffin lid until Edward intervened, and the pall-bearers, black-coated burly men, took responsibility for carrying her until I took a hold. The newspaper, radio and television people phoned us, wrote to us, and some even waited outside our house in their cars for weeks after her accident. Two years later, at the inquest, Billie became a case number for lawyers to argue over and a matter of health and safety discussion. In cyberspace people who didn't know Billie left blogs about her. One commentator called 'Solomon Hezekiah' said that her death, among 1500 others each year by drowning, was being featured because she was 'the beautiful, photogenic child of a television reporter'.

Our Billie was a beautiful and photogenic child but, much more, she was once a living and breathing real person, someone's daughter, a grand little boy's twin sister. She was at the centre of a happy family, a funny, quirky, loving little lass with a lot to live for. Her story is all of our stories, linked to where she was from, to those who shaped her – and were in turn shaped by her – her community and her ancestors.

She lives now in memories and stories, in Heather's paintings and the music Edward makes.

1. Trying to have an adventure

'I don't know what happens next in this story, Daddy.'

This is my daughter Billie. It's nearly ten o'clock at night, past her bedtime, and she's still sitting at the desk in her bedroom with a table lamp on. She has already been in bed, said goodnight, told me she loves me, cuddled up to Anastasia, her favourite teddy, and then tossed and turned, struggling to sleep. After an hour she has decided to get up again to write a story that she says is going round in her mind.

'I'm writing a story about a father and his children, but I don't know what happens next.'

In between I have run a bath and I'm lying in it going over what I need to do before we set off for our short break to Hay-on-Wye first thing in the morning. Billie has never been the best of sleepers. Even when she was four or five she would come to our room to talk about monsters and shadows. There's a shadow called 'Oki' who moves across her curtains. Sometimes she frightens me by coming to our bedroom. I sleep on the side nearest the bedroom door, Heather on the side near the built-in wardrobe. Billie stands over me saying nothing until I sense her and wake with a start.

'What's the matter, love?'

'A monster came.'

'Oh! It's just a silly dream. Come on, let me tuck you in and I'll tell you a nice story.'

'Can you tell me a made-up one? I like them better than book stories.'

Tonight I get out of the bath and go into Billie's room.

'What happens next, Daddy? I need to finish this story.'

'Well, I'll tell you what I do when I'm writing and I don't

know what happens next. You've got some people in your story, haven't you?'

'Yes, three.'

'OK, let one of them remember something. That's how stories carry on. If a character in a story remembers something or wishes for something or does something, it means the story can continue.'

'That's a good idea, Dad. I'll try it.'

Later I get ready for bed and look into Billie's room. She has fallen asleep on her desk, pen still in her hand. I lift her into her bed, put her arm around Anastasia, turn off the lamp and whisper, 'Sweet dreams.'

At seven o'clock in the morning the house is full of activity, all of us scurrying about, packing bags and cutting sandwiches. Edward wants his favourite packed lunch, egg and tomato, chopped together with salt and pepper. Heather fills a flask with tea. Billie can't decide whether to take just Anastasia or Anastasia and Oliver, a doll that looks like a real baby. Marlene, our next-door neighbour, drops us off at Kirkgate railway station in Wakefield. We'll travel from here to Sheffield, to Birmingham, then Hereford, and take a taxi from the station there to a little hotel in Hay called the Seven Stars. I picked this one from the Internet because it has a swimming-pool and the kids love swimming. I've written out an itinerary of train times and connections. Edward asks if he can save it in his pocket. 'Yes, you can, but don't lose it whatever you do!' By the time we change platforms at Sheffield he has lost the piece of paper. What with rushing from one part of the station to another, pulling luggage on wheels, avoiding bumping into folk coming the other way and trying to read the screens, I've let myself get stressed up.

'Do you know, Edward? You're bloody useless!' I glare at him. He glares back, pure defiance. I walk off fast towards the Birmingham train. Edward stays on the platform, still defiant.

Billie starts to cry, frightened that Edward will be left behind. I throw our bags onto the luggage rack, step back off the train, pick Edward up a bit roughly and plonk him on a seat. He carries on glaring. As the train sets off he pretends to ignore me by looking out of the window.

Heather says, 'Come on now, everybody, it's only a bit of paper.'

'Only a bit of paper! We might not get back without it,' I exaggerate, for effect.

Billie reaches out to hold my hand and Edward's. She says, 'You're not bloody useless, Edward, really!'

It makes us all laugh, even Edward. I look him in the eye. He eyes me back.

'Mates?' I say.

'Mates,' he says. 'Can we get the travel chess out?'

At Birmingham we sat next to a woman who was talking to her daughter about Dudley. She spoke in a broad Black Country dialect, and Edward and Billie laughed every time she said the word 'Dudley'. On the way down to Hereford I told the kids that their ancestors came from a place called Netherton, which is an area of Dudley.

Billie said, 'Did they talk like that woman?'

'They probably did, yes.'

'I bet they were funny,' Edward said, and parroted, 'Dudley, Dudley,' all the way to Hereford, by which time we and the rest of the carriage were fed up with him.

The owner of the Seven Stars in Hay turns out to be a fantastic chef and cooks a delicious breakfast. Heather, Edward and I have the full English: poached eggs, back bacon, sausages, tomatoes, mushrooms. Edward is into his stream-of-consciousness humour straight away. 'I say, Daddy, is this bacon lean back bacon?' He then rocks back in his chair until it stands on its back legs. 'Geddit? Lean ... back ... bacon?'

Billie reddens with embarrassment, munches her Glamorgan veggie sausage, and puts her head down so that her hair falls over her face and whispers, 'Is anybody listening to him?'

'He's only having fun, Billie,' Heather explains. 'We're on holiday, love. It's just a bit of fun.'

Edward seizes his cue: 'We might have shepherd's pie for lunch, eh, Dad?'

I know what's coming.

'I heard you were once a spy, Daddy.'

I join in with Edward's music-hall theme. 'I wasn't a spy, Edward, I was a shepherd.'

'Aah! Aah! A shepherd spy!'

Billie groans. 'Can we go swimming after breakfast, Mam?'

Before Heather can answer I tell the kids that it's not a good idea to go swimming after such a big meal. 'You'll sink!'

I'm out-voted. Heather wants to try out the pool, though she's a paddler not a swimmer, and the kids can't wait. The hotel pool is great and has a sauna, which we'd all tried before we had a swim last night. We had a great time. Billie suggested a series of races, using different strokes each time. Edward chose breaststroke, I chose the crawl, and Billie wanted butterfly. 'But Dad and me can't do butterfly, Billie!'

'All right, then, backstroke!'

At the turn I'd decided, when I saw Billie slightly in front, that no nine-year-old girl was going to beat me but I couldn't catch her. She won easily.

After breakfast I pick up the paper to have a squint at it. 'I'll have a swim with you later.'

'Oooh! Daddy! Come on.'

'I can't, not after all that bacon and egg.'

The kids rushed us up to the room, grabbed towels and their swimming costumes and were probably in the pool before I'd opened the newspaper. I read for ten minutes, decided I couldn't be bothered with news on the first day of the holiday and switched on the telly. It was *The Jeremy Kyle Show*, a programme I'd never seen before and haven't since. A woman who had stolen her daughter's boyfriend was trying to explain herself in the face of mock indignation from the show's host. The boyfriend arrived on set to a chorus of boos from the studio audience and then the daughter came on in floods of tears. A slanging match started. I switched the TV off and lay on the bed.

The kids came rushing into the room, followed by a breathless Heather. 'It was great, Daddy! And do you know what? The man says we can even use the pool when we go to stay at that other hotel.'

The Seven Stars had had a vacant room for only one night so we were going to stay at a bed-and-breakfast down the road called Rest for the Weary Traveller on the others. While Heather packed the bags, Edward grabbed the remote and started flicking through the channels. Billie lay on the bed next to me and put her arm around me. 'You're my lovely Daddy, aren't you?'

'I am, darling. And you're my lovely daughter, my cup and saucer.'

We decided to check in at the next place – it was only fifty yards down the road. We rang the bell. A jolly woman shouted downstairs, 'Is that my family?'

We left our bags in the room and set off to explore the bookshops of Hay-on-Wye.

We find a bookshop that has hundreds of those little *Observer's* books, some so rare now that they command prices of fifty or sixty quid. I'm in my glory and Heather is beside herself. She had longed to come here for years because of its bookshops. 'Imagine,' she keeps saying, 'a town with nearly forty bookshops.' We walk into one after another, Heather trying to work out how she's going to make her holiday money last beyond the first day.

After we've been to seven or eight, Edward and Billie are bored. They decide to play games outside. I start worrying because the streets are narrow and I can see them through the shop window stepping on and off the road. I mention this to Heather. She's torn between wanting to do something with the kids and 'just having another ten minutes in this poetry section'. We decide to find the tourist-information office and make a list of other things to do. On the way there Heather tells me that Billie was a bit 'funny' this morning at the swimming-pool. 'A bit distant,' she says, when I ask her what she means. 'When we were getting dry after the swimming she started reminiscing about being a little girl.' Billie had talked about how nicely we had always dressed her.

At the tourist-information office I ask the lady behind the counter about canoeing trips for families. She points to a whole rack of brochures. I pick the first that my hand falls on. It says, *Hay Canoes,* and shows a picture of families having fun on the river. Billie is looking at a picture book about Owain Glyndŵr, Heather is collecting leaflets about local walks and Edward is pestering to have a go on the canoes. 'That man in the Seven Stars says it's fantastic, Dad.'

Outside the office I discuss with Heather what we ought to do next. She says that if I want to take the kids on an adventure she'll continue to browse the bookshops and we'll all meet up later for tea. I get on my mobile and phone the number on the brochure. 'I'd like to hire a canoe for myself and my two children, please.'

The man at the other end of the line offers me the choice of going downstream from Hay, or starting upstream at a village called Glasbury and coming back down to Hay. I tell him I've been looking at a map and think the scenery might be better if I set off from Glasbury. He agrees, and tells me that the whole countryside opens up and we'll be able to see the Black Mountains. 'I'll phone you back in five minutes,' he says. 'What time do you want to set off?' I tell him about two o'clock.

When he phones me back we make arrangements. He tells me that his name is Wayne and that, as well as owning a canoe business, he has a taxi and will pick us up at ten to two at the tourist-information office and drive us to the canoe at Glasbury. He'll do it all in for a special price of forty pounds.

Edward couldn't wait. He kept asking me what time it was every five minutes. We went to a little organic juice bar. Heather blew the froth off a cappuccino. Billie had cranberry as usual and I had to stop myself having a pint of Brains from the hand pump. I'd seen a Ben Webster LP in a second-hand-record shop the evening before so I went to buy it, then some bottles of water and half a dozen Welsh cakes from a little bakery.

Wayne was already waiting in his taxi when we got back to the tourist office. He was tapping his fingers on the steering-wheel and I noticed 'LOVE' tattooed on his knuckles. We small-talked on the way to Glasbury. Wayne told me he'd put weight on since he'd stopped smoking. I asked if he thought it might rain. He wasn't sure, he said, but he thought we'd probably picked the best day.

At Glasbury Wayne helped us to put on our life-jackets and gave the kids crash helmets. Edward wanted a wee – he always wants a wee before he does anything different; he can't even do his piano lesson without a wee first. When we came back from the toilet block Wayne handed me a bunch of forms fastened to a clipboard. 'It's just a health and safety formality,' he said. I thought about reading it, but the kids were eager to get started and I thought it would be embarrassing to stand there studying the small print on a bunch of forms so I signed. Wayne smiled and said again, 'You've picked the best day. You're going to have a lovely time.'

Edward started dancing around and singing, 'Lovely day, lovely day.'

Billie shushed him and said, 'We can't take him anywhere!'

At the river Wayne's mate was holding a red canoe on a rope. He said, 'Have you been canoeing before?' I told him I hadn't, but that I'd been boating on rivers. He said, 'It's easy. Just put your paddle down right to go left and left to go right.'

The water was six or seven inches deep between the shingle and the canoe, so Wayne lifted the kids into it. He sat Edward at the front, Billie in the middle. I looked at him and laughed. 'Can you lift fifteen stone?' He laughed back and said I'd have to get myself in. The canoe was facing upstream. We paddled, made an arc to go downstream and aimed for the middle arch of a lovely old stone bridge. As we came back past the two men, Wayne had his camera out. 'Look at me and smile,' he said. 'I'll take a picture, print it out at home and let you have a copy when you get back to Hay. It'll take you about three hours.'

We didn't know at the time that this was Wayne and his mate's first day in business, operating canoe hire. That they had no expertise in canoeing. That they hadn't, either of them, been canoeing themselves for at least two years previously, and that neither of them had any idea of how fast or deep the river was running at a bend further downstream.

The kids quickly got the hang of paddling the canoe, though Billie struggled a bit at first – the paddle seemed a bit too long for her. Edward, sitting up front, declared that he was the driver. There were one or two moments when I thought it was a bit choppy and the water was running fast over stones, but it was lovely in the open country. Some new lambs were on the bank, there were birds in the air and swans swimming right up to us. Billie marvelled at it all and said, more than once, 'Oooh, Daddy, this is a lovely adventure. I can't wait to get back to school to tell my friends about it.'

I'd asked Wayne which side of the river we should keep to. He told me to stay in the middle, to avoid shallows so as not to ground the canoe, and to follow my nose. We came to a really calm part so I pulled out my camera and took a snap of the kids. Edward had that cheeky eye and Billie a beautiful smile, with her hair all over the place underneath her safety helmet. Much later, when we developed the film, one of the few photos that came out was this one.

We came to a part of the river where the water seemed to flow two ways. Straight on and round a right-hand bend. Wayne had told me to keep going forward so I chose the straight-on option. Months afterwards I learned that the river had formed an oxbow almost overnight when its course changed and we were entering its bottom end. The water slowed almost to a stop and became shallower. I realized I'd gone wrong somehow. I felt a bit of a fool when I phoned Wayne. 'Hello, it's Ian Clayton. I think I've made a mistake and come on to a wrong part of the river.'

'You can't go wrong if you follow the flow.'

'I'm struggling to understand the flow at the moment. The wind's got up a bit and it's pushing us about.'

He asked me if I'd come to a part of the river where it peeled off to the left. 'If you reach that you need to go right round the bend.'

I turned the canoe round and asked the kids to lift their paddles out of the water while I steered us back on course. We came back to the bend and I could hear the water running quite fast round it.

Billie decided she needed to wee. 'Can we stop, Dad, or I'll wet myself?'

'I can't stop in the middle of the river, love. Just wait until we get round this bend and I'll pull up at the bank.'

I tried to steer the canoe into the bend but the power of the water coming down the river was pushing us from the middle to the edges. Then I couldn't steer any more and the canoe was propelled rapidly to the left bank. I don't know whether it was tree roots we hit but certainly there was a fallen tree and we hit it hard. The canoe turned over in the blink of an eye and I was thrown out. I think I went under the water for an instant and then became disoriented. I don't know if I was standing on the river bed or being buoyed up by my life-jacket. I couldn't see Edward or Billie.

I became frantic. The water was trying to push me downstream. I grabbed hold of a branch on the fallen tree. I guessed that the kids must be trapped under the canoe. The water was so fast I couldn't see into it and so cold that it took my breath away. I tried to prop my back against the tree and plunged my arms into the water, moving them backwards and forwards under the canoe. I wanted to go underneath but my life-jacket and the current wouldn't let me. I grabbed and grabbed underneath and then I thought I had them. I thought, I've got two arms, so I pulled.

I hadn't. I had Edward's arm and leg, and he was lengthways under the water. I pulled him up and as he came to the surface he sucked in a huge mouthful of air. He looked me straight in the face and gasped, 'I don't want to die, Daddy! Don't let me die today.'

I tried to reassure him in what I hoped was a calm voice: I told him that nobody would die, that I'm a strong old dad and would get us all out. As I was saying this the current washed him straight out of my arms and swept him down the river. I hadn't been able to hold on to him tight enough. I saw him being battered by the rapids. He shouted, 'Don't let me die, Daddy!' again. I screamed to him to grab a branch. I'd spotted another fallen tree about thirty yards downstream. I didn't see if he was able to hold on to it or not because I turned again to look for Billie.

I couldn't feel anything below the water. I was going numb with the cold. Then I was taken by the current myself. I thought that now I would drown. I tried to swim, but the current was too strong. I hit the next fallen tree with my back. When I looked up I saw Edward holding a thin branch of the same tree with his clenched fists. His legs were flying up behind him in the water. 'I think I'm going to let go, Daddy!' he was saying, over and over again.

I kept thinking, What shall I do now?

I was wearing a thick Berghaus fleece, heavy boots and jeans. These had all become waterlogged and were so heavy I couldn't move. My breath wouldn't come. Edward shouted that his life-jacket was falling off. I could see that the zip had broken open and that the jacket had come off his left arm. It was still hooked over the right and wafting about in the water. I reached out to try to hook it back over his other arm and felt a terrible pain in my shoulder. I thought it might be dislocated. I reared up in the water and banged my shoulder hard against the trunk of the tree, but my arm worked well enough for me to pull Edward's jacket back into place.

'Right – you hang on here, son. I'm going to climb out of the river, take off this fleece and then I'll come back and get you.'

Edward's face was still now. He had turned blue with cold. He didn't speak. He nodded and tried to throw his leg over a branch about as thick as my thumb. I asked him if he thought he could hold on. He still didn't speak but he nodded again.

I edged my way along the trunk of the fallen tree towards the riverbank. In my mind I was trying to work out how long Billie had been under water. It seems ridiculous to say it, but I found an image of my childhood popping into my mind. I was at Graham Royston's tenth birthday party. Graham had a copy of *The Guinness Book of Records*. While all the other kids were playing musical chairs, I sat in a corner reading it. There was a paragraph about a lady from our town called Mrs Matthewman, who was the world's fastest knitter. This came into my mind, along with a fragment I hadn't thought about for nearly forty years, about how a young Norwegian girl survived after being pulled from a freezing fjord after more than twenty minutes. I guessed Billie had been in the river for less than ten minutes. My plan was to strip off my clothes, dive back in, find Billie and hope that Edward could hold on to his branch until I reached him.

The bank was high and steep, and I struggled to climb out of the water. As I threw myself on to the bank my mobile phone fell out of my shirt pocket. I hit the recall button. Wayne answered. I told him the canoe had tipped over and that he needed to phone the emergency services. I then tried to get my waterlogged clothes off. I struggled to do it quickly. The zip on my fleece was jammed, the life-jacket twisted and my jeans belt tangled in it all. I managed to strip down to my underpants and prepared to jump back into the river. Billie was still nowhere to be seen. I was thinking that because she was wearing a life-jacket she was bound to pop up. Edward's eyes were closed.

Then my mobile phone rang. I realized it might be the emergency services trying to get a location so I answered it. I can't remember now what I said. There was a lady at the other end of the line. She asked me where the children were. She advised me not to go back into the river. I threw the phone onto the grass and jumped back into the rapids. I started swimming upstream, at first meaning to try again to find Billie, but the water was too powerful. When I looked up I was further back than where I'd started from. The water pushed me towards the tree Edward was holding on to. His eyes were open again and he looked across at me. I think he knew what I'd been trying to do. He said, ever so quietly, 'Dad, will you try to save my sister first?'

I think I had asked the lady on the phone who I should try to save first. I said, 'Don't worry about Billie, son, she's up there near that tree. She's waiting with the Welsh cakes and once I get you out we'll have a picnic.'

I couldn't pull him through the tangle of branches. I said, 'Edward, you'll have to let go with your hands and I'll pull you to me under the branches.'

'Don't make me go under the water, Daddy – don't make me.'

'I promise, son, that if you're brave I'll save you.'

I got hold of him and said, 'Right, when I say let go, take your leg off that branch and I'll pull you through.'

'Will you, Daddy, will you?'

He was so scared that he was shaking. I pulled him and he came to me. Immediately he started to choke me. I angled my elbow under him and with it shoved him up on my back. I crawled up the fallen tree and managed to throw him on to the bank. I told him to sit still and I'd be with him in a minute. I tried to get back into the water, but it knocked me over again. I thought that if I ran up the bank and dived in further upstream I might get washed towards where I thought Billie was.

As I prepared to do this I saw an ambulance on the other edge of the field that was closest to the river. A man started to run towards us. He reached us and I told him to look after Edward. I said he'd been in the river for a long time and probably had hypothermia. The ambulance man asked about Billie. I told him she was still under the water. He shook his head slightly.

Two policemen came running across. The bigger of the two decided he would wade into the river. The other policeman produced a nylon rope and tied it round his mate. I held the rope while the second copper searched the edge of the water in the undergrowth. The big copper only got five or six yards out into the river when it began to wash him away. I pulled on the rope to keep him steady, tugged him nearer to the bank, then stepped on to a big stone and offered my hand. We clasped each other's forearm and I pulled. He was too heavy for me, so the second policeman reached over and helped me haul him out.

The big copper was shaking but said he would try something else. He'd wade upstream, then try to come back to where we thought Billie was. This time he managed to get across to where the canoe was and lifted it. He said he couldn't see her. His face was stiff with shock. I was shaking so badly now that I thought

I'd black out. The ambulance man was telling me I needed to go to the ambulance.

Some firemen arrived and started to shout orders for everybody to come away from the river. I heard a helicopter hovering overhead. I climbed into the back of the ambulance. Edward was being warmed under a hot-air blanket.

The ambulance took us to a hospital in Abergavenny where we were put into a little side room. Edward lay quietly under another hot-air blanket. He kept looking at me as I sat on a chair, the ambulance blanket still over my shoulders.

Heather had gone to meet us at the appointed time of five o'clock by the river in Hay. As time went by she kept looking at the river and wondering where we were. She had an uneasy feeling that something had happened to us. She waited for perhaps half an hour and then a man walked up to her. She told me that even before he spoke she had guessed he was a policeman. He told her there had been an accident, that he didn't have any details as yet but had been told to take her to a waiting car, which would bring her to Abergavenny Hospital.

As the ambulance was taking Edward and me across the fields near Glasbury, some firemen in a boat noticed that the downdraught from the search-helicopter rotors had parted the water enough for them to see a paddle and a life-jacket. They pulled Billie from the river and tried to revive her in the bottom of their boat. They then transferred her to the helicopter, which flew her to Hereford Hospital.

Heather arrived at Abergavenny Hospital with Detective Colin Fish. Colin was to be our family liaison officer for the next two years until the inquest. I held Heather. I told her I was sorry. I told her over and over again I was sorry. Colin suggested that we should prepare for a journey to Hereford. He would drive us there. He said something about the build-up of Easter traffic. The journey from Abergavenny will remain burned in my mind. I knew in my heart that Billie had drowned. I'd known it in my head probably from the point at which I had turned to join Edward in the ambulance when the firemen arrived. But I said to Heather and Edward, 'Keep your spirits up. Our Billie's waiting to see us at Hereford.'

Edward said, 'Will she be alive, Dad?'

'I'm sure she will, son. Let's all hope for a happy ending.'

Colin was concentrating on manoeuvring the car through busy traffic. I tried to read his thoughts. What did he know about Billie's condition? Did he know if she was alive or dead? He asked if we were warm enough and if he should turn the heater up.

At Hereford Hospital a woman doctor rushed out to meet us in the corridor. She ushered us towards a small anteroom and said straight out, 'I'm afraid the news isn't good.' Edward started to cry.

'Sometimes when a person has been under very cold water for a long time, if we warm them gradually they can respond to resuscitation. I'm afraid this isn't happening with Billie. She's still very cold.'

We were all taken to the room where a male nurse was pressing on Billie's chest. They had been trying for a long time and there was no response. The woman doctor told us that Billie was clinically dead. They asked for my permission to stop trying. I nodded and brushed the back of my fingers across Billie's lovely arched eyebrows. 'What shapes all this, eh, for it to be taken away when she's only nine?'

Another nurse started to remove pipes from Billie's mouth and nose. I asked for a cigarette. A nurse went to her locker and brought me half a packet of Benson & Hedges. I stood at a door near A & E with Colin. 'Do you know, Colin, she was the kindest, most humane little girl you could wish to meet? I went to work in Belarus a few years ago at an orphanage. She gave me some of her best toys to take.' Colin forced a smile. 'She could do anything in sport. She could throw a javelin, kick a football as hard as any lad. She could fight too. She once clocked the cock of All Saints School because he spat some water on her.' I talked like this non-stop while I lit three cigarettes, one off the red end of the last. 'I have a beautiful photograph of Billie next to my computer. I've often looked at that photo and thought, What would I do without you? What shall I do, Colin?'

Colin said my immediate concern must now be for Heather and Edward. They had gone to talk to the woman doctor. I was taken for a check-up. Although I was still numb I had pains in my back and shoulder. The doctor told me I had probably over-stretched some muscles.

Colin drove us back to Hay, to the bed-and-breakfast called Rest for the Weary Traveller that we'd only seen to drop off our bags. The lady who had said that morning, 'Is that my family?' came to the door. She told Colin she would look after us. I stood in her front room in my underpants with the ambulance blanket round my shoulders. She told me to take a hot bath and put some warm clothes on. I had no spare shoes so she gave me a pair of her husband's, which were two sizes too big.

We put Edward to bed. It was past nine o'clock. I talked to Heather about who we should telephone. Colin told us that the press had already been asking for statements for the late-news bulletin and the morning papers. We were worried that our families and friends might hear about what had happened before we'd had the chance to tell them.

We phoned Heather's mother and father. I phoned Tony, my closest brother, who cried, and Brian Lewis, a friend who always knows what to do – I thought he might know what to say to us. He told me later he wished he could reach out down the phone. I left a message for Christine Talbot, my workmate at Yorkshire TV. Then I phoned Jane Hickson, my producer there and one of my best mates. Her husband Michael answered and told me that she was resting with a migraine. I blurted out what had happened. Jane took the phone. She said, 'What do you want me to do? Shall I drive down to bring you home tonight?' I told her we must stay until we knew what arrangements we had to make for Billie.

Heather and I sat on the edge of the bed, and Heather said, 'We'll never be able to hold her again, will we?'

This frightened me. I was still numb and my head was full of images of Billie: eating her breakfast boiled egg, teaching her toys to sit properly, smiling in the canoe and telling me that it was a wonderful adventure. I cast the occasional glance at Edward: he was sleeping with his face towards us. When I was a little boy and heard my mother and father shouting and fighting before I went to sleep, I'd always hoped that everything would be all right when I opened my eyes.

Heather needed to sleep. I sat on the edge of the bed and watched her close her eyes. I stroked her hair, but she told me not to and rolled over. I heard her sobbing gently.

2. In short measure, life may perfect be

I don't cry much. I cried one night when my father was punching my mother on the living-room floor and I watched him do it through a gap in our stairs door. I was still crying when I pulled his head back to get him off her. I cried when I first saw Ingrid Bergman plead to her dowager aunt that she really was Anastasia in that film. I always cry when Jenny Agutter says, 'Daddy, my Daddy!' through the smoke on the platform at the end of *The Railway Children*, and when Hayley Mills watches the policemen take Alan Bates to the Black Maria in *Whistle Down the Wind*. I cried when I watched Featherstone Rovers beat Hull at Wembley in the Challenge Cup Final in 1983, tears of absolute joy. I cried two years later too, when I saw friends who were coal-miners marching back to work at the end of the year-long miners' strike. Bitter tears that time. Tears of anger at the Conservative government and a state that didn't seem to understand or care. Tears of regret. In more recent times, I cried when my friend Muhammed – Miki – Salkic was sent back to Bosnia after trying for nearly six years to obtain asylum in this country.

My granny told me she had special eyes and that she could always tell when the truth wasn't being told. I've always tried to say what I feel. Whether this be right or wrong, that's what I do. It's the end of *King Lear*, when everything comes cascading down and the old king dies of a broken heart.

> The weight of this sad time we must obey,
> Speak what we feel, not what we ought to say.

When my daughter Billie was drowned at the age of nine on a canoeing trip on the river Wye, I didn't cry at first. I didn't cry for three weeks. I was hysterical and crazy with the emotions flowing through me when I phoned friends in the hours and days after, but I don't think there were tears. The first time the tears came was after the funeral when I sat on our settee and thought about what the humanist officiant, Lynn Alderson, had said at the funeral. She said,

We are here today to say goodbye to Billie Holiday Clayton, who died on 12 April at the age of nine. As religion did not play a part in the life of Billie and her family, I have been asked to lead the ceremony today. My name is Lynn and I work with the British Humanist Association. Humanists believe that we can lead good lives without being religious and that we can take responsibility for ourselves and our world and lead the best life that we can. Everyone who knew Billie will be feeling an immense sadness and loss. It was a short life and when a child dies it is particularly hard to bear. Children are our future. We have all been deprived of her future, not just the people closest to her but the community in which she lived and the world on which she would have made an impact, and she *would* have made an impact. She was already showing signs of making a fine young woman. Even at such a young age she has touched the lives of so many. Today we celebrate her life as well as mourning her loss. She will be missed both for her unique self and for all the hopes and dreams she embodied. None of us knows when we will die, but it's important to remember that whenever that is, what is important is not how long we have lived, but the way we lived and that we tried to live our lives to the full. Billie was a much-loved daughter, twin sister, granddaughter, niece and friend.

Lynn then went on to read a poem by Ben Jonson:

> A lily of a day is fairer far in May,
> Although it fall and die that night,
> It was the plant and flower of light.
> In small proportions we just beauty see,
> And in short measures life may perfect be.

Heather, Edward and I decided to sit facing the friends and relatives who had come to Billie's funeral. At all the funerals I had ever been to I had always felt uncomfortable looking at the backs of heads of the ranks of people in black overcoats, shuffling and weeping softly, mumbling their way through half-forgotten fragments of hymns they had struggled with years before at school. Heather wore a vivid red cardigan, a tie-dyed skirt and her red beret with an old Communist Party badge from East Germany pinned to it. She looked spectacular and beautiful. Edward wore some faded jeans, and the sleeves of his checked shirt dangled loose over his wrists. He managed a lovely smile when Lynn mentioned that Billie could be a rascal and talked of their adventures, but his eyes spoke of unbearable sadness.

From the day she was born, people said Billie was beautiful. Edward was a bonny boy, but everybody seemed to want to pick Billie up, to nurse her, to stroke her cheeks. When they came home from the hospital the twins slept in the same wooden crib, head to toe. Every night for the first six or seven weeks I rushed home from work at Yorkshire Television just to stand and look at them sleeping in that crib.

One of my co-presenters at YTV was a lovely flower-arranger called Carl Wilde. He had a fantastic line in very camp humour and I got on with him really well. One night after work he told me he'd got some tickets for the opening of a new nightclub in Leeds and asked if I'd like to join him and a couple of actors from *Emmerdale* for free drinks. I went along but it wasn't really my scene, and I think Carl realized that. He shouted above the gay disco anthems, 'I bet you like back-street boozers full of rough birds best, don't you?' I just shrugged and smiled. 'Show me one of your pubs in Featherstone.'

He drove me in his sports car the fifteen miles from the flashing lights of Leeds to the Top House in Featherstone. I worried all the way what my mates from the Miners Welfare Rugby League Club would make of a bloke who dressed like Jean-Paul Gaultier and spoke like a Yorkshire John Inman. I needn't have worried: everybody in the pub wanted to buy his beer and the women were all over him.

He drove me home in the early hours and asked if he might have a peek at the famous twins. Heather was still up and had Billie on one breast and Edward on the other. She handed Edward to me to wind and Carl asked if he might hold Billie. He rocked her ever so gently and sang a soft lullaby. Then he started to weep, I saw his tears splash down on to Billie's cheek. 'She's the most beautiful thing I've ever seen.'

The following night I bumped into Perry Beckett, one of my neighbours. Perry kept iguanas in a glass tank in his living room, worked double shifts at the Selby coal mines and played rugby in the front row for the Miners Welfare. It was Perry who once admonished the entire team of us at half-time when we were losing an important semi-final. Amid the quarters of orange and patching up of wounds some of the lads were repeating jokes they'd heard on a Peter Kay video. Perry stood up and shouted, 'Listen! There's too much fucking comedy and not enough aggression in this team ... Get some fucking horror films watched before you put your boots on!' On this day Perry shouted across the street to me, 'When am I going to see them babies?'

'Now, if you want,' I replied.

'Right, then. Get the kettle on – I'm just going to get these work clothes off.'

Perry came to our living room and reached into the crib. He

put his huge hands around Billie and lifted her out as if he was holding a bird's egg. He, too, started to weep – more than that: he sobbed. 'Here, tha'll have to hold her a minute. She's too precious for me and I'm too bloody soft.' This was a man well used to crash-tackling eighteen-stone prop forwards and sticking his elbow in someone's face on a whim. 'By bloody hell, she's lovely!'

Rachel van Riel, my friend from the Yorkshire Art Circus, the community publisher I worked for, gave us a beautiful cot for Billie, and Joe Lyman, an old coal-miner, gave us a cot for Edward that had seen better days, but it was a beauty so we cleaned it up and used it.

When they were two, we bought the twins their first beds, and they insisted that we put them in the same room. When they were four they agreed that they were ready for their own rooms, but still insisted on being told the same story from a chair that was placed between the two bedroom doors. Edward always wanted *The Gruffalo* or *The Wide-Mouthed Frog*. Billie loved what she called *The Very Angry Caterpillar*.

To our left Billie's wickerwork coffin rested on a pair of trestle legs in front of the altar in All Saints church – the only building in our neighbourhood big enough to hold all the people who wanted to come to the service. Dean Smith had been out at five o'clock that morning with Andrew Brown to look for some blackthorn blossom. He'd cut two lovely branches and placed them under the coffin. One of Billie's favourite weekends of the year was towards the end of September when we gathered the fruit of the blackthorn to make sloe gin. Only the previous autumn we had all sat cross-legged in our front room and watched *The X Factor* while pricking sloes and placing them in a big glass jar. Edward and I had used two of my gran's old darning needles, while Billie had surprised us by producing from her pocket a fearsomely sharp thorn she'd broken from our favourite blackthorn bush. 'Arnold Millard told me the gin tastes better if you prick them with a real thorn,' she said. She pricked her thumb and fingers more times that night than any princess in a fairy story, but persisted until the jar was full.

Edward's piano had been placed behind us in the church, waiting for him to play a tune called 'When You Grow Up What Would You Like to Be?'. In the rows facing us sat Heather's mother, father and stepmother, her auntie Val and Val's husband David, Sandeep and Manjit, who own our corner shop, and two Muslim mothers from school, whose names I hadn't known until the morning of the funeral. My Bosnian mate Miki Salkic and his wife Alma were nearby, next to our Tony and Gail and our Andrew. Colin Fish, the police liaison officer who had been assigned to look after us, sat at the end of the row, with Geraint and John, the two Welsh police constables who had come into the river with me to try to find Billie. Today was the first time we had seen each other since that day. Behind them were neighbours from every house on our lane, friends from every year of our lives and relatives we hadn't seen for years. My uncle Johnny and auntie Marion had come over from Wakefield – I hadn't seen Johnny since I was a young man and got a shock when his daughters told me he was nearly eighty.

All Saints is a lovely old church. It stands on the very top of the hill that overlooks Featherstone. Since the muck stacks and spoil heaps of the Ackton Hall, Featherstone Main and Snydale collieries were removed and the area landscaped, it looks over the farmers' fields again. On a clear day you can see the hospital at Barnsley and well beyond there to the edges of Derbyshire. As we came into the church, Mozart's Piano Concerto No. 21, the *andante* piano part, wafted from some speakers placed in the churchyard and across the fields. It was beautiful. The last person to have been buried in this churchyard, rather than in the local cemetery up the road, was a well-known strong man and scrap-metal dealer called 'Ossie' Wilkes. The neighbourhood gossips will tell you that not long before he died he paid for the church bells to be cleaned and retuned in a foundry at Whitechapel, London, thus ensuring his place in what, according to the vicar, is some of the earliest consecrated ground in the whole of England. Certainly, there was a church here before the Domesday Book, when a Saxon thane called Ligwulf looked after a handful of hilltop peasants scraping a living off the earth.

The Reverend Nicholas Clews is the vicar, the latest in a line that goes back to Thomas de Thirnum in 1310. He likes the children at All Saints School, where he's a governor, to call him Father Nicholas. I'd had to tell him two weeks previously that we wouldn't be having a Christian funeral. I struggle with the ceremony and I'm neither sure nor certain of the resurrection. When I'd said I hadn't yet found anywhere large enough to hold a simple humanist celebration of Billie's life he offered me the church on the grounds that it was also an important building for the community. He'd known Billie well from school and we agreed that, although he wouldn't be leading the proceedings, he ought to say a few words about Billie's school life.

The incongruities and ironies were not lost on him, and he made that clear when he stood up at the funeral and said, 'Perhaps there are a number of paradoxes here today. This is a secular funeral ceremony set in the context of a Christian building. I am a Christian priest speaking in a secular funeral. And Billie's parents chose to send her to a school with an explicitly Christian foundation.' At which point it crossed my mind to interrupt and say, 'Heather and I chose to send Billie to the school that was nearest to our house and the one where all of her mates and neighbours go,' but manners prevailed. He went on,

It is on behalf of that school community of All Saints that I speak today. There is a danger of putting Billie on a pedestal, of making out that she was the perfect child. I am sure she was not. But from the point of view of the school she was a fine example of all that I hope we stand for. It is so easy for children and adults to be categorized these days, particularly by exam results. In just over a year's time all of Billie's contemporaries will be labelled according to whether they are levels three or four or five in their SATs. Billie will never be labelled in that way. And that in itself is no bad thing, for Billie's qualities are not easily labelled, not easily measured or categorized. What the children of her class remember about her is the way she smiled, the way she cheered people up, the way she was a good friend to others and put them before herself. They remember, as do Heather and Ian, that she was always a bit scruffy, which means she had self-confidence and did not need other people's approval. She had a moral sense and believed that killing animals was wrong. And she acted on that moral sense by not eating meat. She was artistic and had a strong sense of beauty. None of this counts for a great deal in government statistics. But I think that at All Saints School we believe as Christians that it is what you cannot count that really counts. In that respect we are all very proud of what Billie achieved.

I saw Father Nicholas again a few weeks after the funeral. He came to our kitchen one morning on his racing bike. I told him that the reality of the past two months had started to sink in and that I didn't know who I was any more, let alone what I believed in. He said that if I found myself getting angry, then perhaps I should be angry with God. I told him I couldn't be angry with God: I wasn't even angry with the people who had allowed us to go out on the dangerous river after telling us it was perfectly safe for beginners and children.

Not long after that Detective Colin Fish drove up from Wales to see us. He told Heather and me that the two owners of the canoe company had been arrested and questioned and might be charged with corporate manslaughter. He said that they had answered, 'No comment,' to most of the questions that had been put to them.

*

After she had finished the Ben Jonson poem, Lynn Alderson took a sip from a glass of water, breathed in and, from some notes she had agreed with Heather and me, made the most beautiful speech in celebration of the life of our little Billie.

Billie and Edward were born on 9 May 1996, she ten minutes before her twin brother, something which Billie never forgot. She liked to remind Edward that she was his 'older' sister. And in many ways she often behaved like one – she was a bit taller, and often tried to look after him. They have been very close, in spite of bickering like every brother and sister – Edward has always had his twin sister and he will miss her in his own special way. Her story is also his story.

Heather and Ian had been together since they were teenagers and had had eventful and extraordinary lives. There are twins in Heather's family, so it wasn't a great surprise when they learned they were going to have twins, but they were especially delighted to have a boy and a girl. The pregnancy and the birth went well, although Heather tells me that it was lucky she didn't need the gas and air, as Ian pinched most of it! He remembers an immensely strong Heather, talking about Egypt to the midwife. Interestingly, when he went home from the hospital and made himself an egg sandwich, he got a double-yolker – and he hasn't had one since! Edward had to spend a little while in an incubator, but Billie came into this world with her huge violet eyes wide open, and ready to go.

As a baby she was cheerful, but a bit of a rascal, and she seemed to know what she wanted from an early age. Heather's mum, Marion, often looked after the twins and was close to them. Billie and Edward never crawled, they were 'bottom shufflers', until they both suddenly stood and walked perfectly, although Edward did it first on this occasion and Billie within twenty minutes of him.

Billie had a dreamy and thoughtful side, she loved books – stories and adventures – and Ian is a great storyteller; much of his work revolves around that. He took them on imaginary journeys as pirates in a big tank of a pram, careering down the road from Tesco to M&S

– and real ones too: they had lovely holidays as a family, Billie so excited she couldn't sleep at night, and making her endless lists of what to take. They had an unforgettable time in Switzerland, walking and journeying up to seven or eight thousand feet on the Glacier Express – she could be fearless.

Heather found a particular magic in their quiet moments, combing her hair, reading fairy tales ('The Princess and the Pea' was Billie's particular favourite), doing girly things together. Billie would play happily with a piece of driftwood or some stones: she loved natural things and was artistic and creative with them. Her bedroom is full of hundreds of books, and little things and treasures she has collected.

Billie and Edward went to All Saints School. Billie really enjoyed going to school, she liked and got on well with her teachers and she had many friends there. She often stayed over at Hannah's or Lauren's, but she got on well with all the children. She seemed from very early on to have absorbed her parents' sense of social justice and she was instinctively inclusive, never bore grudges and was incensed if she felt someone had been treated unfairly. She hated the images of war on the TV and chose to become a strict vegetarian from the age of three or four. (She was very fond of Heather and Ian's friend Pat, who is also a vegetarian.) She seemed very mature for her age, although she wasn't quite ready to start growing up yet – she still wanted to be a little girl.

She was also a very strong young person and a doer. She was a great swimmer and displayed her certificates on the walls of her room. She was proud of what she could do. She was learning the violin and she would stick at it and go and practise by herself. She could be quite quirky too, especially with language and using words in a way unique to her. Billie adored her collie dog John, a proper dog, but when her friends laughed at the name she had chosen for him she didn't care, just said he looked like a John!

She had a quite formal side to her too, liked setting the table and would do it properly with candles and napkins – the works. Billie was fond of posh hotels and thought things should be done just so! One of their last trips had been to Wild Ginger, a vegetarian restaurant in

Harrogate that Billie had seen in the paper and was bowled over by.

This last holiday at Hay-on-Wye was another adventure with the bookshops and the beautiful countryside. The tragedy of the accident while Ian and Billie and Edward were canoeing is not one that can be rationalized or understood. It is even hard to simply believe and come to terms with. We can all be grateful that at least Ian and Edward survived. They bravely did their best for their beautiful daughter and sister.

There was a pause of the kind that happens on these occasions, punctuated with coughs and murmurs of agreement. Lynn then invited Edward to play his little tribute to Billie on the piano. He whispered to me that he had forgotten to bring his sheet music. I whispered back, 'Can you do it from your memory?' He nodded and a little smile came. He started to play, at half the speed at first, a sort of moderate bossa nova, struggling to remember where to put his fingers next, then it came to him and he started to swing and even ended with a jazzy flourish. It was a piece called 'When You Grow Up'.

I stare into a space beyond the rows of pews where an octagonal ancient font stands. I picture what we grandly call our 'music room'; it's where our hi-fi is, our upright piano and boxes full of little percussion things and sundry other instruments. We have collected rainsticks, rattles and shakers, African thumb pianos, ocarinas, harmonicas in most keys and tin whistles. We hold our family concerts there and make a right old tin-pot row. I'm holding an image of Billie: she looks like the little hippie she was, long flowing Indian skirt, mucky vest, hair all over her face and she's shaking a small egg filled with rice. Edward is banging away on the piano. We all sing:

When you grow up, what would you like to be?
A mother or a father with a fine family . . .

We segue straight into 'The Sun Has Got His Hat On' and then Edward plays 'A Groovy Kind Of Love' and we never know all the words to that one.

In my mind's eye I'm in the tap room of the Greyhound pub in Pontefract now. Big Liza lifts Edward and Billie on to a table and encourages them to sing. Their audience is mainly old blokes reckoning up betting slips, rolling Golden Virginia and ripping apart Templegate tickets. Edward and Billie sing, they're only four years old, but they know a lot of songs off by heart.

> Up the west end, that's the best end
> Where the nightclubs thrive,
> Down into a dive you go.
> There's a jazz queen, she's a has-been,
> Has been Lord knows what.
> Every night she's there on show,
> She dances underneath the magic spells,
> She's full of ale and beer and stout as well,
> She's Fanlight Fanny the frowsy nightclub queen . . .

The old blokes nip their roll-ups and throw flat caps into the air. 'Tha'll allus have the price of a pint with them two,' shouts one.

Liza sweeps them up, one in each arm, and says, 'Come here, mi babbies,' then shouts to the landlord to give them an orange juice and a packet of cheese and onion apiece. These days, Liza cries every time we mention those Saturday afternoons in the pub with bags full of shopping, pints of bitter, glasses of pop and George Formby songs.

When Edward finished his piece he blinked and pulled at his sleeves. People started to applaud in the pews. He smiled the smile of the little boy who had once stood on tap-room tables with his sister to entertain men who spent their Saturday afternoons toing and froing between the pub and the bookies.

Edward is a hero. A stalwart. He's never once complained about what has happened to him. He has never missed a day at school with 'bellyache' since the accident, never blamed any tantrum on what happened, never missed an opportunity to join in, play out or enjoy doing stuff with his mates. A week to the day after the funeral he was ten. It was his first birthday without Billie, coming so close to the day he lost her. Billie had been looking forward to what she called 'my double figures' with great gusto. Edward said, 'Will it be appropriate for me to have a party?'

Heather said, 'Of course it will and it's going to be a special one.'

We arranged with Mark Covell, who was in charge of corporate hospitality at Yorkshire TV, for a tour of the studios. Edward picked four girls and four boys from school to go with him, and they all brought their mams and dads. We toured the sets of *My Parents are Aliens* and *Emmerdale*. The kids loved it, especially when Tim Fee, the big cheese at *Emmerdale*, let them sit on the Dingles' sofa. As we came off the set and into a back corridor we bumped into Patsy Kensit and Shirley Stelfox, the actress who plays ageing busybody Edna Birch. I think Tim had tipped them the wink. Patsy Kensit pouted and said to Edward, 'Who's the handsome birthday boy, then?' Edward blushed, put his hand up as if he was in class and said, 'Me, miss.'

Later on, as we crossed the car park back to the Green Room, I heard Edward telling his mate Liam Oxley, 'I can't wait to get to school in the morning and tell everybody that I've met Edna Birch!'

In the Green Room Mark had laid on cheese, ham and tuna sandwiches cut into triangles. There were crisps and cake and orange squash. One of Edward's mates showed how she could make orange squash come down her nose. The kids burped and giggled all the way home on the minibus, and the mams and dads couldn't wait to tell their neighbours that they'd been into the Woolpack.

When I was invited by Lynn Alderson to stand up at Billie's funeral and pay my tribute I walked to the lectern, shuffled the A4 pieces of paper I'd prepared and went straight away off my script:

I spend my life, don't I, talking about the importance of community? About neighbourliness, about looking after one another, sticking together through the hard times. These last few weeks have been the hardest times Heather, Edward and I have had to endure. The other day I thought I was going mad. But then I realized that all of our friends and neighbours and family members are hurting too. This tragedy has all but broken us, but with the help of our neighbours we can heal. Look around at this congregation. There are people here from different cultures, different countries, different parts of this country. All coming together to walk down a lane behind a little girl's coffin. Billie herself would have loved this coming together, this celebration. If anything will get us through this, it is the thought that our loss is your loss. My friend Arnold Kellett told me that a French poet whose girlfriend drowned in a lake said she was lost not just to him but to the whole world.

There's a musician called Manu Chao who plays what we've come to know as 'world music'. Billie loved him and his songs, one in particular called 'Me Gustas Tu'. In that song Manu Chao simply lists everything he loves. '*Me gusta la montaña*', the mountains, '*Me gusta la guitarra*', my guitar, '*Me gustas tu*', you. In many ways that song was perfect for Billie, combining as it does music with lists. Billie loved music and making lists. She made a list of things she wanted to take the night before we went to Hay-on-Wye. Here's a list of some of the things Billie loved.

Billie loved porridge with Lyle's Golden Syrup on it – she liked to pour the syrup off a big spoon and make smiling faces in her breakfast. She loved having messy hair and scruffy pyjamas on in the morning,

35

and she liked to pad about the house barefooted. Billie loved her dog John. An extraordinary name for a dog – John – but that's the name Billie chose so John he became. On the day before we left for Wales she whispered right into his ear – I watched her and now I wish I knew what secrets she had been whispering.

Billie loved names. She loved her own name, Billie Holiday, and she was proud to tell people it. All of her dolls and teddies had names – and she had a lot. There was a doll I brought back from Belarus that she called Mayuka, a teddy bear with the improbable name Ice Bird, another teddy called Gregory and her favourite, an ugly little teddy she bought in Ireland that became her favourite, called Anastasia. Anastasia went to Switzerland, to a Newcastle United game against Charlton Athletic, to the Cambridge Folk Festival every year and, of course, to Wales.

Billie loved people from other cultures, especially people with brown skin, and sometimes thought that she might like to have brown skin and black hair. I once bought her a book of Sikh bedtime stories. I don't think she ever got round to reading it, but she knew exactly where it was on her bookcase. When Sandeep and Manjit had their new baby boy, Guramrit, Billie decided that the book would make a nice present for them. Billie loved being kind to people.

Billie loved all animals. She loved animals as much as people. Only a few weeks ago she found a lost worm on a path after a rainstorm and gently picked it up and placed it back in the grass. Once on holiday in the North Yorkshire moors she picked up a snake – a viper. When I told her that vipers can bite, she said, 'I know but it won't bite me.'

Because of her love of animals, Billie enjoyed being a vegetarian. She had made her own decision when she was four years old. She loved Linda McCartney's frozen veggie sausages, she loved hummus on toast and cranberry juice – she drank it by the pint and left little red flicks at the side of her lips. She loved grapefruit and I used to arrange the segments on her plate into a shining sun. She liked to eat the sunshine one segment at a time. Billie did eat a little bit of fish and she loved kippers because she associated them with Whitby, and Whitby was one of her favourite holiday places. She once brought a stick back all the way from Whitby. Just a stick, but it was Billie's stick and she kept it in her bedroom. Billie loved collecting things, sticks, stones, coloured shells, and she had loads of hiding places. In the last few weeks I've been discovering all these hiding places and mucky bits of string, and broken shards of blue willow pattern out of the allotment that she fetched home.

Billie loved her violin. She hadn't learned to play much on it yet, but she loved putting it under her chin and rubbing resin onto the bow's strings – she liked to try to play along to Irish jigs she called 'Cambridge music'.

Billie loved tomato ketchup, coloured paper, rubber bands, drawing girls, houses with smoking chimney pots and paths lined with flowers. She loved looking at photographs of herself and Edward growing up. She loved it when it rained and when it snowed. She loved me to call her 'my lovely daughter, my cup and saucer'. She loved the waking-up rhymes I said to her, 'The sweetest lily I know'. She loved it when I called her Lily, but only I was allowed to call her Lily. I once called her it by mistake in the school playground and she said, 'Dad, don't call me Lily in public!'

Billie loved *Coronation Street*, *Dalziel and Pascoe* and *Tracy Beaker*. She loved her hair – she didn't even care when she got nits. She called them 'small creatures'. She loved her legs. She loved being strong and fast. Billie loved gluing things to paper. She loved other children and especially looking after babies. She loved adults and liked to sit at the kitchen table drinking tea and listening to what adults said. Billie liked to be a good girl. Once when she had a bit of bother at school she said to me, 'Mrs Crofts thinks I'm a good girl. I don't want her to think I am a bad girl.' She loved day trips out with her mam and visits to a Japanese noodle bar in Leeds near the Merrion Centre. Billie loved Edward. Especially when he played piano for her. She loved camping. She loved going somewhere.

Above many things Billie loved holidays. She loved hotel rooms. She loved looking through windows she hadn't looked through before. Billie loved mountains and trees and she loved rivers.

Billie just loved and she was loved.

I choked at that and didn't know what to say or do next. I was supposed to introduce the first piece of music – Van Morrison singing 'Sometimes We Cry' – but the music kicked in and I froze. I ended up mumbling a poor introduction over the first verse. Heather retrieved the order of the celebration when the music finished by standing at the lectern and reading 'The Lady of Shalott'. She was the model of calm as she told everyone that one of the last things Billie had done at school was a project about Tennyson's poem. The kids in year five had studied and commented on each verse, and Billie had chosen to take into school a version of the poem set to music by the Canadian harpist Loreena McKennitt. That night when she came home from school, she told us over tea that four of her schoolfriends had cried because of the emotion of the piece. How Heather got through those verses I shall never know. She was measured, clear and looked beautiful as she read:

> Lying robed in snowy white
> That loosely flew to left and right,
> The leaves upon her falling light
> Thro' the noises of the night,
> She floated down to Camelot,
> And as the boat-head wound along
> The willowy hills and fields among,
> They heard her singing her last song,
> The Lady of Shalott.

When Heather finished, leaving her last lines falling like a feather breath across the church pews, she tapped the hand-made papers on which she had written out the words and began to walk back to her seat. After just one step she came back and, almost as an afterthought, said, 'And I've read that for Billie.'

The sound of Sandy Denny singing 'Who Knows Where The Time Goes' then filled the church. I looked at a lot of tearstained cheeks, but my mind was floating off elsewhere. I was thinking about a line that had made people laugh a little bit, the line about Billie not even caring when she got nits in her hair and how she'd called them 'small creatures'. An image of us on our sofa rewound in my mind's eye. When I had been a little boy with nits my granny got out the fine-tooth comb and a piece of white rag. She said you could see the lice better against a white rag. I heard her in that church saying, 'I've got the little bugger,' then crushing the louse with her thumbnail on the flat of the comb. When Billie got lice in her hair I used my gran's remedy. I sat on the edge of the sofa and Billie knelt on the floor in front of me, her head resting on my lap, which was covered with a white towel. As soon as she heard me say, 'I've got the little bugger,' she told me I mustn't crush it. 'Well, what do you think I should do with it, then?' She told me I had to carry it outside and drop it over Dr Forster's, our next-door neighbour's, wall so that it could live in the bushes. She'd once made me do this with a half-dead mouse I'd caught at the back of our washing-machine.

One of Billie's favourite films was the Chaplin silent *The Kid*, the one in which the tramp befriends a little lad who goes round throwing stones through windows in the neighbourhood so that later in the day Charlie can go and repair them for a bit of brass. There's a scene in it that made us both cry. It's the bit where the authorities come to take the kid away from Charlie and to a children's home. The kid holds his hands out pleading, over-acting in the way that silent actors do, and Charlie tries to wrestle him back.

Billie had her own scruffy-old-bloke mate and she saw a lot of Charlie Chaplin in him. Arnold 'Sooner' Millard was a rogue of the most lovable kind. He dressed in the mismatched clothes of an old bloke who was given jumpers and coats by neighbours. He even once came up to our house for his dinner in a T-shirt with 'Frankie says Relax' on it. Where the hell he'd got that from I'll never know. Arnie drank beer by the gallon, like the old sailor he was. He taught Billie to snort phlegm and spit when she had a cold. He bounced her on his knee and recited poems and parodies that only he seemed to know.

> There is a Jacky land far, far away
> Where all the Jacky pigs run, run and play.
> When they see the butcher come,
> You should see them run, run, run.
> He'll cut three slices off their bum
> Three times a day.

On Saturdays we used to take Arnold shopping on the pretext that he was helping us. He loved to push Edward and Billie's big double buggy. We bought him a quarter of homemade potted meat and slices of brawn at John Hill's, the butcher's. When Billie found out that brawn was cooked pig's head she was outraged, but never judged Arnold for that – I don't think she even questioned him about it. Once she told him that if ever his sister Flo got fed up with doing his washing, her mammy would do it. Heather bit her lip and hoped that would never be the case.

We all loved Saturday-afternoon lunch. I used to make lentil, leek and tomato broth with pieces of cheese on toast to dip in it. Arnold would attack it like a man possessed and end up with soup stains all over his jacket. One Saturday he said he was sorry but he couldn't manage the soup and asked if we had any Andrews liver salts because he felt a bit 'stomachy'. Billie looked through our medical cupboard and found a tin right at the back that I think had once belonged to my gran. It was at least five years past its sell-by date, but Arnold said he never took any notice of sell-by dates. He downed the liver salts in one and belched, then announced to Billie that he felt 'champion now'. Three days later he died in Pontefract Infirmary with severe complications after an operation to repair his intestines. His family allowed me to be with him as he passed away. I stroked his hair and looked at his tattoos. I didn't know what to say to Billie and Edward so I told them he'd gone to a crematorium and hoped that they wouldn't ask me what a crematorium was.

That Christmas when Billie wrote her letter and list for Santa she decided to write one to Arnold as well. I asked her how she would post it. She said that of course she would post it through the letterbox at the Green Lane club. She thought he still might be in there because Pluto, his little dog, sat there every day still, waiting for him. I still have the letter on a file in my computer.

Dear Arnie, my Daddy says that you are in a crematorium with a fairy and an angel.

You said it was alright if I said 'Bloody Hell'.

You taught me how to do tic-tac like a bookie at Pontefract Races.

You only said Pardon Me if you did a really loud trump.

I once had a taste of your beer and it was a secret.

You always let me have a bite of your sandwich when you came for lunch after the supermarket.

When it rained we splashed in puddles.

You said that my best dolly was called Billy, when really she's called Lilly and you said my brother Edward was really called Jennifer.

I helped you to wash your dog.

You told me a song about a butcher who slices bacon from pigs' bottoms.

When I got head-lice in my hair, you said that you had some as well.

You let me try your flat-cap on when my Daddy told you not to.

And you bought me a kite for my birthday. When I fly it in the sky, it reminds me about you.

When Sandy Denny's song finished we lit four candles for Billie. Our next-door neighbour Peter lit the first. He loved Billie. He liked to watch her running and jumping, and often told me that he thought she would make a great athlete. 'Look at them bloody legs – she's all power.' Every now and again he comes to lean on our gate and likes to tell the story of how he once watched Edward and Billie fencing with two canes. Edward must have caught Billie a stinging whack and she became angry and said, 'If you do that again, I'll shove this stick straight up your arse.' Another time they had made a train in our yard out of some cardboard boxes that were left out. Edward was the driver, of course, as he always liked to be. Billie was pretending to make tea with some toy cups and saucers. 'Shall we set off, Billie?'

'Do you want another cup of tea?'

'No, thank you, else I'll have to stop at every station for a wee.'

Peter tells this story and laughs every time as if it's the first.

Peter lit his candle and Lynn said, 'This candle represents our grief. The pain of losing you is intense. It reminds us of the depth of our love for you.'

Edward lit the second candle. 'This second candle represents our courage to confront our sorrow. To comfort each other. To change our lives.'

I was third. 'This third candle we light in Billie's memory. For the times we laughed, the times we cried. The times we were angry with each other, the silly things you did, the caring and joy you gave us.'

Heather struck the fourth match. 'This one we light for love. We light this candle that your light will always shine as we enter this sad time and share the day of remembering with family and friends. We cherish the special place in our hearts that will always be reserved for you. We thank you for the gift your living brought to each of us.'

The coffin was carried out of the church to Neil Young's song 'Unknown Legend':

> Somewhere on a desert highway, she rides a Harley-Davidson
> With her long blonde hair flyin' in the wind

It was the first time Edward had cried. He held my leg and wept huge tears. The funeral directors had placed the coffin in our music room for half an hour before we left for the church. For two hours or more that morning he hadn't let it out of his sight. We opened the lid so that people could say their last goodbyes. We had dressed Billie in her favourite T-shirt, one with a rainbow on it and the slogan 'Be Happy'. She wore her Cambridge Folk Festival patchwork trousers and nothing on her feet. Billie was always a barefoot warrior. Heather placed her woven friendship bracelets by her side along with some shells and coloured stones.

When the time came to close the lid, Edward decided that he would do it and secure it with wooden dowel pegs. The funeral director thought his gesture was magnificent. Edward followed the coffin out of our house and stayed close to it right through to the end of the ceremony. Now, as the coffin was being carried out of the church and we waited while the people filed out behind it, Edward was being separated from his twin sister. Only on a handful of occasions since they had gone to separate incubators had this happened. He cried. He roared. I tried to comfort him and rubbed his arm.

Lynn welcomed us to North Featherstone cemetery. She reminded us to take a moment to notice our surroundings in this beautiful place, the trees, the sky, the flowers, the birds, a natural reminder of the cycles of life; there are endings but always new beginnings as the seasons come and go. As she spoke a swallow swooped low. She remarked that it was the first one she'd seen that year.

Everyone linked hands to say a final goodbye. Lynn told us

to remember that Billie's life was filled with love and respect and that we should recognize the unique person she had been and how she had touched the lives of others.

In sadness, but without fear and with love and gratitude for Billie's life, we commit her body to its natural end, to the earth which has sustained her and from which all life comes. Her spirit goes free of the earth, clear in the sweetness of her liberty. Commit to your minds all that Billie meant to you, and what she held dear commit to your hearts.

Lynn then read from a poem by Kathleen Raine:

> Let her be safe in sleep
> As leaves folded together
> As young birds under wings
> As the unopened flower.
>
> Let her be free in sleep
> As the flowing tides of the sea,
> As the travelling wind on the moor
> As the journeying stars in space.
>
> Let her be healed in sleep
> In the quiet waters of night
> In the mirrors pool of dreams
> Where memory returns in peace,
> Where the troubled spirit grows wise
> And the heart is comforted.

She then quoted Brian Patten, 'A person lives for as long as we carry them inside us, for as long as we carry the harvest of their dreams,' and read an adaptation of some words from C. Day-Lewis:

Her laughter was better than the birds in the morning, her
   smile
Turned the edge of the wind, her memory
Disarms death and charms the surly grave.
Early she went to bed, too early we
Saw her light put out; yet we could not grieve
More than a little while,
For she lives in the earth around us, laughs from the sky . . .

Billie's schoolmates, Hannah, Lauren, Amy and Ben, came
forward to sprinkle little handfuls of earth into her grave. As we
came away I looked over my shoulder and nudged our Tony
to look behind as well. The first swallow of summer was still
skimming around where we had been standing.

In the Featherstone Old Working Men's Club we ate vegetarian quiche and supped pints of Guinness. We told stories
about the miners' strike, about famous rugby matches we had
played in and others where we were spectators. We talked
about who was working and who was looking for work.
Heather's sisters had a bit of a tiff. Edward and some of his
mates got hidden under the tables. Some people who had
seen stories about Miki Salkic and his family in the *Pontefract
and Castleford Express* asked him if he would be able to stay
or be sent home. Heather and some of the others went on to
the Bradley Arms when the club closed. I gave the caterers a
cheque, and Edward and I put our arms round each other and
walked home. We had a game or two on the bagatelle board
that our next-door neighbour Dr Forster had found in his attic
and brought round for us as his way of distracting Edward
in our early days of grief. Then we went up to bed. As we were
going upstairs Edward said, 'Did you see that swallow?' As
I tucked him in, he asked for a story.

This is the story of the nail soup. On a cold and rainy night a long time ago, a traveller came to knock on the door of a little cottage on the edge of some woods. He was wet through and shivering, but he could see a little candlelight through the window, so he knew somebody was in. He knocked again. A croaky voice shouted, 'Go away!'

'Please open the door. I've been travelling all say and I just need shelter from the storm.'

'Go away before I put a spell on you.'

'Please let me in, I'm frozen to my bones and I need to see a friendly face and a warm fire.'

The door creaked open ever so slightly. An old lady looked through the gap, her face pressed on the jamb. She saw that the traveller had a friendly face and she told him that he could come in, but just long enough to dry his cloak.

The traveller sat down by the fire and took off his sodden boots to toast his toes. He took off his cloak and hat and hung them on the mantelpiece. Steam rose up. The old lady told him that people round here thought she was a witch and nobody usually came. The traveller was pleased that she had chosen to open the door for him and wondered if she had eaten supper yet. The old lady told him that there was no food in the kitchen. So the traveller said he would make nail soup. The old lady said she had never heard of such a dish. The traveller picked up one of his boots and removed a nail from its heel. He asked the lady to fetch a pan of water. They placed the pan of water on the burning coals and the traveller dropped the nail into the pan when it started to bubble.

'We must let it simmer for a few minutes and it will be the nicest soup you ever did taste.'

After a few minutes, the traveller stirred the soup with a wooden spoon, brought the spoon to his lips, blew on it, sipped a little bit and declared, 'Oooh! It's delicious. Perhaps all it needs is a little onion. What a pity we haven't got one.'

The old lady said she would look in the pantry to see what she could find. She came back with a little brown onion. The traveller chopped it and dropped it into the pot. He stirred the soup, brought the spoon to his lips, blew on it, sipped a little bit and declared, 'Oooh! It's delicious. Perhaps all it needs is a little bit of carrot. What a pity we haven't got one.' The old lady went to look in the pantry again. She came back with a mucky old carrot. The traveller scraped it, chopped it and dropped it into the pot. He stirred the soup, brought the spoon to his lips, blew on it, sipped a little bit and declared, 'Oooh! It's delicious. Perhaps all it needs is a little celery and maybe a tomato or two.'

The lady found a stick or two of celery and some ripe tomatoes. The traveller chopped them and dropped them into the pot, stirred the soup, brought the spoon to his lips, blew on it, sipped a little and said, 'Oooh! It's delicious. If only we had a handful of herbs and some salt and pepper.' The old lady shuffled off again to the pantry. She found some fresh parsley and basil, a sprig of rosemary and even some scraps of fat bacon left over from breakfast that she'd saved to give to the birds. The traveller stirred in the mixture of ingredients, brought the spoon to his lips, blew on it, sipped and now he declared, 'The nail soup is ready.' He ladled it into two wooden bowls and, with some chunks of rough brown bread that the old lady remembered she'd saved on a shelf, they dipped and sipped until their bellies were full. The old lady agreed with the traveller that it truly was the most delicious nail soup she ever did taste, a meal fit for the king himself!

After a while when the fire burned low, the traveller began to snooze in his chair. The old lady tapped him on the shoulder and told him that such a fine cook should not sleep in a chair. 'I have made you up a bed. Come and take your rest.' She showed the traveller to her spare room where she had placed a piece of freshly cut lavender on a plumped-up pillow. The traveller slept and dreamed under a beautiful patchwork quilt and woke the next morning when he heard the birds singing in the tree outside his window. He ate an apple for his breakfast and hugged the old lady on her doorstep before, with a swish of his cloak, he turned and went on his way.

Later that morning when the lady was washing the dishes she found in the bottom of her saucepan the little boot nail. And in the evening she decided to make another pot of the delicious nail soup. Because it was a fine and clear evening, this time she took her pot out into the field, lit a fire and soon the pot was bubbling. One of the local farmers went by and asked what she was doing. When she told him about the nail soup, and perhaps it needed a little onion, he said he would see what he could find. He came back after a little while with an onion, and his brother came too with carrots and potatoes. Before long, news of the supper spread round the village and more people came with leeks, and pearl barley, and swedes, and bread, until everybody round about was joining in. They all sat down to the tastiest meal that anyone could remember.

'I like them sort of stories, Dad,' Edward said, and turned over.

'I love thee, son.'

'I love thee too.'

Billie's bedroom is right next to Edward's, divided by a plasterboard wall. As I came out of Edward's room, I looked into hers. She looked back at me from a photo on the wall, of her in her school uniform with her hair tied back. Her last school photograph.

3. Wired to the moon

My dad had sent word with my youngest brother Andrew that he would like to come to the funeral. I sent word back with our Andrew that he was not to bother. In the last thirty-five years I have seen my father no more than half a dozen times. It doesn't bother me that much and I don't suppose it bothers him either.

When I first started courting Heather back in 1978 I thought I ought to introduce her to my mother and father. They had divorced messily four years before. My mother went off to live with Jimmy, my dad's youngest brother, in a terraced house opposite Pearson Park in Hull, and my dad got a council flat on the edge of the city centre. He managed to find himself a series of 'girlfriends' who paid for his colour-television licence and for trips to Blackpool boarding-houses.

We took the train to Paragon station in Hull and walked the half-mile through the central shopping area to where I'd been told he lived now. By complete fluke my dad happened to be walking down Prospect Street. Bizarrely he was pushing a broken lawnmower. I said to Heather, 'See that man there? It's Sid, my father.'

'It never is!'

We quickened our pace and walked up behind him. I tapped him on his shoulder and said, 'Now then.' He spun round, flinched and put up his fists. He blinked two or three times, then stared without saying anything.

'It's me.'

He still said nothing. Kept his fists on either side of his face like a middleweight. Then a bell rang somewhere in his memory. 'Tha's in disguise. Tha's got a beard on.'

'Don't kid me. You didn't know me, did you?'

'Well ... I thought tha was a bloody mugger. You can't be too careful, these days. Who's this, then?'

I said that this was Heather, my girlfriend. He wiped his hand on his overalls – my father has worn bib-and-brace overalls since 1961 – shook Heather's hand and said, 'Nice to make your acquaintance, Hazel.'

We were looking at his broken lawnmower. He told us he had found it round the back of a wall and he was going to mend it. I asked him if he fancied going for a drink, said we were on our way to see my mother but we had half an hour. He asked me if I had a bottle of poison in my pocket, then laughed an hysterical high-pitched laugh and slapped Heather's shoulder. Heather blushed.

'Are you a punk rocker, love?'

We walked to a pub called the Zoological Arms at the corner of Spring Bank and Beverley Road, near to the furniture shop called Everything But the Girl that would later give Tracey Thorn and Ben Watt their band name. My dad embarrassed Heather all the way there, pushing his broken lawnmower and singing '2–4–6–8 Motorway' to her. Every Saturday afternoon shopper turned their heads to look at us. In the pub Heather and I had a pint and my dad had a half of mild.

'Bloody hell, lass, supping pints, eh?'

When my dad found out that my mother was having an affair with his brother he followed them one night and attacked them. He bashed Jimmy's head on the iron railings round a church wall. He was like that at times, but mostly he liked to make up very childish jokes, throw back his head and laugh like a madman. My grandmother said that he was wired to the moon and at certain times of the month you had to watch your back with him. She also said he was a simple bugger and sometimes called him 'the cod-eyed dog'. I've never known anybody else to be described as a cod-eyed dog, but it fitted him.

I can't remember now what we talked about in the pub, but my dad was eager to get home with his lawnmower and watch the *World of Sport* wrestling hour. He finished his mild, belched, looked at Heather, said, 'Manners,' and told us, 'I shall have to get off.' He made for the door and then, as an afterthought, leaned back inside. For a reason known only to himself, he stared at us and began to recite.

> When I was out walking with my uncle Jim
> A kid came round t'corner
> And chucked a tomato at him.
> Now, tomatoes don't hurt when they come in the skin
> But this bugger did –
> It came in a tin.

He laughed his hysterical laugh and off he went. Ten seconds later he popped his head round the door again.

> And remember, if they bite, squeeze 'em tight,
> Then they won't come another night.

This time, he really did go. Through the window, I saw him pushing his lawnmower across the Beverley Road. I hardly dared look at Heather.

'What the hell was he on about?' she said.

'Bed bugs.'

'Is he right in his bloody head?'

'I did try to warn you.'

We walked across the park to where my mother lived with Jimmy. Heidi, their daughter, the girl my mother had longed for after having us three lads, would have been three or four years old at that time. She was playing in the backyard. We sat there on some deckchairs, sipping tea and eating buns. Heidi liked Laurel and Hardy, and Jimmy had painted them on the yard wall with some leftover emulsion. I told my mam that we'd seen my dad in town. She asked if I'd tried to shove him under a bus.

After that I saw my mother occasionally when she visited my gran for Sunday dinners. I didn't see my dad again for ten years. Then one day something came over me and I decided to visit him.

Not long after I had gone freelance with my writing work I found myself at a community-programme unit's Christmas party with some BBC people in London. I got talking to a young woman who told me she was working on a Radio 4 programme called *First Person*, a fifteen-minute slot given over to authors writing stories in the first person to read their work. It was late at night, I'd had some plonk and, in my excitement, I told her I had just such a story ready to go. She asked me if I thought it might be suitable for the slot she was working on.

'More than!'

'OK, I'll give you a call in a few weeks' time and we can sort something out.'

By the following morning I had forgotten most of what I'd said and the names of most of the people I'd met. When the woman from Radio 4 phoned me at home about a fortnight later I struggled to make sense of what she was asking.

'The story you said you thought might be suitable for *First Person*, do you remember?'

'Oh, yes, right, love, got you now. I'll send it down to you later in the week.'

What I should have said was that I hadn't got a story ready, that I'd fibbed to impress her because I was at a BBC party and that I'd forgotten most of the evening because I'd drunk far too much champagne, which I don't even like to start with. Instead I put the phone down and went over to a little table on which I kept an ancient Olivetti typewriter. I wrote 'First Person' and 'Ian Clayton', then sat there for half an hour and smoked three roll-ups. I looked round the room for inspiration. I dredged my memory, remembering that I'd been sitting there not too long ago at the height of the anti-poll-tax campaign. I'd been at that typewriter when I'd heard footsteps on the bottom stair. Thinking it was my brother Tony, I'd hidden behind the door and said, 'Boo!' just as a bailiff reached the top step. He fell halfway down the stairs with the surprise and I pushed him down the rest and out of the door.

'I've come to place a restraint-of-goods-and-chattels order,' he said, standing, dishevelled and wet, in the rain in the yard.

'Tha's what?'

'I said I've come to . . .'

'I heard what tha said, now piss off!'

'I can fetch a policeman.'

'Fetch one, then. But if you think I'm going to pay the same amount of poll tax for a two-bedroom flat above a shop on Station Lane as Lord St Oswald does at Nostell Priory you must think I'm simple.'

He never came back. I took my poll-tax protest all the way to Castleford Magistrates Court, but when the magistrate told me I'd still owe the money even if I went to jail I gave in and paid up with as much loose change as I could find.

Under the heading 'First Person' I started to write about the campaign and how, on the day I had been in court, I had been shepherded into the dock with a streetful of people from Featherstone. The clerk read out addresses, 17, 19, 21, 23, 25, 27 and so on, all from the same road. It was funny and poignant at the same time, solidarity by postcode.

I wrote two paragraphs, rolled the paper out of the typewriter, screwed it up and lobbed it. The ball of paper hit my bicycle, the old Pashley policeman's bike that I always parked at the top of the stairs. I decided to go for a ride on it and find inspiration in the fresh air. At the bottom of Station Lane I turned left, passed the Junction Pub, the crematorium and went into Pontefract. I carried on through Knottingley, beyond Kellingley colliery and into the open countryside to where the old West Riding turns into East Yorkshire. I pedalled and sang,

'Lola', 'Honky Tonk Women', 'Ging Gang Gooly', 'Fog On The Tyne' and 'Ride A White Swan'. I stopped at the Brewers Arms in Snaith for a couple of pints, got talking to an interesting old bloke and had four or five. Outside when I remounted the bike I fell off, jumped up, looked round to see if anybody had noticed me and got back on again. Instead of heading back west and home, I carried on east and towards Hull. It's fifty miles or more to Hull from Featherstone on the old road. I thought if I pedalled quickly enough I could be at my dad's house for teatime. I pressed on. When the Humber Bridge came into view I was still singing, 'Riding along on a pushbike, honey'.

I carried the bike up on to my dad's balcony, paused for a breath, then knocked on his door.

I heard a hoarse shout from inside. 'Rent . . . spent.'

My dad opened the door about the width of his eye. 'Now then, what's thy want?'

'I've come on my bike.'

'What for?'

'I was out riding and I thought I'd carry on.'

'Oh, tha did, did tha? Does tha want to come in?'

'Well, I haven't come all this way to look at the busy lizzies on your balcony.'

'Come in, then, and make me a pot of tea if you're making one for yourself. Sugar's in that basin.'

We sat opposite one another in a sparsely furnished front room with a tropical fish tank lit up in one corner, a telly in the other. 'I can see you're admiring my fish. Them little ones near that windmill are harlequin tetras and them others are neon tetras. That sucker fish near the gravel eats all the shit and keeps t'tank clean.'

'Have you got any biscuits?'

'Biscuits? What does tha want biscuits for?'

'I'm a bit hungry.'

'Well, there's a fish-and-chip shop on Spring Bank, but it's not open yet. You can get some on your way home.'

My dad started walking up and down singing 'Whispering Grass'. He always sang 'Whispering Grass' when he didn't know what to do next. 'I've just fitted a new needle on to my record player. Do you want to listen to my Ink Spots records?' I told him I wasn't bothered just now. He reached under his television and held up a videotape. 'Want to watch a blue 'un – Swedish?'

'Why the bloody hell would I want to sit here watching a porn film with my father?'

'Well . . . I just wondered.'

I finished my mug of tea. 'Right, I'll get off, then.' I stood up and put my coat back on. As I was doing this, a parrot in a cage in the kitchen said, 'You can fuck off!'

My dad laughed his high-pitched laugh. 'I learned him how to talk. Good, eh?'

I rode back across the city and thought about the story I would write when I got home, the story that, a few weeks later, I read on Radio 4's *First Person* programme.

My dad was born in the middle of the 1930s depression, one of four lads. His father died after a night of heavy drinking in Wakefield city centre. Sometimes my dad told me that he had his throat slit because he had been cheating in a game of cards in a cellar under a pub. I don't know, I think he made that up. My dad never went to school, never learned to read or write – my mother always filled in his sick note when he was off work.

While he was still a teenager he went to work on the waltzers at the fairgrounds. He courted a woman called Joan Peace, who, he claimed, was a direct descendant of the notorious Victorian criminal and violinist, Charlie Peace. He used to arrange to meet her inside the pictures because he was too tight or skint to pay for her ticket. During the interval he would ask her if she wanted an ice cream, then advise her not to have one because it was too cold out. She chucked him and then he met my mam at Bridlington.

The pair of them came back to my gran and grandad's house in Mafeking Street and my mother told her parents that they wanted to get married. My grandad threatened to give my dad a bloody good hiding. My gran had to wash a suitcase full of my father's stinking shirts, a whole summer's worth of unwashed clothing. My grandad continued to threaten my dad with a bloody good hiding most weeks for the next ten years or more.

My parents rarely did anything together. Their nights out were so few and far between that they could sit in the front room and recount exactly what had happened on the rare occasions when they did venture out to the pictures or pub.

'Do you know what the silly bugger once did with your mother's best gloves?' This was the opening line to one of my gran's favourite stories about my dad. 'They were coming to the bottom of Station Lane late one night and the slack set-up swine chucked both gloves up on to the roof of the chapel. For nowt. But I made him go down on the Saturday morning with his window-cleaning ladder to find them. He came back and said his ladder wouldn't reach. They were lovely gloves an' all, fur-lined.'

My dad spent most of his spare time on his allotment, where he kept hens for their eggs and rabbits for the pot. He grew cauliflowers and cabbages, which I helped to harvest and then pushed in an old wheelbarrow round our neighbours' houses. Sold them door to door for pennies. I chopped sticks for firewood as well and bound them into bundles with wire before selling them. 'Everybody wants firewood, lad,' he'd say. 'Just count all them chimney pots round here.'

My dad told stories, squatting with a cigarette cupped inside his hand, when he wanted a rest at the allotment. He told me he had once chopped a cockerel's head off with his spade and that it had run around for half an hour with its head off. He also told me I had to beware of rats when I moved the sacks of hen meal. 'A rat will spring up at you and go for your throat if it's cornered.'

I think the story was meant to warn me to keep away from rats, but I was always impressed by it. I liked the idea that a little animal would hide, then fight its way out of a tight spot. I've always liked stories about coming out fighting when your back is to the wall.

My dad took a job at a local factory that made cardboard boxes. He hadn't been there long before he was badly crushed when a huge roll of wrapping paper fell on him. He ended up with a fractured pelvis and back injuries. The doctors told him he had to sleep flat on a board. We unscrewed the hinges of the door that separated our kitchen from our living room and he slept on that for months. When the company offered him a thousand pounds' compensation he couldn't wait to grab it. Despite advice from my grandad that he was probably due a lot more, he took the first offer and, with the cheque cleared in someone else's bank account – my dad didn't do banks – he bought a caravan at Withernsea and a terraced house in Hull.

The house in Hull was no different from the one in Featherstone. Two up, two down, no bathroom, no central heating, no garden. We bathed once a week in a tin tub in the kitchen. I took my bath after tea and listened to the Top Thirty on a transistor radio that I placed on a kitchen chair. While David Bowie sang about 'Life On Mars' I washed my mucky neck with dark green blocks of Fairy soap. One Sunday night I fainted as I got out of the bath – I think a combination of hot water and the cold kitchen caused it. My dad panicked, ran to the phone box and called the only person in our family with a private telephone, my auntie Laura, sixty miles away in Pontefract. 'Our Ian's collapsed, I think he's dying!'

Auntie Laura was more sensible. When she'd established that I'd merely fainted she told him to give me some sweet tea and not to bloody exaggerate.

Not long after that my dad built what he called a bathroom. He knocked a hole in the kitchen wall through to the back yard, then built a brick shed that linked the kitchen to the outside lavatory. He bought a second-hand tub and ran a waste pipe from the plug hole to the grate in the corner of the yard. We filled the bath from a hosepipe connected to the geyser next to the kitchen sink. We were one of the first in our row to have such a bathroom. It was 1973, squealing girls were queuing to see the Bay City Rollers outside the ABC cinema, I was about to embark on my O levels at Hull Grammar School, by then a comprehensive, and on a Sunday evening in the autumn of that year the whole family took it in turns to soak in their first bathroom experience. My mother bought a bar of Wright's Coal Tar soap and told us to lift it out of the water and put it in the soap dish when we weren't using it.

The last time I saw my dad, he didn't see me. He came to knock on our door just after the twins were born. I pretended not to be in and, through the bedroom window, watched him walk off with one of his girlfriends. About half an hour later I got a phone call from Pete Green, landlord at the Top House. He said, 'I've got an old couple in the tap room. The bloke says he's your dad and he's come over from Hull to see you and the kids.' I told Pete to tell him that I'd taken my family out for the day.

When I think about my father now, I have an image of him standing in the headmaster's office at Hull Grammar in his rolled-over wellingtons and stinking overalls. He has his hands forced deep into his pockets and eyes the headmaster from under an overgrown fringe of sandy hair. The headmaster wears a black cloak and a frown.

'What's to do, then?' my dad says.

The headmaster tells him he's concerned about the level of violence I had displayed on the rugby field the previous Saturday. I had played at scrum half for my school against a touring team from the London Oratory, a gang of posh, lank-haired schoolboys. I had been bitten, kicked and nearly had my balls pulled off in a tackle before I'd lashed out, kicking their number eight under the chin. 'It will not do, Mr Clayton.'

'What won't?'

It was like observing a conversation between two aliens, neither of whom could speak the other's language.

Slowly and precisely, the headmaster recounted the events on the rugby field. My dad listened with his head down and a slight smile on his chops. When the headmaster finished my dad looked him straight in the eye. 'Well, me old love, I'm a bit disappointed if the truth be known.'

'And why might that be?'

'Cos I've allus told him to get first 'un in if he ever gets in any bother. Anyroad, don't fret, old cock, cos when I get him home I shall see to it that he gets a proper hiding.'

At home my dad told me that my punishment would be to wash the pots for a week, dry them and side them, then added, 'Before tha does owt else, nip to the shop and fetch me ten Player's No. 6. And don't bloody embarrass me like that again. Tha knows I don't like talking to school teachers.'

Our local swimming baths was called Lister Baths. It was named after the Earls of Masham, the Cunliffe-Listers, who owned the coal mines and much of the land in Featherstone. When I was about three my dad took me to the baths and dived in at the deep end with me on his back. When he came up he swam to the side and left me to struggle back by myself. I don't know if I can remember this now – I can sometimes recall water feeling hot inside my nose and coughing as I held on to someone's arm, but I don't know if it was on that occasion. I do know that my gran told the story many times of how my father nearly drowned me, that he was a stupid, simple bugger who wasn't right in his head. And my dad would say, 'It's the best way to teach somebody to swim.' He claimed he was a better swimmer than Johnny Weissmuller because he had swum in rivers as a child at a place called Bottomboat near Wakefield. My dad told bizarre tales about his childhood, about bike rides to the seaside and how they filled their tyres with grass if they got a puncture in order to get home. He said that he blew a trumpet for a rag-and-bone man because he was the loudest blower in the West Riding and everybody knew he was coming.

Once in Blackpool I watched him run down to the sea and belly-flop straight into the waves. He scratched all his front on the sand and shingle, came back perishing, shivering and blue with cold, and announced, 'That's very healthy for you. I don't get colds in the winter through doing that.'

4. The democracy and irony of graveyards

The cemetery manager let us choose our own spot for Billie's grave. There's a part of North Featherstone cemetery in the top corner that has no headstones, just grass that gets cut every now and again by a council worker who drives a mini-tractor with a lawnmower at the front. Under this grass lie the bones of children and poor people, whose families couldn't afford a permanent marker. Children who were killed in coal mines, children who died of diarrhoea, typhoid and cholera are here. In the 1880s Featherstone had the worst infant-mortality rate in the country. Houses were being thrown up quickly without proper sanitation to house a massive influx of mine-workers. Children were being born and dying, sometimes within months of their birth; forty-eight deaths of children under the age of one were recorded in 1887 alone.

One of my neighbours is a lovely former primary-school teacher called Jenny. She sometimes gives me a lift back with my shopping from Tesco. If I see her on her way to church she always stops to ask how I'm going on. She knew Billie well from school. I like talking to her and remembering Billie. She once told me that people find it much more difficult to talk about the death of a child now than they used to. 'At one time,' she said, 'most families had experienced the death of a young family member, so they knew better how to talk about it.'

I once leaned on a wall in that cemetery and watched a kestrel hovering over the wheatfield that runs along the side. A man came up beside me and made me jump when he said, 'They buried the king of the Gypsies against that wall, y'know.' I told him I'd never heard that story. He said, 'It's true, though.'

'When was that, then?'

'Oooh! You're going back some years. Maybe just after the war.'

People round here do that. Stories never seem to have a specific date. They just happened before or after a war, 'round about the time of the big strike' or 'a long time ago'.

'The Gypsies came from all over in the middle of the night, from all over, and they dug the grave themselves and burned his wagon on them fields. When the council found out what they'd done, they said he'd have to be dug up, but they couldn't find anybody to do it. So I think he's still there. If you look, you'll notice that from time to time somebody leaves flowers there, wild flowers, and nobody knows who it is.'

For months Heather, Edward and I visited a bare patch of earth to place flowers. Hannah, Jessica and Lauren, three of Billie's mates from year five at All Saints School, left teddy bears and butterflies. Edward left a little purple tin with Harry Potter sitting cross-legged on its lid. Inside is a message that reads, 'To the best sister in the world'.

Heather told me that she sometimes dreamed she had dug the earth out of Billie's grave so that she could give her one last hug. She frightened me when she said that. 'Don't be stupid, Ian. I told you it's just a recurring dream.' Heather last saw Billie alive in the back of the taxi that was to take us to the place where we were to join the canoe. She didn't kiss her or hug her then, just said, 'I'll see you later this afternoon. Have a lovely time.' She has often told me since that Billie looked sad in the back of the car.

On the morning after Billie died, Heather went to the mortuary at Hereford Hospital with Colin Fish, the detective who was looking after us. I decided I couldn't go. I don't know why. Fear, perhaps, shock certainly. I was being sick a lot too. I stayed with Edward. He spent the entire day playing the computer-game version of 'Who Wants To Be A Millionaire?' on the TV in the front room of the bed-and-breakfast where we were staying.

'Dad, will you be my phone-a-friend?'

'Yes, of course I will.'

'All right, then. Which cricket club play games at –'

'Edward, Edward, I can't think about quizzes at the minute.'

'But you said you'd be my phone-a-friend.'

I tried to picture Heather walking into a cold room to sit by Billie.

When Heather came back she told me that the nurse who showed her into that room told her to try not to touch Billie. Billie had a kind of white neckerchief on that was smudged with blood. Her long fingers had turned into little bird-like claws and those lovely ruby-red lips were colourless and thin. Heather talked to her: she said we were so sorry that this had happened. That we loved her and would always think about her. After ten minutes, Heather became aware that Colin and the nurse were waiting beyond the window. She stroked Billie's hair and left the room.

Billie stayed on her own at Hereford for nearly a fortnight. I contacted Granville Brooks, the local joinery firm and under-taker that had arranged the burials of my gran and grandad. They sent a van down to Hereford to bring her back and then she lay in the Room of Repose across the yard from the joinery shop until the morning of the funeral when we brought her home to lie in her open wickerwork coffin in our music room.

Edward couldn't understand all these arrangements. He had wanted to bring Billie back to Featherstone the day after she had drowned. Our good friend Jane Hickson had driven down to Hay-on-Wye on the Thursday afternoon to pick us up. We packed our things into her car. Before we set off I swung my legs out of the passenger-seat door and unlaced the borrowed shoes to return them to the bed-and-breakfast lady's husband. As I was doing this Edward said, 'Are we going to Hereford now?'

I looked at him. 'Why? Do you want to see Billie?'

He said he wanted her to travel back in Jane's car. His bonny little face and big brown eyes looked so certain that this was a perfectly normal thing to do.

'I'm sorry, but the authorities say we aren't allowed to do that, Edward.'

He was shocked. 'But she's our Billie!'

I looked at Heather. 'Somebody else has to bring her home, Edward.'

He said again, 'But she's our Billie. It's up to us!'

We had headed north out of Hay. I put my hand through the gap between the front two car seats and searched for Heather's hand. After about a mile, she broke the silence and said, 'You're holding my hand too tight!' I let go and stroked Edward's knee. He moved his leg out of reach and said, 'Will she come home tomorrow?'

One night, not long ago, Edward wanted to watch a DVD. He searched the shelves and said, 'What's *Midnight Cowboy* about?'

I said, 'It's an eighteen. I'm not sure you should be watching that.'

'I didn't say that. I said what's it about?'

'Well, it's about a cowboy from Texas who goes to New York to seek his fortune and makes friends with a homeless tramp.'

'I'd like to watch it.'

'It's an eighteen!'

'You let me watch some other eighteens. A lot of Clint Eastwood's films are eighteens and they've got cowboys in 'em.'

'All right, then. You can watch it if you let me fast-forward the bits that I don't think you need to see.'

He offered me a high-five and said, 'Deal!'

I put the DVD into the player. Edward grabbed for the

remote like he always does and threw himself on to the settee. I started to sing, '"Everybody's talking at me, I don't hear a word they're saying, only the echoes of my . . ."'

'Do you have to spoil it by singing loud?'

'I thought you said I had a good voice.'

'You're all right, but you're too loud and I want to hear the film.'

We sit in silence and watch the opening sequence unfold.

> I'm going where the sun keeps shining
> Through the pouring rain
> Going where the weather suits my clothes
> Backing off of the north-east wind
> Sailing on a summer breeze
> Skipping over the ocean
> Like a stone

During the scene where Jon Voight and Dustin Hoffman are shivering with cold in their tumbledown apartment and trying to improvise a meal out of left-over scraps, Edward said, 'Why don't they do the lottery?'

I tried to hide a giggle behind my hand. Edward had that incredulous look on his face again. 'I can see you're bloody laughing at me. You'd laugh if your arse was on fire!'

'Stop bloody swearing.' I laugh again.

Towards the end of the film Edward was falling in and out of sleep, propping himself on five cushions on the settee.

'I think you ought to go to bed.'

'No. I want to see the end. Are they in Florida yet?'

'Nearly.'

'And that's where it ends. They get to the sunshine!'

'Well, you'll have to see.'

'Oh! Tell me. What happens?'

'Wait and see.'

'What's up with Ratso? Is he dead?'

'Yes, he's died.'

I tried not to look at Edward, but I knew he was shedding little tears from those big brown eyes. 'Are you all right, Edward?'

'Course I am. I'm just rubbing my eyes cos I'm tired.'

The credits rolled to that lovely music played on the harmonica by Jean 'Toots' Thielemans.

'Will you carry me upstairs like you used to do with Billie?'

'I'll try, but you're a big lad now you're twelve.'

'I thought you were supposed to be strong.'

'Come on, then, Cheyenne Bodie. Fireman's lift or piggy-back?'

'Fireman's.'

'Right, then!'

'Dad! You're hurting me belly!'

I threw him on to his bed. 'Look sharp, before your mam comes home. She'll want to know why you're still up at eleven o'clock.'

'Dad!'

'Yes, lad?'

'Is Jon Voight allowed to bring Dustin Hoffman to Miami when he's dead?'

'Well, it's just in a film, Edward.'

'Yes, but would the authorities allow it in real life?'

'I think so. Because they were best mates.'

'Oh! Right, then.'

I gave him a hug and said what I say every night as I leave his bedroom, 'I love thee.' He always comes back, 'I love thee too.' That night he didn't. He was already half asleep when he said, 'Jon Voight put his arm around Ratso and hugged him when he died.'

'Yes. He did, pardner.' I stood at the bedroom door for a half a minute or so. As I turned towards the stairs, Edward said, in the sleepiest voice, 'I love thee too.'

★

North Featherstone cemetery dates back to the mid-Victorian era when rural workers left their muddy patches of land in the countryside to find work in the coal mines. Their bones lie here. Many never found the fortunes they came to seek by digging black gold. They died young: trapped by machinery, buried under roof falls, some shot by the military after a local magistrate read the Riot Act to a crowd of picketing workers.

Edward and I come here two or three times a week. We like to explore the old stones in the Victorian part just through the gates. It's probably not the most appropriate thing to do, but we play a little game between ourselves of who can find the most unusual or interesting name. I found Zillah Waller and Lizzie Polkinghorne. Edward found Abednego Jepson. Recently Edward has started to cheat and make up names.

'What about that one, Dad, Fanny Shufflebottom?'

'Where's that?'

'Oh! We passed it the other day, and I can't remember where it is now. I think it was near Esau Wood and Lilac Fartlepant.'

'Give over, you're making them up.'

'I'm not, Dad. I'll show you next time,' he says, with a look of mock indignation on his face.

We pick up the two-litre plastic milk cartons that blow about all over the place on a windy day. People bring them so they can water flowers on their loved ones' graves and leave them by the tap for other people who might need a watering can. The problem is, everybody thinks they're the only ones to have thought of it and as a consequence North Featherstone cemetery is filling up with them.

The inscriptions on the blackened stones tell the story. The biggest one in the cemetery is a huge sooty piece of sandstone. It towers above all the others almost in the middle of the Victorian section.

THIS MONUMENT WAS ERECTED BY
FEATHERSTONE MAIN LODGE.
IN TRIBUTE TO BROTHER MINER
CHARLES GREENHOFF
KILLED BY A FALL OF STONE AT
FEATHERSTONE MAIN 1875

It then goes on with a chilling verse of advice to all onlookers:

Death did him short warning give.
Therefore be careful how you live.

You don't have to look far for stones to dead miners or warnings. Just a few yards away there's another:

The master cut the flower.
The gardener held his peace.

And another:

THOMAS LIGHTBOUND,
AFTER AN ACCIDENT AT FEATHERSTONE MAIN 1910

JOSEPH WESTWOOD, 12 APRIL 1892,
KILLED AT FEATHERSTONE MAIN

WILLIAM DYAS, 16½,
FATALLY INJURED 1910 AT ACKTON HALL COLLIERY

BERNARD WESTBROOK, ACCIDENTALLY KILLED
FEATHERSTONE MAIN, 2 JANUARY 1928, AGED 16 YEARS

CUT OFF IN EARLY BLOOM OF YEARS
WHICH CAUSED MY PARENTS FLOODS OF TEARS.
WHOSOEVER THOU MAY BE,
DEATH HATH A DART IN STORE FOR THEE.

Then there are the graves of the two men who were shot by the South Staffordshire Light Infantry in 1893: James

Duggan, a coal-miner, was once arrested for throwing stones at people who, on polling day in 1888, cast their vote for the Conservatives, and James Gibbs, a Sunday-school teacher from Altofts, a village nearby. On James Gibbs's stone it says:

THE BELOVED SON OF ROWLAND AND MARY,
WHO WAS SHOT THROUGH BY SOLDIERS WHO
CHARGED THE LOCKED-OUT MINERS AT
LORD MASHAM'S COLLIERIES.

GONE NOT FROM MEMORY OR FROM LOVE
BUT FROM A WORLD OF STRIFE,
SWEPT BY A RIFLE BALL FROM EARTH
TO LIVE AN ENDLESS LIFE.

On James Duggan's headstone it says directly: 'Through a gun-shot wound by the South Staffordshire Regiment'.

With both the democracy and irony that graveyards bring, you need to walk only a few paces to find the family plot of Alfred Holiday, once the agent for Lord Masham. Lord Masham owned a lot of the land in Featherstone and therefore what lay underneath it. His Ackton Hall colliery was one of the biggest in the British Empire and his spoil heap grew so high that, according to my old mate Arnold Millard, 'The ministry put lights on it to warn low-flying aircraft.'

From the early 1890s until his death in 1905, Alfred Holiday lived at Featherstone Hall on the hill that overlooks the colliery land. He was a member of the Plymouth Brethren and regularly preached the gospel at the crossroads in North Featherstone. It was Alfred Holiday who called on the local constabulary to bring the military to Featherstone in September 1893, which resulted in the shooting of Gibbs and Duggan. Some of the older people in the area will tell you he was so ashamed of what he had done that for years after the incident he only travelled in a covered carriage, and that he died of a broken heart while leaning on a five-bar gate up the road. His son, Roslyn, who became a councillor, and his grandson, Purcell, who died in infancy, are buried with him, as is his daughter-in-law, Amélie, a Swiss lady who loved the arts, helped redesign Featherstone Hall and built a glass aviary bigger than a lot of local people's houses, in which parrots and macaws flew about freely.

Alfred Holiday built the Gospel Hall from solid Ackton Hall brick, and when Billie and Edward were born, Heather and I converted it into our home. I can look over my wall today at Featherstone Hall, and see the stables in which he kept his covered carriage and horses and the parrot house too.

About six months after we buried Billie, friends and neighbours started to ask Heather and me, 'When are you going to put a stone up?' The truth was, we didn't know. We didn't want one of those black granite blocks with gold lettering that look as though they've been picked out of a catalogue. We wanted something small – special, if you like – that said something about who Billie was. No 'Rest in peace', no 'Sadly missed', no warnings about 'death's dart looking for us all'.

One day I found myself at Ampleforth Abbey, the beautiful home to Benedictine monks and a Catholic public school on the edge of the North Yorkshire moors. I was to present a documentary for ITV about the work of Father Rainer, a monk there who looks after the vast orchards; he makes a powerful cider and a very expensive apple brandy. As part of the programme we were to film him taking a mass at the church in the village nearby. I arrived early on the morning of the service and wandered around the churchyard looking at the gravestones. Two in particular caught my eye, quite small pieces of white Portland stone, arched at the top and with exquisite carved lettering that had been coloured in muted reds and blues. One was a memorial to a girl who had died in her teens.

After the service the congregation filed out of the little church and shook hands with Father Rainer. I joined the queue, offered him my hand and said, 'Do you know who carved those beautiful headstones?' He said he thought he had the address of the mason and that as soon as he found it he would email it to me with the phone number.

We made a lovely little film. There's a great sequence with Father Rainer pressing his apples and a beautiful long shot of him and me walking the length of the cloister, him in his habit and me in jeans, with the sun streaming through the windows to land on the stone flags. They were a bit worried about allowing the shot, because it would have involved Jane, our director, entering an area where women are forbidden. In the end we compromised and she stood outside, behind the door, while we did our walk.

A few days after we finished filming I had an email from Father Rainer. The stonemason was called Martin Jennings and I rang him. 'Hello, my name is Ian Clayton. I was at Ampleforth last week and I admired two pieces of your work in the churchyard.'

A gentle voice at the other end of the line thanked me.

'Well, I'll come straight to the point. I'm looking for someone to carve a headstone for me. I wondered if you might like to do it.'

There was a pause while Martin Jennings took in what must have seemed an abrupt request from a stranger with a thick Yorkshire accent at the other end of the line. 'I don't really take on private commissions for headstones. I'm actually a sculptor and I do quite large public works.'

'But you carved the headstones at Ampleforth.'

Another pause. 'Yes, but they were quite special ones, for people whose families I know.'

'OK. Well, I think mine is a special one.' And then, I don't know why, I blurted out to this stranger the story of how Billie came to drown on the canoeing trip in Hay-on-Wye.

A third pause. This time I tried to fill the gap. 'I'm really sorry I burst out with all that. It's just that sometimes when I'm that road out I can't help it and I just –'

Martin Jennings interrupted me: 'Did I read about this story in the *Daily Telegraph*?'

'You probably did. It was in quite a few of the papers. The *Telegraph* was one of the papers that said crowds of Easter holidaymakers were on the riverbank as I dived back in to see if I could find Billie. None of that was true. Nobody was there until the police and ambulance men arrived. It was just Edward, Billie and me.'

Martin said something softly about how terrifying it must have been. And then, 'It's quite an expensive job to carve stones like the ones you saw. I could put you in touch with some stonemasons who might be able to do it for a better price.'

'No. I've set my heart on you doing it.'

'Right, then. I'll do it for you. Have a look at my website to get some ideas and rough out a design. Send it to me and I'll get back to you with my own thoughts and designs. Make sure to tell me exactly what words you want to use.'

'Where am I phoning to, Martin?'

'Oh! Blenheim Park in Oxfordshire.'

'Aw! Right, then, cheers!'

When I put the phone down I looked at Heather. She was ironing Edward's school trousers. 'Don't you dare leave me out of this,' she said. 'I want to know what you're up to. Who's Martin Jennings?'

I told her to leave the ironing a minute and come to my computer. We Googled him. We discovered that Martin Jennings is one of Britain's finest sculptors, with work in collections all over the world. He sculpted the Queen Mother for her hundredth birthday and had done a bronze of Sir Roger Bannister. His monuments include a Gulf War memorial in St Paul's Cathedral and a stone to Nicholas Knatchbull, godson of Prince Charles, who was killed in Ireland at the age of fourteen with his grandad, Earl Mountbatten of Burma. In November 2007 his statue of John Betjeman was unveiled by the Poet Laureate,

Andrew Motion, at St Pancras station after the refurbishment there was completed.

I swivelled in my computer chair. 'What do you think, Heather?'

'I'll tell you what I think. I think it's going to cost a lot of bloody money, but it'll be worth every penny because it's for our Billie, so don't you dare change your mind when he tells you how much it'll be!' She gave me that Heather smile with the little dip of her head that say, 'Mark my words.' She went back to finish ironing Edward's school clothes.

'What are we going to put on the stone?'

She told me to get a writing pad and a pencil. 'You can put, "A child of nature. Budding artist, violinist and humanitarian."'

'That's it, Heather! Leave it at that. That's perfect.'

'What about dates?'

'Shall we put May the ninth, 1996, to April the twelfth, 2006?'

Heather thought for a little bit. 'No. Because that shows she was still nine and she was looking forward to being ten.'

We decided that if we just had '1996–2006' she could have been ten. And we left it at that.

Within a few days Martin had drafted some design ideas that we liked straight away. Then we added a verse from Sandy Denny's song:

> Come the storms of winter
> And the birds in spring again
> I have no fear of time

Martin suggested that unless he made the stone much bigger he wouldn't be able to fit it all on so we decided that the things about Billie should go on the front and the Sandy Denny verse should go on the back. It was early November and we told Martin we'd love to have the stone in place for Christmas. Edward had already decided that on Christmas Day we would cook a good breakfast, then visit Billie's grave and unwrap our presents. We didn't hear anything for more than a month. Then an email came from Martin. 'I hope I didn't promise you Billie's stone for Christmas.'

I hit the reply button straight away. 'I guess you're busy Martin, but we were really looking forward to putting Billie's stone in place.'

Fair play to the man: he wrote back and said, 'I'll do my best.'

The week before Christmas Martin got in touch to say the stone was ready.

We chose a day in the week leading up to the Christmas holidays and Edward took the morning off school. He said he wanted to dig the hole that the stone would slot into. That morning the washing-machine broke down. It flooded the kitchen and the repair man arrived just before Martin did. I had wanted to make a special lunch for Martin. I'd forgotten to ask whether he was a vegetarian or not, but in honour of our Billie, I made a big pan of tomato and lentil soup, Billie's favourite, stepping over bits of washing-machine and the repair man's legs.

Martin arrived in a baseball cap and overalls. We had the soup with pieces of Cheddar cheese on toast, like Billie used to do. Then we went in Martin's car to the cemetery. The stone is beautiful: an arch of white Portland stone with the carving picked out in reds, blues and gold. Edward helped, as he'd said he would, to dig the hole for the stone. I had to turn away. Edward said, 'What's up?' and I told him something had blown into my eyes. Martin paused to straighten his back and I pointed out some of the things you can see from North Featherstone cemetery. It's on top of a hill, about the last hill in West Yorkshire before the lowlands and the Vale of York to the east. You can see the white tower of Leeds University, and Wakefield Cathedral's spire to the south-west. To the east over the fields are the cooling towers of Ferrybridge power station.

'My mate Harry Malkin calls that a "cathedral of electricity".
And look over there, Martin.' He followed my finger to the
north-east. 'That's Castleford, and do you know who was
born in the back-streets there? Henry Moore. But you can't
visit the house he was born in any more. The council knocked
it down because they couldn't get the new dustbin lorry round
the corner.'

After Edward had gone to school for the afternoon, and Martin
had set off for Oxfordshire to beat the traffic, I went back up to
the cemetery with Heather. We stood in front of the stone for
ten minutes holding hands. When Heather wanted to come
home I asked if she minded if I stayed a bit longer on my own.
And I did. I know, because they've told me they do this,
that Heather and Edward like to talk to Billie. Heather tells
Billie about buying nice clothes when she's out shopping and
Edward tells her what her mates have been doing at school.
Once on a cold, frosty Sunday morning not long after we
placed the stone, I left Edward to say his few words. I heard
him say, 'Try to come back one day, Billie.'
    I never know what I want to say, I just try to picture Billie
giggling her almost baritone giggle. On the day we put the
stone up I sat cross-legged on the damp grass. Henry Moore
must have been still in my mind. 'Billie, when Henry Moore
was a little boy he used to go to Sunday school and one day a
preacher came who hadn't been before and said, "Boys and
girls, I'm going to tell a story this morning." And he told them
a story about Michelangelo who was the greatest sculptor in
the world. This Michelangelo was working in his studio, which
opened out on to the street. He was carving the face of an
old man. He stepped back to admire his work, when a man
walking past stopped and said, "Excuse me, but if you mean
that to be the face of an old man, wouldn't it have a tooth or
two missing?" Michelangelo agreed with the passer-by, took up
his chisel and knocked out one of the teeth. "And the moral of

that story," said the preacher to the children, "is that even if you're the most famous artist in the world, you're never too old to learn." The young Henry Moore was fascinated by this story, not because of the moral but because there was such a man called "the most famous sculptor in the world". And he promised himself at that very moment, when he was only six years old, that one day he would be the most famous modern sculptor in the world.'

I wanted Billie's voice to come into my head. Those deep tones of hers. 'And one day, Daddy, if I practise hard enough, I'll be a famous violin player and I'll play my violin at Whitby Festival and Cambridge Festival and I'll make lots of people happy.'

I looked around to see if anybody was watching and placed a sea shell on the earth in front of the stone. It's a shell that Billie once brought back from Southwold.

The wind and rain can be quite wild at times on top of the hill at North Featherstone. Local people have a saying, 'It's an overcoat colder up at that cemetery.' After less than a year the paint on the lettering started to fade. Martin said he would call in the next time he was passing and redo it. He did so when he was on a visit to some aunts in Ampleforth. It was a cold and rainy day at the back end of September. We went to examine the stone and he said he would rub it down, but he would have to come back another day because of the weather. On our way out of the gates I picked up a conker. 'Here, Martin, hang on to this.'

Years ago I met an elderly photographer called Geraldine Underell who had once taken morning walks on the beach in Cornwall with the sculptor Barbara Hepworth. One morning Geraldine Underell picked up a pebble that had been well washed by the waves and gave it to Barbara to remind her of the moment. She told me that Barbara Hepworth looked at the pebble and said, 'Why do I bother to carve stone when nature does it better?' She slipped the pebble into her pocket and said, 'It will remind me of something I have to do.' Martin slipped the conker into his pocket and had a similar thought.

The following day was a beautiful, sparkling autumn day. I wished I'd arranged for Martin to come up from Oxford a day later. Martin must have thought the same. Unbeknown to me he stopped with his box of paints on the way back from Ampleforth and made a beautiful job of repainting the carving. He sent me an email. 'I called on my way home. I left the conker on top of the stone as a signature. I don't suppose it will have survived the wicked weather up there.' I took the dog for a walk and found the conker. I placed it inside Billie's shell.

5. A head like a toyshop

My shed is in a corner of our yard where the dog goes to cock his leg. It has bitumen felt on the roof and on that, going soggy in the rain, there are some torn pieces of mouldy bread that have been thrown there for the starlings to bicker over. Some old green curtains that once belonged to Doris Pyatt hang at the shed windows.

Doris was shuffled off to an old people's home more than twenty years ago, talking to herself about a policeman she'd had a crush on in the years before the war. She'd lived with her two sisters, Hannah and Mabel, who worked in the mills at Bradford. I once saw Doris stamp on a mouse that ran out of her house. She squashed it with her little black polished shoe. All the kids in our backs formed a circle round the dead mouse and made animal noises. Peter Goodfellow said the mouse wasn't dead yet because he could see it twitching its nose. Margaret Cording said she could see its heart was still beating. Doris picked it up by its tail and threw it into her dustbin. She walked back across the yard to her door, wiping her hands on her wraparound pinny, and said, 'At one time the council would have given me twopence-ha'penny for that.'

I rescued the green curtains when they cleared Doris's house, those and a zinc wash-tub with the word 'soap' moulded into a little shelf attached to its rim. It collects rain that I use to water the garden in dry spells. I also have the button hook that Doris used to fasten her little black polished shoes.

When I was a little boy I played in Doris's house. I helped her to Brasso the shell canisters brought back by her father from the First World War that she had as ornaments on her mantelpiece. I played at hide-and-seek, and once I crept upstairs and tried to hide in the big old drawer of a Victorian dressing table. I climbed in between the pants and vests and lay there in the must and mothballs till I fell asleep. In my half-dream I could hear Doris, 'Let me see your raggy arse'; she was going to cut off my tail with a carving knife. I jumped out of the drawer and tried to tidy it up. There was a single nylon stocking like a draught excluder and it was full of old white five-pound notes. I shoved it under the vests and big pants, sneaked back downstairs and peered through a knot hole in the stairs door. Doris was winding wet pillowcases through her mangle. I tiptoed up behind her, tapped her on her left shoulder, ducked to the right and when she spun around 360 degrees, I said 'Boo!' She looked at me for a long time and threw her hands on to the top of her head, 'Lors! You're going to stiffen a body like that!' I think 'Lors' is a corruption of 'Lord above'; folk like Doris still spoke an ancient language. I don't know what happened to the stocking full of white fivers.

Inside my shed there is a black bicycle, a 1952 Pashley, which still works. A man called Jim Travis gave it to me. He was the secretary of the Bygone Bikes Club, and had a penny-farthing too. He died sudden, as they say round here.

At the back of the shed is my gran's once beautifully polished dining table. It sat under the window at number three Mafeking Street with four chairs round it. That table and those chairs were her pride and joy. Woe betide anybody who marked the table with a hot mug or put their feet on the spells of the chairs. The table has an in-built cupboard at its heart. In this cupboard were kept our family's only two books: a maroon leatherbound dictionary that my auntie Alice won at Sunday School in the 1920s for good attendance, and a self-help book called *Better Sight Without Glasses*. When my gran died I couldn't bear to see the table and chairs thrown into the skip, so the chairs stay in our yard, slowly rotting in the weather, and the table waits at the back of my shed, like a thought on hold, with all sorts stacked up on it; half-used cans of paint long since skinned over, old Oxo tins full of screws that will never bite into wood, a fireside rug slowly being eaten by moths, and some brightly coloured buckets and spades that Billie and Edward built sandcastles with at Bridlington.

My head today is like my shed – full of washed-away castles, deflated tyres, thoughts I'm trying to cling to and broken toys I really ought to throw away.

There's a song by John Prine that I love to listen to:

All the snow has turned to water,
Christmas days have come and gone,
Broken toys and faded colours
Are all that's left to linger on.

Broken hearts and dirty windows
Make life difficult to see.
That's why last night and this morning
Always look the same to me.

I put it on, and then a CD by Lal Waterson and Oliver Knight. I love their song 'Some Old Salty'; 'He's got a head like a toy shop . . . Hull Fair, waltzers, bopping to Brenda Lee'. Just like my dad back in the middle of the fifties, spinning girls around on the waltzers.

Today I am forty-nine years old. It is 4 September 2008. This morning I opened my presents at the breakfast table. In between mouthfuls of sausage and toast Edward was eager that I should unwrap the parcels. He had to leave for school at any minute and wanted to see my reaction before he set off. I unwrapped some socks that Heather had bought in TK Maxx in Wakefield yesterday and a bottle of ginger shampoo from the Body Shop; I only wash my hair once a week but I do like a nice shampoo. My dad told me that you wash all the 'goodness' out of your hair if you wash it too often. He only washed his once a fortnight. Edward had bought me a card with a photo on it of Vinnie Jones grabbing Paul Gascoigne's knackers. The caption reads, 'Bloody hell, Vinnie! Lineker keeps nicking my crisps and you keep pinching my nuts!' Edward likes jokes about 'nuts' and 'asses' and 'nice juicy pears'. He's a walking *Carry On* film – he mimics Charles Hawtrey, 'Oooh! Hello, madam,' and Kenneth Williams, 'Oh! No no no, Matron!' Edward is twelve. When I was twelve I saw *Carry On Henry* at the Star cinema in Castleford with my auntie Alice. We both laughed about Sid James whipping out his chopper.

I take the dog for his walk down Richard Copley's fields. Some hired hands from other farms have been helping to bring in the bales of straw. The youngest lad brags that each acre of the biggest field has yielded three and a half tons of wheat. I say, 'And it's nearly two hundred pounds a ton now, isn't it?' He rethinks quickly and, in typical farmer fashion, says, 'Aye, well, it's not that price now, it's dropped down again and, besides, with all the rain it'll take some drying out and that gas burner we dry it with costs some money.'

When I get back, Heather has put out John the dog's water bowl and his dinner. In the middle of the pile of food there is a heart-shaped dog biscuit. Billie always left a heart-shaped biscuit in the middle of his bowl. She loved that dog. She named him John before she saw him. On Christmas night I went and knelt next to her bed. She was five and had painted-on Christmas eyes that were trying to stay open. 'What would you say, Billie, if I told you that I think Santa's going to bring you a little puppy for Christmas?' She sat up in bed and said, 'I would be very pleased, Daddy, and I would call him John.' Billie could never understand why people laughed when they asked her for her dog's name and she told them, 'John.'

Billie had some eccentric ideas. She thought that if you told her a joke it was just for her. I sat at the kitchen table with Edward and Billie once and started to tell them a joke about little noses running in our family. Billie shushed me and whispered, 'Don't tell it in front of Edward – he'll spread it round All Saints School.'

Both Edward and Billie loved that school. Edward prided himself on never having had a day off all the way from nursery to year four. Somehow he contrived to catch chickenpox during the half-term holidays. Billie wasn't so organized. She caught chickenpox from Edward and spent the following week in bed scratching herself through her beautiful blue pyjamas. Our friend Brian called and Billie came halfway down the stairs to see who was at the door. She rested her chin on the banister rail and smiled. When Brian saw her he jokily remarked about her spotty face and she fled back upstairs, vowing not to come out of her room again until every spot had disappeared.

I'm spending this birthday filtering snapshots of memory through my head. Edward and Billie are being born. Billie is the first: she opens her eyes; they look like violets. A nurse and a doctor take her off to a corner of the room and stand with their backs to me. I don't know whether I should go over to see what they're doing or continue to stroke Heather's hair and murmur words of encouragement. A Chinese midwife sternly tells Heather that she must start to push again. Heather looks at her and says, 'No! I've pushed enough. I'm going to have a rest now.' The midwife looks at me, then at Heather, and says, 'The head is in place so you must push.' The male doctor decides he wants to make a cut; I hear the sound and want to faint. Heather tells me to stop stroking her head so hard and then tells the doctor, who is Egyptian, that she once spent the night sitting in Cairo airport shooing away feral cats. Edward starts to come out. I'm expecting to see the back of his head, but instead I see his crumpled face. Billie came out in a forward crawl. Edward is here doing backstroke. Another midwife tells me later that nurses call this 'face to pubes'.

Edward and Billie are eighteen months old now and they

don't know how to walk yet. They've worked out that by shuffling everywhere on their backsides their hands are free to examine things and open cupboard doors. I have fastened child locks to every one, but they know how to undo them. They have developed an alarming habit of banging their heads on the floor when they want something.

We are in Menorca on a pleasure boat that cruises Mahon harbour. The tour guide announces that, after Pearl Harbor, Mahon is the deepest natural harbour in the world. Billie is drawn to the water rushing past the boat and she keeps leaning over the side. She's terrifying me so I hold her by her reins and legs. I'm relieved when she comes to sit on my knee.

She does it at Whitby too, this scary behaviour near water. Every time we go to the folk festival we have a little ritual. Most mornings we go and drink mugs of tea at a little wooden hut near to the fish market. Billie insists on rushing headlong across the quayside and stopping just before she topples off the edge into the mucky water in the harbour twenty feet below. In some dreams I'm climbing down ladders let into the harbour wall trying to catch her before she hits the water.

On our third day in Menorca Billie starts to be sick. The day before yesterday I had watched her sucking *aioli* from her grubby fingers and encouraged her to use a knife and fork to eat her rabbit. She put her knife and fork in the wrong hands, which she would continue to do for the rest of her life. Then when she thought I wasn't looking she carried on eating with her fingers, dropping food on the wooden table and picking bits out from between the planks.

She was sick all that day and the next. We took her to a local doctor, who advised us to give her plenty of water. She spewed it back up. I took her to a clinic in Ciutadella; the doctors there said she would have to stay in hospital because her body was completely dehydrated. We were due to fly home the following day. The doctor said he couldn't allow Billie to fly. The insurance company told us they would pay for only one parent

83

to stay with a poorly child, so Heather flew back to Manchester with Edward, and I stayed with Billie in the clinic and slept on a steel-backed chair. Before she left us, Heather said, 'She won't die, will she?' I told her not to be so daft and that we'd be home within a couple of days. Billie stopped being sick on the next day and passed the bug to me. On the afternoon that we were supposed to fly home, I was on all fours in the lavatory throwing up and Billie was crying for her mammy.

A doctor came in with his clipboard and wanted me to cancel the flight. I told him I couldn't bear another night in the clinic. He gave me a bottle of water with 'something in it' that he said would probably get me home. At the airport I felt as if I wanted to die and Billie started to bang her head on the marble concourse in Departures. I had to crawl around the floor after her as she shuffled and banged. I put my fingers, palms up, on the floor to cushion her forehead.

It's midday on the forty-ninth anniversary of my birth. I want to go upstairs and take out envelopes full of photographs that plot our family history. I want to spread them on the kitchen table and tell myself the story that joins all the dots. But I can't bring myself to do it. There are lovely photos of Billie and Edward on the walls in the kitchen, the living room and the music room, but I can't open the envelopes to look at the ones we chose not to display. Instead I allow these random images to come into my head and disappear, to be replaced by all the pub-quiz trivia I seem to hold. This head that is a shed, a toy shop. I can recall the entire Featherstone Rovers team that beat Hull at Wembley in 1983, but I can't remember where I've left my clean shirt.

We're in Switzerland on board the Glacier Express train that is taking us from Chur high in the Alps down to Brig near the Italian border. Billie has seen a ghost. She is seven years old now and she sees ghosts. She can't sit still and she's crying. When I ask her why, she cries some more and says she doesn't know why she's crying. She stands on her seat and looks at the snow on the mountains that are flashing by and cries. She doesn't like tunnels in the way that when I was a child I didn't like piers. I always thought I would fall through the gaps between the planks into the sea. Billie likes trains, but she doesn't like getting on to them or getting off. She has to be sure that Heather, Edward and I are safely on or off before she joins us. She doesn't want anyone to be left behind, and once we're on the train she likes us to stay in our seats and not wander off down the corridors. When the train comes to a tunnel, she holds all of our hands, by insisting that we make a pile of hands in the middle of the table.

At Kandersteg, high in the Oberbernese Alps, we decide to walk in the mountains above our hotel. Billie and Edward have seen snow on the summits from our balcony and Billie wants to touch the snow in June. We climb and climb. The rain is heavy in Switzerland at this time of year, and the path up is very slippery. The rain is running towards us as we climb. We pause to rest near a waterfall. I'm frightened that we might fall. 'I'm sorry, but we can't go any further today. It's too dangerous.'

Billie starts to cry. 'But, Daddy, you told us we could touch the snow!'

I get firm. 'No! We have to go back. We're all dripping wet – we'll catch our death of cold.'

Heather is relieved – I think Edward is too – and we turn to go back down to the village. Billie stands staring at the waterfall and above to the snow, defiant eyes glaring. It takes me ages to coax her down from the mountain with promises of ice cream and *apfel strudel*. She refuses to speak to me properly for hours after. She repeats her mantra whenever I try to initiate a conversation: 'You said I could touch the snow!' She lets her lovely hair fall over her face so that I can't see her eyes. She pulls her hands inside her sleeves and folds her arms round her knees to make herself disappear into a corner of our hotel room. On her left wrist is a sweatband, red with a white cross on it, like the Swiss flag. On every photo we take on that holiday Billie is wishing to touch snow and showing her wrist-band to the camera.

Billie and Edward are nine now. We walk John down Richard Copley's farm track. Edward is telling us about Homer Simpson. Billie announces that Edward will become a potato pie. Edward says, 'What do you mean, Billie?' We establish that she means a couch potato, like Homer Simpson. She has an eccentric way with words. While we mull over this funny image, Billie declares that she will become a farmer when she grows up and ride around on a fine black horse called 'Dijon'.

I can see Billie and Edward sitting on a step that leads into our library. They would be five. Earlier this week they have been having the forty-yard dash at school to see who will represent All Saints at the local sports gala. Billie won her race and Edward came second to last. Billie has been picked and Edward hasn't. For the first time the twins will not be doing something together. Edward has spent all week trying to understand why Billie has been picked and he hasn't. On the day before the gala they sit on the step to our library. I earwig their conversation.

'Billie! I should be in that race.'

'No, Edward, you shouldn't, because you're not as fast as me.'

'But I didn't hear the teacher say, "Go," and that's why I got left behind.'

'So you'll have to try harder next year.'

'I can't understand it, Billie. We're twins, we should be the same.'

Billie pauses and puts her head on Edward's shoulder. 'Let me tell you something. I know we're twins, but sometimes twins can be different. It's like you're a fire engine and I'm a strawberry.'

'What do you mean?'

'Well. They're both red but they're different!'

Seven years on from that little bombshell I look across from my chair at the table in our kitchen and I can see them. I see them both look round when I chuckle. Billie with those eyes that smile and Edward confused and saying, 'It's not bloody funny!'

I see Billie in her red duffel coat now and her ankle boots. She's carrying her violin to school. When she becomes a farmer she's going to play it to her cows. A farmer violinist, who paints in her spare time, and when she has her holidays she'll take toys to children in poor countries because her toy box is over-flowing and children in poor countries don't always get nice toys, only wooden ones made by their grandads who carve them with a rusty knife – at least, that's what happens according to Billie.

I'm about to embark on a journey to Belarus, to make a television documentary about the plight of orphans in state-run children's homes there. Before I go Billie asks if there is room in my case for some toys. She goes to her room and brings down her best toys and teddies, even the Steiff teddy that cost me a fortune at Hamleys in London's Regent Street. 'Billie, I can't take your lovely things. Why don't you bring me some of the ones you don't play with?'

'Because it's obvious! If I don't want my worst toys, why would any other children want them?'

Today, on my birthday, I open a parcel. This parcel is not a present, but I will make it into one. This parcel is an evidence bag that the police in Brecon gave to me at the inquest into Billie's death. It contains her bonny red cardigan, the cardigan she took off and placed in a watertight barrel before we embarked on our canoe trip. I have had this brown evidence bag for months now. It's secured with thick brown gaffer tape and I haven't been able to bring myself to open it. Today I will. Today it is a present to open alongside socks and shampoo and cards that say, 'To Dad from Old Ted', the nickname I use for Edward.

When I open the bag and pull out the cardigan I don't cry as

I'd thought I would. I hold it to my face and smell it. I feel in the pockets. There is a tag in one that reminds me we bought it for Billie at the Cambridge Folk Festival. In the pocket on the other side there's a little screwed-up tissue. I hold that to my nose as well. Heather looks across the kitchen at me. Her cheeks are wet and her eyes are brimming. She doesn't say anything and I don't say anything back. I walk to her and she to me, and we hold the cardigan between our bodies while we have a hug. Later, Heather takes the cardigan and hangs it on the bedpost in the room that was Billie's bedroom. I throw the torn brown-paper evidence bag into our waste-paper recycling bin.

When Edward comes home from school he gives me a kiss on the side of my hair, catches me in the eye with the zip of his coat and says, 'Have you had a nice birthday, Dad?' I tell him I've had a lovely birthday and that my head has been full of memories. He looks me up and down and says, 'Can you remember when we leaned on that wall at Whitby and Billie saw a kingfisher?' I want to ask him how he came to remember that, but before I can he's running upstairs to get changed so that he can play in Joseph's back garden and talk about the latest episode of *Family Guy*. He has moved from Homer Simpson to Peter Griffin.

Edward is a happy boy. He loves jokes and telling stories. He laughs a lot. Not long after Billie's funeral he asked me if I thought he would die while he was still a boy. Very matter-of-fact, straight out with it. I told him he wouldn't. That he would probably have a long life and that he might even get some of Billie's years added on to his. He seemed pleased with that.

We walk down from the Whitby Folk Festival campsite to the Whitby Fisherman's Rowing Club. It's the Sunday morning of the first weekend of the festival. In the rowing club, children of all ages will play jigs and reels, and we've been invited to watch. On the way there we rest by a wall that overlooks a stream that empties into Whitby harbour. Billie asks me to lift her up because she can't see properly. As I do so, she says, 'Look at that, Daddy. What is it?'

The blue-and-orange plumage of a kingfisher zips past flying upstream.

'It's a kingfisher, darling.'

Edward wants me to lift him up now. 'Let me see it, let me see it!'

'Wowee, Daddy,' Billie continues, 'a kingfisher!'

Edward can't wait to be lifted up and tries to jump on to the wall. He bangs his chin and falls down.

'It's gone now, Edward,' shouts Billie. 'And, besides, it was my kingfisher. You'll have to get your own.'

All the way down the hill Billie wants me to tell her about kingfishers so I dredge up from memory everything I read in my *Observer's Book of Birds*. 'The kingfisher lives near rivers and makes its nest in holes in the riverbank. It lays its eggs in a nest made out of old fish bones.'

'Wowee, Daddy, imagine that. I bet it was a bit smelly.'

'In the olden days people called the kingfisher the halcyon bird, because they thought it could calm down the wind and the sea, and that it could even make its nest on the sea because in those times everything was peaceful and serene and lovely.'

'Wowee! I wish I could be a halcyon bird and rest on the sea!'

When I think about Billie under the water I try not to think about her being trapped. I think of her as a mermaid. She's swimming to a little fairy grotto full of coloured shells and stones. It's a way of trying to let go without letting go.

The missing is the hardest part of all. For months after Billie drowned I had these nightmares in which I was thrashing about in the river trying to change the end of the story. I would wake up wet through. The nightmares have nearly stopped but the missing carries on.

I sat in my friend Sandra Hutchinson's car one day in a

car park in Wakefield. Rain was teeming down so we waited and talked. I told her about my nightmares and the missing. She told me that after her parents and brother died she found it helped her if she placed them somewhere when she thought about them, so when they came into her mind they were in a place called Nida. This is the southernmost village on the Lithuanian side of the Curonian spit, a massive strip of sand in the Baltic Sea. 'Whenever I think of my parents and brother, I think of them in Nida,' she said, and I could see they were in her mind right then.

I made a television programme at a place called the Bar Convent in York. It's Britain's oldest lived-in convent. In the couple of days I spent there I made friends with a ninety-five-year-old nun called Sister Gregory Kirkus. She was fabulous. She was the convent's archivist and librarian, she had a right old glint in her eye and she did the lottery in secret every Saturday, trying to win the fortune that she knew would secure a future for the place she had been connected with for more than sixty years. She was a brilliant educator and a great thinker. I sat in the library with her, surrounded by antique books, and she told me about her life.

'I went up to Cambridge in the 1920s.' It was the first and only time anyone had ever told me that they had gone 'up to Cambridge'. In those days women at Newnham College were still obliged to wear a hat to lectures. She told me about the years she spent as a headteacher and how, long after the age when most people retire, she had set up the library at Bar Convent. Then she started to take down books that were beautifully bound in kid leather, some of them more than four hundred years old. She told me I should hold them to feel the history, then asked me to read from them to her as her eyes were fading. I muttered something about expecting to have to wear white gloves.

'Oh, no no no!' she said. 'A little grease from your hands is good for the leather.'

Later she showed me the most important relic in the convent's chapel. It was the tiny preserved hand of St Margaret Clitherow, a York martyr, who had been pressed to death under a door that was piled up with stones. One of her supporters cut off her hand before the authorities had taken her body away. Margaret Clitherow was a relative of some of the gunpowder plotters – Guy Fawkes was a York man.

Sister Gregory stayed in my mind, though I never saw her again after the filming. Her colleagues told me she was delighted with the little documentary we made with her.

She died not long after Billie, on the feast day of St Margaret Clitherow. I phoned her colleague, Sister Mary, at the convent to offer my condolences. Sister Mary told me that in the last months of her life Sister Gregory had said many prayers for our family and talked and thought about me often. I resolutely refuse religion, but I was deeply moved by this. I often think about Billie in the same moment as Sister Gregory – I don't know why. Neither Billie nor I would have had anything in common with her: our backgrounds, beliefs and faith couldn't be further apart. Yet for a few minutes in an ancient library I saw Billie in Sister Gregory. Those ancient hands that lovingly handled the books, the little girl's laugh, the humanity.

At first after Billie's death I lay on the settee crying a lot. Then one morning I listened to an old ballad 'The Unquiet Grave'. It's a song that's been done by everybody from Shirley Collins to Kate Rusby. It deals with mourning a loved one and warns not to shed excessive tears as this will impede their journey onward. The story exists in many forms and in many parts of the world. In the Grimms' tales a dead boy appears to his mother and begs her not to weep any more because he can't rest in a wet shirt. In another saga the tears turn to blood, and in some Indian versions, they burn the dead. In her sleeve notes to *The Power of the True Love Knot* album, on which her version of 'The Unquiet Grave' appears, Shirley Collins tells us there is an ancient belief that mourning can drain life from the living and swell the river Styx so much with tears that it becomes impassable. The dead can only return then as ghosts to tell their loved ones to stop crying.

I am damned by my ability to remember everything – whole conversations, entire scenarios. It drives me mad. Heather remembers things in shapes and colours. She remembers smells, certain clothes and furniture. I recall the words, the looks on faces, body language, even what was playing on the radio or jukebox at the time. It hurts.

I went to visit Billie's bench today. It's a hard wood seat, wide enough for six junior-school bottoms. It's anchored into a flagged area in front of year five's classroom facing out on to the tarmacked playground at All Saints School. This was where Billie played ball with the Bethanys, the Olivias, the Chantelles and Alishas. It was where she sang her school playground rhymes and ditties.

> Cauliflowers fluffy and cabbages green,
> Strawberries sweeter than any I've seen,
> Beetroot purple and onions white,
> All grow steadily day and night.
> The apples are green, the plums are red,
> Broad beans are sleeping in a blankety bed.
>
> My boyfriend gave me an apple,
> My boyfriend gave me a pear,
> My boyfriend gave me a kiss on the cheek,
> And threw me down the stair.
> So I knocked him down in Italy,
> I knocked him down in France,
> I flung him over Blackpool Tower,
> And he lost his underpants.
> I made him wash the dishes,

I made him wash the floor,
I made him wash the baby's bottom in 1994.

The bench is wet and I wonder if I should sit down on it or not. What am I thinking? What's a wet arse at this moment in time? I sit down under my umbrella. I look round to see if anybody's listening and I start to sing.

We four Beatles of Liverpool are,
Paul on a bicycle, John in a car,
George on a scooter pipping his hooter,
Following Ringo Starr.

Billie is dancing with Edward on the grass forty yards away. They sing back to me.

Teacher, teacher, I declare
I can see your underwear.
Is it black or is it white?
Oh, my word! It's dynamite!
Kick the table, kick the chair,
Kick the teacher down the stair.
Five . . . four . . . three . . . two . . . One!
Now I've gone!

A few days into the new school term after the Easter break Heather brought home the contents of Billie's desk. On top of the pile was a painting. It showed mountains, a river with a right-hand bend and the word 'Rapids' repeated five or six times.

The locals in the pub up the road clubbed together in the days after Billie's funeral to buy this bench. There's a little *faux*-brass plaque on it that says 'Billie's Bench' in a typeface you see in Walt Disney movies. At the time I had mixed feelings about accepting it because I had been on a bit of a downer about the pub. Some people who had joined the British National Party had infested the tap room. I knew one of them very well – I'd even been to the Bradford Mela, or festival, with him and we'd tried various curries on a sunny afternoon and watched Fun-Da-Mental power their way through a really aggressive set of red-hot dub. But after a nasty evening of heated arguments in the pub I declared I would never go in there again and I still haven't.

My friend Max Morley, who went to see Bob Dylan at Blackbushe with me in 1978, tells me whenever he sees me that I'm cutting off my nose to spite my face. I know I am. He says, 'Tha's depriving decent people of thi company.' I saw him helping his blind sister-in-law home after a family christening party there and in beer he told me, 'Tha's a tosser.' It hurt. Because it was true. Sometimes my principles make me into a tosser. Two weeks after that I got a call on my mobile from my friend Jess Gardham, a York singer-songwriter. She said, 'I'm about to start playing in the garden at the pub near you. Are you at home?' I told her I was, but that I couldn't come to the gig because I'd barred myself from the pub. When she asked why I was embarrassed to tell her that it was because some BNP people went there. Jess is black. She said, 'Well, why have they asked me to play there?'

'I don't know. Though I know it's not that there's anything wrong with the pub itself. It's a great pub and the new landlord is a lovely man. I talk to him when I walk my dog down the fields.'

'Well, I'm playing in the garden so you won't have to go into the pub.'

This tosser who cuts off his nose to spite his face went to the garden and enjoyed it. I shook hands with five or six people I hadn't seen for a long time and bumped into Jess's aunt, who said she'd send me some photos of Billie playing on a round-about that she'd taken at a folk festival when the kids were five. Jess sang her song 'Ocean Eyes'.

Ocean eyes your mystery defeats me
In the depth of your kingdom white horses ride the waves
Ocean eyes you navigate my feelings and you calm my
   monsoon mind
Ocean eyes I'll float on your forever
And your current will carry me along

Then she sang me her version of the Black Eyed Peas' hit 'Where Is The Love?'. She knows I love her interpretation of that song. I'm glad now that I went.

The damp on the bench is striking right through me. I stand and walk round the building to the office. The school secretary has a book to give me. Mrs Crofts, the headteacher when Billie and Edward were here, has retired now and wants me to have it. It is the remembrance book that parents and schoolfriends signed in the days after the Easter break when Edward returned to school without his sister.

Olivia has written that Billie's teeth were like individual diamonds. Shane has written that he will never forget Billie's smile and that he admired her for never giving in. Kyron put, 'Billie helped me with my schoolwork when I was struggling. I will miss and remember her. Love from (class friend)'. Some parents wrote about Billie's beautiful blue eyes and silky hair. A teacher said that our loss was an asset to heaven.

On top of Edward's piano there is a class photograph taken in 2005. Billie is in the second row of four, sitting on a long gym bench behind Edward. Her hair is tied back in the French plait that only Heather could do. Her red and white tie is slightly skew-whiff. She is showing her diamond teeth, and her eyes twinkle. I try to imagine, when I see the other girls coming home from big school blowing bubble gum and texting on their mobile phones, what Billie might have looked like now. She'd been looking forward to going to St Wilfrid's. Every time I took her there for after-school swimming lessons, she peered through the canteen window to see what was on the lunchtime vegetarian menu. She once told me that they had Mexican vegetarian dinners at St Wilfrid's.

I walk once more into the school playground. In my mind's eye Billie is skipping round and round. She is singing again.

> See, see my playmates
> Come out and play with me
> Under the apple tree.
> Slide down a drainpipe
> Into a pot of gold.
> They will be best friends for ever more.
> More! More! Shut that door.
> This is the end of chapter four.

6. A tailgate ripper at Sharlston Pit

'Don't ever let owt get you down!' That was one of my grandad's favourite sayings. He said it a lot. He said it when I dropped and smashed a jam-jar full of tadpoles in our backs when I was about seven. He said it when I told him I'd failed my eleven-plus at George Street School, and when I came home with a badly broken nose after I got headbutted in an amateur rugby league match at a pit village called Upton. He said it to my gran time and time again when he came home from Sharlston Pit with hardly any wage to give her because he'd stopped at the bookie's on the way home and got skint. He said it when we thought there was nothing to eat during a strike, then produced half a stone of fresh fish wrapped in newspaper and laughed his baritone laugh. He'd been given the fish by some students while he was picketing at the gates of Sculcoates Power Station in Hull.

He probably said it to me the night he died in Pontefract General Infirmary, but I can't remember. I was so shocked by his frail appearance that night that I remember hardly anything. My grandad was unusual for a coal-miner in his day: they were mostly short, stocky men with powerful upper-body and arm strength. My grandad was tall, over six feet, slim and lean but with huge, poker-fingered hands and a chin full of bristles like iron filings. I hadn't seen him for nearly a fortnight until that evening in the hospital. I went with Heather, and it hurts me to admit it now but we nearly walked past his bed. 'That's not your grandad,' Heather whispered.

In many ways she was right. This wasn't the grandad I knew, but an emaciated old man, croaking and gasping his last few breaths, coughing up years of dust and Woodbine smoke into a pot beaker at his bedside table. In his younger years he had been a champion sprinter over a hundred and two hundred yards, a light–heavyweight boxer who had won the title on the troop ship that carried him out to El Alamein. He was a tailgate ripper at Sharlston Pit. They were the men who removed rock above the coal seam and set rings to support the roof as the face advanced. He devoured what he called ''oss work', then supped his pints and bet his wages and got up at a quarter past four every morning to do it all over again.

On that night when Heather and I visited him he could barely speak. He kept moving his head from side to side on the propped-up pillows and asking for my gran. 'She's having a night off from visiting, Grandad. She's exhausted. It's getting too much for her to come twice a day on the bus.'

The nurse had left a dish of bright pink blancmange with a little teaspoon next to it. He hadn't touched it.

When they rang the bell for the end of visiting time I leaned over to whisper that we'd come again tomorrow. He touched my arm ever so gently. It was a shock. My grandad never touched anything gently, except my gran, and once I'd seen him cradle a pigeon with a broken wing. I told him I loved him. I'd never said that to him before – nobody told Ted Fletcher they loved him, except my gran.

We came to my gran's house. She was eager to know if he seemed any better. I lied to her and said he was looking a lot brighter and mentioned that I thought he might even be home in time for Christmas. We stayed for a couple of hours, drinking Bournvita and eating home-made scones. As we were putting our coats on to leave, the living-room light bulb popped. My gran said, 'Leave it, I'll see to it in the morning.'

I said, 'Don't be silly. Let me get the stepladder and I'll change it now.' I went into the cupboard under the sink. She had above a dozen bulbs stacked neatly next to bar upon bar of Fairy soap, wash leathers and dishcloths. It was siege mentality, developed through years of strikes, no work and gambled-away wages. Just as I was changing the bulb, the doorbell rang. Heather answered the door to two local bobbies.

'I'm sorry, Mrs Fletcher, the hospital have sent us to let you know that your husband Edward passed away about ten past nine.'

My gran dropped down on to the settee. She keened and wailed.

At the time, Heather was working in a factory and had to be up early so she went home to bed and I stayed until my gran said she wanted to sleep. We talked about holidays in Blackpool and the times they had seen Frank Randle on the pier and Charlie Cairoli at the circus. She told me how once, during the war, Grandad had visited her at home. He was riding a motorbike and guiding a convoy of lorries from Scotland down to Stow-on-the-Wold in Gloucestershire, and one of their designated stops was at a pub called the Crofton Cock, near Wakefield, only about four miles from my gran's house. My grandad waved the convoy through, then made a detour to Mafeking Street. Gran said she heard the motorbike coming while she was pegging out some washing and said, 'I wondered what the bloody hell it was. When he came round the corner I was flabbergasted.'

Some time after that she learned that my grandad was in a barracks near Chester, about to embark for Egypt, and decided to pay him a visit. The furthest she'd ever been from home before was to her aunt's farm near York. She took a train to Manchester and arrived just as the air-raid sirens were wailing. In the shelter, she found herself next to two young school teachers, a married couple about the same age as herself. When the all-clear sounded the teachers invited her to stay the night at their house and gave her supper. She told me the sheets she slept between were the most spotlessly clean white sheets she had ever known. The following morning she made it to the barracks. 'I thought it might be the last time I ever saw thi grandad.'

More than forty years after this, I met an old man in the tap room of the Railway pub in Featherstone. He had come back from Pontefract races skint. He was nursing half a pint of beer and said, 'Buy a drink for an old soldier, young 'un.' I liked his way and bought him a pint when I got my own.

'Were you really a soldier, then?'

'King and country, young man, king and country.'

'In the war, eh?'

'Yes, lad, Royal Army Service Corps – El Alamein, Qattara depression, Italy, I saw some stuff.'

I told him my grandad was in the Royal Army Service Corps and that his name was Ted Fletcher. 'I don't suppose you knew him?'

'Knew him? Knew him? He was one of my buddies! Lived up Mafeking Street. His wife was a beautiful girl – Hilda, they called her.'

'Yes, that's my gran and grandad.'

'Well, bugger me, it's a small world! Do you know, your gran came all the way to Chester during the blackout to see him? I was on duty at the gate when she asked for him. I had to tell her to wait while I fetched him – he was confined to barracks for being pissed up and fighting.'

I never told my gran that story.

My grandad survived the war to go back down the pit. He worked there for another thirty-odd years and became a firebrand socialist who disliked lazy people and bosses with equal venom.

I spoke to Mick Appleyard who had been the union delegate at my grandad's pit at the time it was closed down. Although my grandad would have been an old man ready for his retirement when Mick was still an up-and-coming union activist, Mick remembered him well as somebody the men looked up to.

'Now let me tell thee something about thi grandad, Ian. I don't think that man ever told a lie in his life. He was straight as a die. He was stubborn, yes, and awkward, yes, because he was wage militant. If anybody tried to take a penny off him that he thought he'd earned he'd be up in the bloody air. But he was a damned good worker and he thought that if somebody said yes they should mean yes and bloody no should mean bloody no. People like thi grandad,' said Mick, 'are what is known as the salt of the earth. They might have lived in back-to-back houses, but when they told anybody anything they told them face to face.'

Mick remembered when my grandad instigated a downing of tools over a dispute about carrying explosive powder. 'He was bloody adamant. He said that they had enough to carry without bags of powder.'

The powder was put into bags that had been fashioned out of old conveyor belting by a saddler. The bags were heavy, especially if you had to carry them a mile before you got to your work. On this day my grandad must have been 'that way out' and stubbornly refused to pick the bags up. None of the other lads dared defy him so they joined him in the stand-off. Mick reminisced: 'We were nowt but bloody pack mules. You might have boring bits, picks or shovels, an oil lamp on your belt, and then they wanted us to carry powder as well.'

I told Mick a story that my grandad liked to tell, about the time he was called into the under-manager's office to explain why he had insulted a fellow worker by telling him he wasn't a man. Both my grandad and the man he had belittled were called in.

The under-manager said, 'Is it true, Ted, you said he's not a man?'

'Yes.'

'What? He's not a man?'

'Yes, he's not a man.'

'Well, what is he, then?'

'I don't know, but he's not a bloody man.'

The other man never spoke, just stood there.

'Right, then. I want you to tell him he is a man and let's have done with this.'

'Look, I'm telling thee that this bloody thing here is not a man in my eye and nowt tha says will make me say he is one.'

'Then I have no alternative than to stop your lamp until you see sense.'

Stopping a miner's lamp was a serious matter. It meant my grandad could not go down the pit and therefore not earn. He still wouldn't give way.

'He is not a man and thy ought to be ashamed of thiself for defending him.' My grandad jabbed his finger at the manager.

The manager swiped away my grandad's hand. 'Don't you dare point your bloody finger at me!'

My grandad's lamp was stopped that day, the following day and the day after that. Each day my grandad and the other man were called into the office; each time he was asked to back down; each time he wouldn't give in. My gran was beside herself with worry, when every day my grandad came home spitting and cursing. She begged him to give in. Told him he'd made his point. Even told him to apologize and keep his fingers crossed behind his back at the same time. My grandad would not budge an inch.

On the Friday the under-manager called him in again. 'Right, then,' said the boss. 'I've come to a decision. I've decided that you're not to talk to one another and you, Ted, are not to say he isn't a man ever again. If you agree to that your lamp is back on.'

My grandad nodded. The other man walked out of the office. My grandad made to turn to collect his lamp. As he got to the door the under-manager called him back. 'But, after all, he is a man, isn't he?'

My grandad shook his head and made his way to the lamp room.

'That's thi grandad all over,' Mick Appleyard said. 'By hell, he was a stubborn bugger! Him and Horace Hill and a little stocky bloke called Lou Marsh always worked together.

They were always tailgate rippers or centre-gate rippers. They breathed some bloody muck and dust in, them lads.'

Mick then asked me if we'd had my grandad examined for dust when he died. 'He must have been full of it.' I told him that my gran didn't want him cut open. Even the thought of a big compensation payout couldn't bring her to have a post-mortem. I remembered that Dr Islam had said each time he visited and saw my grandad coughing that he ought to be compensated, but even then he was stubborn. 'I don't want any bugger cutting my insides, not even when I'm dead.' What he would have made of the compensation people get for industrial deafness and vibration white finger I wouldn't like to guess.

I often think about my grandad. I loved him and have taken great inspiration from him throughout my life. But one thing I've never been able to square is the idea of him wasting his money on gambling. Why would someone work like a horse all week down a hole, then gamble his hard-earned wage on cards, dominoes and horses that never won? I asked Mick about this.

'He liked a few pints in the Kibble before he went home.' The Kibble was the Sharlston Colliery Miners Welfare Club. It was so called because 'kibble' is the name for a small wooden tub used underground, and when it was first built someone said, 'It's no bigger than a kibble.' 'Aye, he liked a few pints and a game of crash. It was just something that was in him. Some blokes round here liked gambling that much they'd bet on two flies going up a wall.' Mick made no attempt either to understand or to justify it: it was just the way it was.

He went to a drawer and pulled out some ancient maps of underground workings. Geological surveys, seams with wonderful names like Silkstone, Beeston, Flockton, Kent and Haigh Moor. He sighed. 'I can dream about how it all was, Ian. It's gone now. The whole culture of the British working class has altered. For every job in a pit there were at least three more in other industries. There was that feeling of being together.

An injury to one was an injury to all. Common interests, dreams and aspirations.' He talked about 'Bull Week' when miners worked like mad to earn as much as they could for their holidays. Then the whole town would decamp to Blackpool for a fortnight. You'd bump into people on the pier whom you worked alongside during the rest of the year. Seaside landladies welcomed back men and their wives who might have stayed in the same digs for more than thirty years.

My gran and grandad always stayed with Mr and Mrs Calloway in a boarding-house at the back of Blackpool Tower. They took their own sheets and spent many happy hours watching the laughing man at the entrance to the Pleasure Beach.

'Do you know why they called it Bull Week, Ian? It was from the days when they took the bull to market and everybody had a good time off the money they got for it.'

I asked Mick about his regrets for what happened to the coal-mining industry.

'I've been through this in my mind so many times. We should have known it was coming. When working people started coming to Kellingley Pit in the 1960s from Fife and getting off the trains with their picks and shovels, we knew it then. Mick McGahey [the leader of the Scottish miners union] once said he had seen with his own eyes the destruction of the Fife coalfield. "At least in England," he said, "if a child has nothing he can rely on his family to give him something. In Scotland you can't do that because nobody has anything, and I'll tell you now, it's creeping down. And it's not about closing pits, it's about closing workforces, closing towns and villages, closing people, if you like."'

I mentioned to Mick something that stayed with me about my grandad. During the big strike Thatcher came on television and said, 'In the Falklands we were forced to fight the enemy without and today we fight the enemy within.' My grandad was disgusted and hurt by that. He had fought in the desert for his country and mined coal for near on fifty years. I remembered him telling me that when Churchill died he wanted to have a street party to celebrate. My grandad, like a lot of coal-miners, despised Churchill. In turn, my gran despised Lady Astor, the first woman MP, who, she said, once wanted to know if miners came up from underground every day. When Margaret Thatcher dies, I shall have my own street party on my grandparents' behalf and, in the words of Elvis Costello, 'Tramp the dirt down'.

7. Crumbs of comfort

There's a bloke in our local called Peter. He's a well-spoken, intelligent man, who read history at St David's College, Lampeter University, probably the only man from round here who ever went there. Peter is always on a mission. Since he retired from his job marking exam papers, he has made it his business to help people. He fetches the landlord's paper every morning, walks people's dogs when they're on holiday, brings malt whisky for an elderly neighbour. He's constantly backwards and forwards to town bringing shopping, putting money in Post Office savings accounts. He's a scribe too. If any of the older end need a letter writing to the council, it's Peter who pens it, the prose always elegant. You never spend long in Peter's company: he'll down a pint, exchange pleasantries and then he's off. He never speaks to me about Billie – I believe he finds it too painful.

Not long after she died, I stood in his company at the end of the bar. He took out a snuff tin. 'Have a pinch, Ian.'

I told him that if I did I'd sneeze. I always do with snuff.

'That's good. Clear the passages!'

'What is it? Rumney's?' Actually, Rumney's is one of the few snuff brands I know, mainly because Phil Paver and the lads at Ackton Hall pit used to tease a man called Sammy Gascoigne by singing a parody of Jeff Beck's song 'Hi Ho Silver Lining'. They sang 'Hi ho Sammy Gascoigne, everywhere we go, we see his snuff tin shining, but we don't make a fuss, because it's Rumney's plus'.

Peter said, 'It's a special snuff, Wilsons of Sharrow, Crumbs of Comfort.' He smiles and sets off on another mission, Aldi and Netto's busiest customer.

*

When you lose a child it's like you're a sky on a clear night. Full of twinkling fragments that seem to be close together but are really millions of miles apart. You're salt spilled on a tablecloth, scattered grains, once contained, now all over the place. How do you start to piece all this back together? It's like that Tom Waits song, 'Tom Traubert's Blues', when he says, 'No one speaks English and everything's broken'. The character in that song has, through alcoholism and travelling back alleys, come to a place that he doesn't know, a foreign country. I feel like that. I have become a refugee, an asylum seeker in a land I don't know. I want to pull around me things that are familiar. I start with the duvet and the patchwork quilt on our bed, but I've never been one for lying in bed longer than I need to sleep. And I don't want to sleep. Sleep only brings nightmares and sweating.

I bump into a former soldier, a lad I knew years ago and haven't seen for ages. He's walking through the outdoor market at Castleford, lost in his thoughts. I tap him on the arm and say, 'Hey up!' He looks at me and doesn't know what to say so he tells me he's been on a trip to the Caribbean. This soldier lost close friends on the yomp to Port Stanley and later in a horrific car crash on a night out with the lads. He's had his own nightmares. After two or three minutes he says, almost under his breath, 'I'm sorry to hear about thi loss.' I say something about having to stay strong and trying to do what's right for Heather and Edward. He tells me about his fears of going to bed at night.

I try lying on the settee and crying. I try going to the pub. One Friday afternoon in the Shoulder of Mutton there's just me, Robbo, Dave the landlord and Martin Oxley. We talk about the decline of the English pub tap room, the smoking ban, the influx of Polish workers, and then Billie. Dave remembers her once cheekily remarking that he looked like an 'egghead' after his barber had gone a bit too close. Martin tells of how he'd once lifted her on to his shoulders to get a better look at a Romanian gypsy band called Taraf de Haïdouks when we danced wildly to the violins. I start to cry, not the gentle weeping I do on my settee, but out loud, the sort you never do in front of beer-swilling big blokes in an old tap room. Dave wells up too, and walks off to the best room to polish his glasses. Robbo puts his head down and sighs, whispering, 'Dear oh dear.' Martin Oxley puts his arm round my shoulders and squeezes me towards him. I end up with the side of my face pressed into his beery beard. 'We're with you, lad,' he says. 'We're all with you.' He shouts Dave back into the tap room. 'Fill these three pots, Dave, and get thiself one.'

Dave pumps pints of Batemans XXXB into the glasses, then says, 'Can tha remember during t'strike, Martin, when I dropped on thee at the bus stop?' He opens up the tale he's told a hundred times to the rest of us.

'It was six months into t'strike. I dropped on Martin at a bus stop near Stan Brookbank's garage. I asked him where he was going. He said, "Anywhere." I said, "Where's yer dog?" He said, "I've walked its legs off." I told him to get in the car at the side of me and he came and helped me to rewire my boat. Tha'd steak for thi tea that night, didn't tha, Martin?'

Martin nodded and smiled. There wasn't much steak for tea during the miners' strike. Plenty of liver and stuff in tins that were sent over to the soup kitchen from Russia.

After the patchwork quilt and the pub I find comfort in the kindness of friends and neighbours and people I only know by their faces. Perhaps I know their uncles or brothers, but I don't always know their names. People pick me up and offer me lifts when they see me standing at a bus stop. Lesley and Angela, whom I worked with at Yorkshire Art Circus, offered to come and help us with the housework in case we didn't feel like facing the ironing. Les Bowkett stopped me while I was walking the dog and told me he'd got some little wallflowers he'd like to put on Billie's grave.

Steve Huison, a mate who works as an actor, phoned out of

the blue and asked me how Edward was getting on with his piano.

'He's fine. He practises for half an hour every day – he'll be as good as Jools Holland by the time he's fifteen.'

Steve mentioned he'd a little project in mind for Edward to get his teeth into. It turned out that, by a convoluted route, he had in his kitchen drawer a harmonica that had once belonged to John Lennon. It'd been there doing nothing for more than twenty years. He wanted to give it to Edward. I thought he might want to get in touch with Julian Lennon and give it back. Steve's cousin had been at Ruthin College in Wales with Lennon's son by Cynthia, his first wife. At that time in the late 1970s Julian had cut a bit of a lonely figure and become friends with Steve's cousin. According to Steve, Julian had all sorts of bits and bobs that had once belonged to his dad. He'd given Steve's cousin the harmonica and now Steve wanted to pass it on to Edward.

'He can do what he wants with it. He can keep it, or if he fancies trying to track down Julian Lennon he can give it back.'

One Sunday morning Steve drove over to our house. I made some coffee, and while we sat at the table sipping it, he reached into his pocket and took out a little brown-and-gold silken bag with a drawstring top.

'That might be one of Yoko's, y'know, Edward,' I joked.

'No, it's just a bag I've put it into,' said Steve. He took out a battered Hohner Blues Harp in the key of E. I couldn't wait to touch it. I put it to my lips and played a very wonky intro to 'Love Me Do'. Edward took it off me and tapped it on his knee. He turned it over and over in his fingers but didn't attempt to blow it. When he thought we weren't looking he slipped it back into its bag, carried it over to his piano and placed it on the top in front of a photo of Billie in year four.

'What do they call John Lennon's son, Dad?'

'Julian.'

'I might try and write a letter to him when I'm a bit older.'

After Steve had left, Edward said, 'Is he a proper actor, him, Dad?'

'Of course he is. He was once in a film with me.'

'What was it called?'

'*Prometheus.*'

'What's that about?'

'Oooh! It's about all sorts. It's about what happened after the miners' strike. It's about the Greek gods and the destruction of industry.'

'I bet that's a bloody laugh! What do you do in it?'

'I get melted down in a factory and made into a statue. Would you like to see it?'

'Maybe when I'm older.'

A few months later Edward was flicking through the TV channels. He stopped on a scene from *The Full Monty*, the one in which the red-haired stripper has decided to commit suicide by putting a pipe from his exhaust into his car. Edward laid the remote on the coffee-table, looked across at me and said, 'That's him who gave me John Lennon's harmonica!'

Steve plays Eddie Windass in *Coronation Street* now. Edward is reminded of John Lennon's harmonica nearly every weeknight.

I find comfort in building a nest of books, CDs and DVDs. I have become almost addicted to Amazon and Abe Books and HMV Guernsey, to a CD warehouse somewhere in California called CD Connection, to a left-wing bookshop in Sydney. I make nightly searches of the Internet with my credit card ready to buy books that I never get round to reading, CDs that I leave the cellophane on, DVDs I've yet to watch. Wayne, our postman, knocks every morning on our door with armfuls of little cardboard boxes and Jiffy-bags. Heather's fed up, she says, of piles of stuff all over the house that gather dust. Piles of CDs, DVDs and old books. Piles of ironing and washing. Piles of unread newspapers and magazines. Piles of games and toys that I buy for Edward and he plays with once. And dust. Dust that occasionally gets flicked from one corner of a room to another.

Heather and I both find comfort in the bottle. We rarely drank alcohol in the house before Billie died unless it was a party. The occasional bottle of wine with a nice meal. Home-made sloe gin and Advocaat snowballs at Christmas because that was what our parents and grandparents had done. Now we drink every night. We criticize each other for drinking and smoking too much, then we drink some more and roll our Drum roll-ups. I only realized how much we were drinking when the council delivered green recycling boxes for glass and plastic. When I took it down to the yard on bin day I noticed there were as many beer and spirit bottles as there were milk cartons.

'At least it's good-quality beer!' Heather reckons – Duvel, Hoegaarden and Leffe from Belgium. Warsteiner and Düsseldorf Alt from Germany. Staropramen from Prague and Sierra Nevada Pale from America. An international beer festival on our settee while we're watching Louis Malle films. Then it's Laphroaig and Ardbeg before bed or Miki Salkic's homemade raki sent over from Bosnia.

I first came across the story of Miki Salkic when I took Edward for his piano lesson. Edward has had piano lessons since the age of four. In the autumn of 2005 there was a bit of a to-do in the *Pontefract and Castleford Express* about an asylum-seeking family from Bosnia who were living in a council house on the Willow Park estate in Pontefract. On the counter in the music shop there was a photocopied article from the paper about the plight of Miki Salkic, his wife Alma and their teenage daughter Tina. Eileen and Darryl, who run the music shop and school, were trying to drum up support for Miki and his family and their attempts to start a new life in Yorkshire. Eileen told me she thought Miki was a lovely man. 'He comes in to buy strings for his acoustic guitar.' She wondered if I might be able to help in any way. I said I'd have a think. At the time my mate Jane Hickson and I were drawing up a list of people we hoped to feature in a new series of the documentary I presented for ITV Yorkshire, a programme called *My Yorkshire*. The idea of the series was that we would build up a patchwork collage of the region using the varied voices and stories of people living there. In the past we had featured the former Archbishop of York, who took us to Flamborough, his favourite place on the coast because it reminded him of his childhood trips. We did a programme with Lord Lofthouse, a former coal-miner who campaigned tirelessly on behalf of miners with respiratory illnesses, and another with Ian Charles, the Trinidadian who founded the Chapeltown Carnival in Leeds. I talked to Jane about looking at Yorkshire through the eyes of an asylum seeker. She liked the idea and we arranged to meet Miki and his family.

We arrive at the Willow Park estate one Wednesday evening, knock on the door and listen to bolts being slid back. Miki greets us with a firm handshake and a big smile. He's an imposing figure, tall, raw-boned and athletic. He told us later that he'd once played as a centre-half for the Yugoslavian under-21 football team in the days of Tito. The house is sparsely furnished with a steel-framed settee on loan from the council, a portable telly that's on too loud and a small coffee-table on which are placed ashtrays and little glasses of homemade slivovictz. Miki likes to chain-smoke and asks us if we mind. He nods an acknowledgement to his daughter when she tuts, and says, 'I have made promise to my Tina that when these problems are over I will stop to smoking.' He speaks in a thick Eastern European accent and apologizes for his lack of English. 'I try every Tuesday and Thursday to learn English at St Mary's community centre.'

I ask him to tell the story of how he and his family come to be living on the edge of a council estate in Pontefract.

'First thing, before talking, we will eat. Alma, please bring food.'

His wife appears from the kitchen and shyly shakes our hands. She is beautiful, with black hair, and very tall. Her eyes are tired and sad; they tell stories even before she speaks. She brings platefuls of sliced meats and a warm flaked-pastry mince pie that Miki calls 'Bosnian Pie'. We eat and wash it down with thimble-sized glasses of raki. I share Miki's harsh Bosnian cigarettes.

Miki tells us that first he was in London, then 'dispersed' to Wakefield and that the local authority had found him this house in Pontefract. 'When we came here the house was not looked after. The garden was overgrown and full of rubbish.' He thinks that the previous occupants had been asylum seekers from Asia, who had been made unwelcome by some local people. 'My first job was to clear this garden.' He points through the window. He has made a rockery from all the stones he gathered, cut the grass to make a lawn and built benches and a wishing well from discarded wood. The neighbours' kids have a trampoline – I can see them bouncing high above the wishing well.

He tells me that he has tried hard to make friends with the neighbours. He points: 'A man over there was throwing out his lawnmower one day. I told him that I am an electrician and that I might be able to save him some money by mending it. He was going to Argos for a new one and the old one only had a loose wire.' The neighbour on the other side is a retired miner with breathing problems. Miki helps him with his garden and Alma cooks him the occasional dinner. 'I hope people in this neighbourhood like me now. I try to be a good neighbour.' Alma mentions that every time they go into town to do the shopping they walk the mile and a half back uphill with carrier bags biting into their fingers because Miki won't allow taxis. 'If they see asylum seekers getting out of taxi, they think I am getting more money than them.' He dashes over to a little bureau in the corner and takes out a sheaf of social-security payment slips. 'This is a record of all the money I have been paid by this country in the last four years. If I am allowed to stay here I promise I will pay all this money back!' He waves the slips. 'I mean this, will you believe me?'

I tell him that of course I believe him.

Miki and his family have made great efforts to be accepted into their adopted community. As well as lessons in English at the community centre, Alma has completed a course in child-care and Miki one in basic electrics. He hopes to find a job as an electrician, but is unable to work until his status is reviewed. Tina attends the local comprehensive school, speaks English with a strong Yorkshire accent and is one of the most popular girls in her year. There is talk of her becoming head girl when she moves into year eleven.

'Do you miss Bosnia?' I ask them.

Alma and Tina go off to the kitchen to bring even more food and Miki breathes a deep sigh. 'Bosnia is destroyed.' He mentions that back home he had built a successful business and was a high-flyer in the Chamber of Commerce in the Tuzla area. After the first Gulf War he had worked as an electrician in the power stations of Iraq, saved his money and, back in Bosnia, had bought a clothes boutique and a café.

'This was a very good café. People from all backgrounds, Muslim, Orthodox, Serbian, Croatian, came to drink coffee, raki, and play music. When civil war started who do I fight? When my customer all come from different side, do I fight them? No! I will not fight. I am humanitarian. I believe all humanity.'

Miki tells Jane and me some horrendous stories that evening about the civil war in the former Yugoslavia. About running between neighbours' houses to avoid the shrapnel thrown up by nights of shelling. About carrying terrified neighbours' children to the safety of cellars just before bombs landed. And about the inevitable corruption and collusion of local business people. He says that at one point during the height of the war he had swapped his car for a sack of flour so that Alma could bake bread.

It was surreal to sit for a couple of hours in a council house in Pontefract with a family who had seen so much horror in a European war that had taken place only a couple of hours' flying time away. When we talk in the car afterwards, Jane and I wonder whether we can do justice to a story of these proportions in fifteen minutes of regional TV.

'When did you realize you had to get out, Miki?'

'In my café one a day a drunken soldier came and told me I must hand him a bottle of whisky from the top shelf. He said he would not pay because he was a brave soldier. I told him he could not steal from me. He took out a grenade and said he would destroy the café. I don't know why I did this, but I reached out my hand and gripped the soldier's fist, the fist that held the grenade. I told him, "Pull out the pin", that if we must die now, we would all die together. The soldier hesitated. He stared at my hand and face. Then he laughed. He said, "Not today," and went out of the café.'

Miki takes out from an old wallet some photographs of happier times. Him and Alma sitting by a lake before the war, smiling. Then a photo of his father and him when he was a little boy, his foot resting on a football.

'Ian and Jane,' Miki says, and sighs again, 'I am Muslim. I am Muhammed Salkic. I believe in all peoples – my father taught me well. He was a good man, humanitarian, and he taught me to be humanitarian. He lies now in Muslim cemetery at Lukavac, my home town. One day if real peace come to Bosnia, if I not make my home in England and go back, I invite you to my home. I will show you lake where I spend good times. I show you my father grave in Muslim cemetery. One day!'

I have been in the company of Miki and his family only since about six thirty this evening and it isn't yet nine o'clock, but I feel like a close friend. I think I already know that one day

I will spend time with him by the lake above Lukavac and Tuzla.

'Ian and Jane.' Another sigh. 'I know more about John Lennon than mosque.' Miki reaches for his guitar. He plays a sad, sad song, a *sevdalinka* from Sarajevo.

We leave him and his family with their over-loud telly showing *The Bill*, and on the two-mile drive between Pontefract and Featherstone we talk about how we can make a film called *Miki Salkic's Yorkshire*.

Our boss at ITV Yorkshire called us in to discuss progress on the new series. We talked her through the list of people we thought were definites: Sister Gregory, the elderly nun in York who looked after the archive and library at Britain's oldest lived-in convent; Kate Rusby, the folk singer some know as the Barnsley Nightingale; and Hawarun Hussain, a Bangladesh-born health worker who was helping Bangladeshi women in Bradford to run an allotment project. When we got to Miki, eyebrows were firmly raised.

'How long have you known him?'

'We met him while we were researching this series.'

'So, he's a Bosnian Muslim asylum seeker, who was a conscientious objector during the civil war in Yugoslavia and is now living on a council estate in Pontefract?'

'That's it.'

'What about the people in his neighbourhood? What do they think about him?'

'He's very popular. The people at his local community centre are campaigning for him to stay. He's very well liked.'

'OK. How do you know he's not a war criminal?'

'Well ... I've thought about the possibility,' I lied, 'but I don't think he is.'

'And what makes you believe that?'

'Instinct.'

'Well, then, it's up to you. If you trust your instinct, make a programme about him, but it shouldn't be about the war in Yugoslavia. It should be about his experiences in Pontefract. And don't worry, I've got faith in your judgement.'

I came out of that meeting worried. The thought that Miki might not be who he said he was had never crossed my mind. I felt a bit naïve. I'm always one for trusting what people tell me before I know different. Jane and I discussed it and decided to go ahead. No way could Miki be a war criminal: his stories had been told from the heart – and, besides, war criminals don't sing sad songs accompanying themselves on acoustic guitar.

Miki Salkic and his family made a lovely programme with us. We set part of it at the ruins of Pontefract Castle where Miki liked to walk. Pontefract Castle has been in ruins since the English Civil War. Cromwell's cannons did some of the damage, fired from the hillside not too far from where Miki now lives. The people of Pontefract did the rest when, after the war, the cry went up, 'Down with the castle!' Even today, more than three hundred and fifty years after the English Civil War, you can find boundary walls in Pontefract gardens built from the stones of its castle.

We made another part of Miki's film in his neat garden. He spoke of how he had been attacked and beaten in his home town after the Bosnian war for refusing to fight in the military. 'They said I didn't deserve to live there.' He laid out his photographs. 'These are the only reminders I have of my former life.' He came to a crumpled black-and-white picture of his dad. 'He taught me that we are human beings, we are not animals. If we need to do battle, we should do it not with weapon but with intelligence.' Another photo shows Alma swimming in a lake with baby Tina. Alma holds her above the water like a little mermaid with inflatable wings.

We talk about their coming to Pontefract. 'People in this community have been so kind to me. I was very surprised. I came to this house – it already had a fridge and table and chairs.

All people in this neighbourhood say, "Hello," to me even before they know my name.' He then told me that on the first day Alma had cried. He had thought she was upset, but she said she cried because of all the kindness.

'Do you like living here now?'

'I have been told that people in Western countries are not friendly. In Pontefract I have found that not true. People here have helped me so much.'

Miki picked up another photo and said, 'Look at this one. This is beautiful Mina.' Mina was a little girl from a Serbian family, supposedly Miki's enemy. In one night of heavy shelling, Miki carried her and two of her friends into a car and drove them to shelter. Just as he got them out of the car, a shell landed directly on it. I said to him, 'If you were one minute later you would have all been killed.' He looked at me, still holding the photograph. 'One minute, Ian? No, fifteen seconds. We would have been killed fifteen seconds before. This is what happens in wars.'

We became close friends after the filming. Miki, Alma and Tina were delighted with the piece when it was shown on the telly just before Christmas in 2005, but in the spring of 2006 they were starting to feel uncertain that they would be allowed to stay. One night we had them over for some dinner at our house. Miki was worried that at any time a knock might come at his door and he would be told that his asylum application had failed. I asked him what he would do. 'I will invite the policemen in and make some tea and then I will have to pack my suitcase and leave. I do hope that my Tina is allowed to stay to finish her school and GCSE.' Alma dabbed away a tear. The idea of her family being separated again was too much for her to bear. There had been a point during the Bosnian conflict when the shelling had become so bad that Miki arranged for her to take Tina into hiding with relatives in Croatia. Unable to bear the separation, Alma had crossed the mountains with Tina, a babe in arms, to be back with Miki. They had sat on the balcony of their apartment to watch the bombs falling, wondering if one would fall on them next.

After dinner Tina went to play with Edward and Billie in our music room. Billie quickly established a rapport with Tina and they drew pictures of girls with plaited hair skipping among trees laden with apples. After the family had left, I picked up one of the drawings. A little girl was skipping with a rope, a typical Billie drawing, and to it Tina had added a speech bubble coming out of the little girl's mouth, saying, 'Please help me!'

Before she went to bed Billie wanted to know why Tina and her family might not be allowed to stay in England.

'Because the government has to decide who can live here and who can't.'

'But if people are kind and they've got lots of friends and they live in a nice house they should live here.'

'I know that, Billie, and you know that, but sometimes the authorities don't and they make wrong decisions about people's lives.'

'The government should look after people better, then,' said Billie, and took herself off to bed.

Billie's death deeply affected the Salkic family. They came to our house the day after we got home from Wales. Ironically they arrived about the same time as Clare Morrow, my boss at ITV who'd had faith enough in me to make a film with Miki.

Miki simply said, 'I know, Ian.' It was enough. He turned to Heather. 'I know one thing. I know you must be strong. You must be strong for you, for Ian and most for little Edward.'

He came with Alma to look at Billie lying in her coffin on the morning of the funeral. He held his index finger and middle finger together and kissed the tips, then gently placed those fingers on Billie's forehead. Under his breath he said something in his own language. I never asked him to translate for me.

The last time I saw Miki in England we sat on his homemade bench in the garden, sipping Turkish coffee and raki. Alma had a hospital check-up to attend in Wakefield and Tina was at school. We were like two old codger mates, sipping and saluting and putting our arms round each other's shoulders. 'I think the time will come soon, Ian, when I will be sent back to Bosnia.'

'What makes you say that, Miki?'

'I have a feeling. One morning soon the police will come. My kettle is ready.'

It was nearly six months since Billie's funeral. We talked about trying to put yourself back together. 'Always be strong, my friend, only be strong.' He held his big hand over his heart. 'I must always be strong after the war. I saw terrible things.' I don't know what Miki saw, only the things he has made himself tell me. I can see in his eyes that he still holds a lot in, things he'll probably never tell. 'Strength and humanity': those are the two most important things.

I told him about something that happened at the school gates on the morning I took Edward back to school after the accident. A young Hindu mother who had only ever smiled at me before came up and said, 'Good morning.' I said, 'Hello.' She told me that rivers are very important to Hindus, that they are the life force and are considered female. The Goddess Ganga rides the river on the back of a crocodile. She suggested that Billie had been taken to a spiritual place by the river.

'We have a lot to learn from other people's culture,' said Miki. 'We can do many things as people if we listen to the culture of others. In Lukavac the imam knows that even though I never go to the mosque I am still a good person.'

A few days after we'd sat on Miki's bench philosophizing and putting the world to rights, I got a phone call at eight o'clock in the morning. Miki's neighbours told me that before dawn three Black Marias with policemen in protective gear had arrived. They had smashed Miki's front door with the type of hammer they used to break into drug-dealers' houses, dragged Miki, Alma and Tina out of bed and told them to gather their things. They were first taken to a police station in Leeds and then separately to an immigration centre somewhere in Bedfordshire.

Miki phoned me the following day. He said that Tina had been almost hysterical most of the time and that Alma couldn't stop crying. They had been treated quite well and the rooms they were staying in were clean. The Bosnian Embassy official who had issued them with temporary passports had smirked at him and said, 'Don't worry, Mr Salkic. After all, you are going home.'

I told Miki that Heather, Edward and I would never forget their kindness, humanity and friendship towards us in what had been difficult times for both of our families.

'One day, my friend,' Miki said, 'we will be together again and we will sit by a lake near my home town and drink a raki together. Until that day, stay strong, and I promise that we will too.'

I put the phone back into my top pocket. I took out the dog's lead and we went for a walk down Richard Copley's path across the fields. I leaned on a gate and broke my heart.

8. Angels flying too close to the ground

Heather took three months' compassionate leave from her job at the children's home where she was now working. When she went back she found fulfilment in looking after three Kurdish teenagers who had been dropped off the back of a lorry on the A1 near Ferrybridge power station. Their parents had paid for them to flee Iraq and they had spent weeks in lorries crossing borders until, in the middle of one night, they had found themselves wandering around the car park at a Granada service station in Yorkshire. Because they were still juveniles they fell under the care of the local authority's children's services and ended up at the home where Heather works. Heather became fascinated by their manners, their culture, their dignity and the way they carried themselves. Ever since she had lost her own daughter, we had worried about how looking after other people's children would affect her. The Kurdish lads gave her a real sense of purpose and a focus.

She also decided that she wanted to paint, to channel her emotions and memories. We had bought Billie a portable easel and a set of paints the Christmas before she died. She never really got round to using them and they lay gathering dust in a corner. Heather decided that she would use them and set up the easel behind the settee. Within weeks there was paint all over the living-room floor, splashed on the back of the leather three-piece suite and half-worked-on canvases stacked against every wall. She painted most evenings in poor light when Edward and I were watching the telly. If the volume was too high it disturbed her concentration. The poor light meant she couldn't see the colours properly.

'If I'm going to treat this seriously I need a place of my own to paint in.'

'Why don't we buy a shed for the backyard then and you can paint to your heart's content in it?'

The shed came to us by a very strange route. Two people who have been dear to us since our loss have been Ken and Chris from our local record shop, I first knew of Ken around thirty years ago when he imported copies of 'Anarchy in the UK' from France to sell on his market stall at Pontefract. We became close when I took the kids to his shop every Saturday morning to buy their videos and DVDs. Ken helped Edward to collect a full set of James Bond movies while Billie selected things like *Bend It Like Beckham*, Harry Potter and *Narnia*. He loved Billie for her manners and looks. Ken played rugby league for Castleford back in the late sixties: he's a big tough guy, who cried in the street when we talked about Billie in the weeks after.

One morning a young teenage lass took a load of Sugababes and Madonna CDs to trade in at Ken's shop, plus a cardboard box full of old LPs.

'What's these in this box, then?'

'Oh! They're just some of my grandad's old records. I don't want them. Will you give me something for them?'

They were mainly Beatles and Bob Dylan albums. Ken and Chris don't sell vinyl any more, but Ken thought the covers might look nice framed up for sale as pictures so he gave the young lass a few quid for them.

I happened to be in the shop later that morning and Ken showed me the handful of LPs. 'They'll make nice pictures for bedroom walls, don't you think?'

I thumbed through the pile: *Blonde on Blonde, Sgt Pepper, The White Album, Highway 61 Revisited* and, at the bottom, *Please, Please Me*. I turned the cover over and read the back, 'Serial number PMC 1202, sleeve printed by E. J. Day, mono'. I took the record out of the sleeve. The vinyl was near mint, with its black-and-gold Parlophone label with the magic words 'Dick James Publishing'.

'Do you know what, Ken? I think you've dropped on a piece of treasure here.'

'Is it worth something?'

'If it's what I think it is, I should say so.'

'Chuffing hell, I only gave a few quid for it.'

I told him I'd take *Please, Please Me* and the others to a dealer I knew in Huddersfield. He said, 'Get what you can for them.'

Wall of Sound in Huddersfield is a serious record collector's shop. The best-condition copy of Elvis Presley's first LP I ever saw was in here. Elliot, who runs the place, looked through the cache of Beatles and Dylan records, realizing they were nearly all first pressings. I had deliberately left *Please, Please Me* at the bottom. His eyes lit up when he came to it. 'I suppose you know how much it's worth?'

I grinned.

'OK, then. Let's have a look.' He spaced the records out on the counter top, about a dozen in all. He pointed to each in turn. 'I'll give you a tenner for that, twenty for this one, I can go to thirty for that and that one, and forty for these. Now, *Please, Please Me* . . . will you take two hundred for it?'

'Nope.'

'All right, then, two fifty?'

'Nope.'

'Well, look, I want it for this shop. It'll be an important talking point as much as anything else, but I'm in business as well. I can go as far as three hundred, but that's it.'

We shook hands on that. I saw it under plastic on the wall with the rarities some weeks after for six hundred pounds and not long after it had gone.

I think Ken would have been happy with a tenner apiece for his records, but I would have felt terrible guilt if I'd done that. I phoned him and told him about our good fortune. We went halves.

A week later we went to a shed manufacturer in the shadow of Pontefract's biggest liquorice factory and ordered a custom-built shed with plenty of windows. Heather, with a grand ironic gesture, calls it her 'studio' and I call it 'The *Please, Please Me* Memorial Shed'.

For nearly eighteen months she was in it every day painting. She has created some lovely vibrant abstracts that are about rivers flowing and becoming tangled in life, living, childbirth and womanhood. They are emotional pictures, and where she gets the strength to tackle them I don't know. I'm awed by what she does.

When Heather had her first exhibition in a little gallery at Castleford, Edward and I were so proud. Our friend Brian Lewis spoke at the opening. He said he could see influences from Edward Munch and Monet to tee up a joke that reminded everybody that 'Where there's Munch there's Monet!' There won't be many artists who can sell eighteen paintings at their debut exhibition, but Heather did. The brass paid for her canvases, paints, the wine, nuts and Twiglets. It was a bit surreal watching our mates sipping Pinot Grigio and munching away at a gallery opening. I suppose we ought to have ordered a barrel of ale and some pies, but there you go.

Heather called the exhibition after a Willie Nelson song, 'Angel Flying Too Close To The Ground'.

My Heather is the most down-to-earth person I've ever known. I joke that I've known her since she sat on her front doorstep in a mucky nappy. Heather was brought up in a row of terraced houses in Halfpenny Lane, Pontefract, only a couple of miles from where I grew up. Whenever we visited our auntie Laura we walked to Pontefract down Halfpenny Lane, which links Featherstone to Pontefract. I have very early memories of walking past the terraced houses on Halfpenny Lane; I would be four, maybe even three. Families always sat at the open doors, parents and grandparents sipping beakers of tea, and dozens of grubby-faced kids with bread and jam and saggy nappies. The people who lived there all kept barking dogs and budgies in cages. I must have gone by Heather's family home at number 179 dozens of times before the rows were knocked down in the middle of the 1960s and everybody moved to the council estate at King's Mead.

I fell in love with Heather in the Blackmoor Head tap room in 1978. We met there during the winter after she'd come home from working the summer season in a posh hotel in North Devon. We listened to Sex Pistols' records on the jukebox and I pretentiously recited Persian love poetry to her in between 'Anarchy in the UK' and 'Pretty Vacant'. She wore a pink mohair jumper, which I used to make fun of, and Dr Martens boots. Heather could drink pints in pace with the lads and once won the yard-of-ale drinking competition on a bank holiday Monday. We made tap-room plans to travel the world together, to buy books of poetry, to build a huge record collection, to throw the best parties in our own apartment and one day to settle down and start a family. I felt so proud to be Heather's chap. Sometimes I couldn't believe my luck. Heather is beautiful, with lovely wide-set chocolate-coloured eyes and a heart-shaped face.

We walked barefoot in temples in India. We sat cross-legged and lit joss sticks on Oriental rugs in Haight-Ashbury in San Francisco and bought second-hand bookcases from junk shops all over Yorkshire to store our growing collection of books.

Heather had left Pontefract Girls' Secondary Modern at sixteen with a couple of CSEs. She came home from school on the Friday, packed a suitcase and, on the Saturday morning, travelled to Woolacombe in Devon to take a job at a hotel there. By Sunday lunchtime she was waiting at tables, doing silver service. She worked at the Woolacombe Bay Hotel for five consecutive summers, though she was nearly sacked during her second season when the manager objected to her blue cockatiel hairstyle. She was summoned to the office and told, in no uncertain terms, 'This hotel does not employ punk rockers.'

When we settled back in Featherstone in 1982, she took a job in a clothing factory called Gaunson's. She operated a Hoffmann press, which ironed gentlemen's trousers. She told me that from the start the manager seemed to have it in for her. I lost count of the number of times she came home upset and said, 'I can't do right for doing wrong with that man Myers.' One night, she came home and told me that if he said one more thing to her out of place, she'd be packing in.

'Then what will you do?'

She said she wanted to go to night school to get some O levels.

The following day Myers opened his mouth once too often, and Heather told him where he could stick his job. She went off to enrol at night school. She got two O levels in six months, in English and sociology. Then she started a two-year full-time course at a college in Castleford, and was awarded a diploma in Higher Education. She went on to take a degree in social policy at the University of Leeds. I promised her that wherever I was working on the day of her graduation I would come to the ceremony.

That week I was with some Scottish musicians in Buckie, five hundred miles away on the Moray Firth. I took the early flight from Aberdeen, and rushed into the hall at Leeds University just as Heather was going up to shake hands with the Duchess of Kent, who was then the Chancellor. I couldn't contain myself and shouted, 'Good old Heather Parkinson!' Everyone in the room, including the Duchess, looked round, and Heather went as red as a Tetley beer mat. I managed to spend a couple of hours with her and her mam afterwards, then dashed back to Leeds-Bradford airport for the return flight to

Aberdeen. I even made it in time for the dress rehearsal of the performance we were putting on the next night in Buckie town hall. It cost me nearly as much to make the journey as I earned that week but I wouldn't have missed it for a gold pig, I was that proud of her. Within weeks of her graduation, Heather took up a post as a residential social worker in children's homes.

I was thirty-six and Heather thirty-five when Edward and Billie were born. We'd been together for eighteen years, already longer than both our sets of parents had managed to stay married. We pegged terry nappies, two sets, to our washing line at our new family home. The spotless white nappies blowing on the line made us so proud, so full of joy. We were four. A happy family now of two boys and two girls.

9. The music that ordinary people make

In a place called Nabs Wood near Silkstone Common in South Yorkshire, Les Young is leading a project to rebuild a dry-stone wall. It forms a boundary to the wood and is over a mile long. The current wall has probably stood for more than two hundred years and is in a very poor state of repair. Les has made it his ambition to renew it and runs courses in dry-stone-wall building, teaching volunteers and would-be wallers the techniques. His team expect to complete five or six yards of wall over a weekend course, so it might take ten or even twenty years to finish the project. Les admits that he might be in his seventies or eighties when the last stone is dropped in. He's doing this work as both memorial and tribute to something that happened in those woods a hundred and seventy years ago.

Nabs Wood was the site of a small coal mine called Husker Pit, which had two entrances, a shaft and a drift. On 4 July 1838 a terrific hailstorm blew across South Yorkshire. Such was its ferocity that it put out the fire in the pit-top steam engine, which powered the winding mechanism and ventilation, trapping underground the workforce, who were mostly boys and girls. The forty-odd children, between the ages of seven and seventeen, became terrified: they had heard massive thunderclaps, which they believed were underground explosions, and rushed *en masse* to the drift to try to escape the pit. A beck running alongside the pit burst its banks and the water gushed down the drift towards the children who were making their way up the tunnel. It smashed into them and pinned them against a ventilation door. Twenty-six boys and girls drowned that day. Victorian society read about the disaster in *The Times* at their breakfast tables and was scandalized. For many it was their first knowledge that children, some no more than babies, were labouring in the bowels of the earth in appalling conditions.

Boys and girls were employed first as trappers. They sat for up to twelve hours a day with a piece of rope attached to ventilation doors. Their job was to pull open the door for the hurriers, pushing tubs, to come through. The trappers were in complete darkness for the duration of their shift. Some old coal-miners will tell you that the expression 'Not worth a candle' has its origins in these little lads and lasses who were deemed so low in the pecking order that it was wasteful to allow them a light. The hurriers were slightly older and stronger, boys and girls who pushed the tubs with their foreheads and were bald at the front of their skulls.

An inquiry into work practices in the mines was instigated, and headed up by Lord Ashley (later Lord Shaftesbury). Four years after the Husker disaster, the Mines Act forbade the employment of women and girls, and boys under ten underground. Queen Victoria herself is said to have given two hundred pounds towards a distress fund.

Of course the landed gentry and toffs who owned, yet rarely went near, the coal mines were never held responsible for what happened in their pits. And when you start looking into these things within the pit communities you're met with sad acceptance. A big memorial stone at All Saints Church in Silkstone tells its own tale. The children who died at Husker weren't even given the dignity of their own graves. Their bodies were wheeled to the cemetery on rough wooden handcarts and lined up in communal holes, the girls laid at the feet of the boys. A carving on the memorial quotes Matthew's Gospel: 'Therefore be ye also ready'. The whole terrible event was blamed on 'an act of God'.

Les Young hopes his dry-stone-wall memorial will last for another two hundred years when it's finished. 'I don't want those children to be forgotten,' he will tell you. I asked him how he came to be involved in the project. 'When I first moved to this district I was walking my dog in the woods. I don't know why, but something came over me and I sort of knew that something terrible had happened there.' It was only when Les started talking to his new neighbours that the connection between his uneasiness in the woods and the story of Husker became clear.

In parts of Yorkshire the dry-stone walls chime so perfectly with the landscape that it's almost as though they grew out of the soil. They didn't. They were put there by rough hands. Les's are creating something that will go far beyond enclosing a bit of land. As he says, 'After all there aren't many crafts where you can make something that will still be there for your great-great-great-granddaughter to touch.'

I like the idea that stories can be passed on in stones, in water, in carvings. The great American folklorist Alan Lomax once said, 'It is the voiceless people of this planet who hold in their memories the generations of human life and wisdom.' He referred mainly to the music that ordinary people make.

Before we buried Billie, Heather and I talked about what we should place beside her in her coffin. Heather put in some friendship bracelets, since she always wore a lot of them – 'You have to wear lot of friendship bracelets when you've got a lot of friends,' Billie once said after I pointed out that her arms were almost tattooed with them. We also placed some coloured stones and shells in there. I wondered aloud if we ought to put in her violin too. Heather was adamant. 'No! It might come in handy for somebody else one day.' The thought, at that time, that another person might play Billie's violin startled me. I didn't want that. But as time has gone on I'm less precious about Billie's lovely things. We gave some of her clothes to the local hospice shop, occasionally we give her books to other children as presents and some of her toys have gone to a nursery across the road.

When my bosses at ITV gave me a cheque for one thousand pounds not long after Billie's funeral, we were already making plans for a lasting memorial. In lieu of flowers at the funeral people threw coins into a bucket. We collected nearly nine hundred pounds, which we divided equally between an urban farm project in inner-city Sheffield, the NSPCC and Billie's school. These three causes said a lot about Billie – her love of animals, of children and of learning. Money that came in afterwards seeded another project.

Heather and I were sitting on the settee one night listening to Eliza Carthy, and I remembered I had a DVD somewhere of the Waterson Family in an old black-and-white documentary made in the sixties. It's a wonderful film about the power of music and how culture thrives with a bit of nurturing in the most unlikely circumstances. The film is set in the scruffy backstreets of Hull, full of smoky chimneys and wet streets. Behind the curtains of a terraced house off Hessle Road, Norma, Lal and Mike Waterson sit, smoke cigarettes, cuddle babies and discuss old songs and poetry. Anne Briggs, the iconic wild child of the folk revival, is visiting and she tries to explain the relevance of traditional music in a modern society by saying that the 'now' is the half-remembered past. Contemporary folk singers have picked up the threads of the tradition. They're all in their early twenties, yet somehow they have found a path to cultural expression and a way to share it with others.

Billie and Edward had been exposed to all sorts of music since they shared a pram. One Christmas Edward did a lovely impression of Marc Bolan's 'Hot Love' in a wig borrowed from the wardrobe department at ITV Yorkshire and a red satin shirt for an audience of four-year-olds at nursery. Billie fell in love with the fiddle-playing of Norma Waterson's daughter, Eliza Carthy, at the Cambridge Folk Festival one year. She decided that one day she, too, would play the violin at Cambridge. I took her to buy her violin and the music-store assistant showed her all sorts of instruments for little girls – one was metallic blue, another green and there was even a vibrant pink one. Eyes half-closed and her jaw almost set, Billie admonished me. 'Daddy! They're not proper violins! I want a wooden one that I can polish.'

So a proper wooden one she got. She loved that violin. I watched her one day when she didn't know I was there. She put her fingers on every millimetre of each string and plucked, listening to each different sound. She placed it under her chin, moving it around until she was comfortable. She kissed it and whispered to it. It was a lovely moment and I had to tread carefully as I walked to the next room so that I wouldn't disturb a floorboard and alert her that I had been watching.

Our home town has a wonderful male-voice choir, and a number of members are retired old coal-miners. There used to be a brass band at Ackton Hall colliery, but that went when the pit shut. There are one or two working-men's club singers, who perform Céline Dion songs to backing tracks, but apart from that there is little music in the town. I discovered that just one peripatetic teacher visits the four junior schools to teach strings. I guessed that behind the curtains of the terraced houses there might be huge numbers of kids with a burning ambition to play an instrument.

We set up an account called 'Billie's Violin Trust', put the thousand pounds ITV had given us into it and added a thousand pounds from our own savings. Featherstone Male Voice Choir did a fundraiser for us alongside the Trinity Girls Brass Band from Wigan and put in nearly another thousand. A man called Roy Hampson, who sells Al Bowlly and Dorothy Squires CDs on the market, organized a fantastic Palm Court orchestra concert, and the Black Dyke Mills Brass Band played for us at Halifax parish church. The heavy-metal guitarist Graham Oliver of Saxon threw in his hand and a comedy/vocals duo called ESP, which stands for Ellie and Steve Parker – Steve's dad, 'Tetley' Dave Parker, says it stands for 'Eggs, Sausage and Peas' –, did a marvellously anarchic fundraising evening at the Willow Park Social Club.

Initially we'd thought we might buy one or two violins each year for children in local primary schools, but within weeks, through the generosity of people in our town and nearby, and people we didn't even know, we had raised more than ten thousand pounds. Folk started stopping me in the street and giving me fivers. One local businessman dropped on me in Pontefract market on his way to the bank and told me to follow him. He drew out five hundred pounds from his bank and gave it to me in a brown envelope. He told me he remembered Billie playing in the beer garden at the back of the Bradley Arms and was always struck by her lovely smile and eyes. He swallowed and took out a clean white handkerchief.

We didn't want the responsibility of holding on to all that money and worried that if the project got too big we wouldn't be able to administer it properly. I found out that the local authority in Wakefield has a Music Services Department based in an old school there. It's run by an amazing woman called Geraldine Gaunt, a classically trained pianist who, with enthusiasm and more energy than I've ever seen in one person, encourages musical expression in local youth. I had a meeting with the immaculately dressed Geraldine. She smelled of Jo Malone perfume and had a no-nonsense air that I admired straight away. Within minutes of the meeting starting we had arranged what to do with the money and decided to have an annual memorial concert at St Wilfrid's School sports hall. At the first, 'Fiddles and Flutes', a folk ensemble of teenage flute and violin players, would play, our Edward would do a solo turn on piano, St Wilfrid's jazz band, a combination of sixth-formers and teachers, would join us, and Wakefield Youth Choir would round the whole thing off with a song I was to write called 'Billie's Song'.

Thanks to Geraldine, the concerts – known as Billie's Violin – have become a living and breathing entity. The two concerts we have done so far have been attended by nearly eight hun-

1 and 2. My two early inspirations. My grandad Ted Fletcher, with his mates at the Central Working Men's Club: he's the one with his tie over his pullover, and his dad is in front of him with the big flat cap. And my gran with her mates in the backs at Mafeking Street; my gran is furthest right.

3 and 4. Two shots of Station Lane, looking south from the railway line. *Top*, 1960s, the lane I remember from my childhood (*Francis Frith Collection at www.francisfrith.com*), and *bottom*, the lane today. (*Roy Hampson*)

5. Featherstone Rovers coming home after winning the cup in 1973. I was fourteen and my grandad lifted me on to his shoulders. We stood in front of the shop to the left of the photo.

6. Ackton Hall Colliery dominated our landscape until it became the first pit to be shut after the 1984–5 strike. The town of Featherstone lies beyond the pit wheels. (*Frank Waude*)

7. Ackton Hall colliers march back to work at the end of the year-long strike. (*Tony Lumb*)

8. Me at Bridlington, summer 1960.

9. Me in the late 1970s, not long after I met Heather.

10. Me on a visit to Mafeking Street, the street where I was born. (*Roy Hampson*)

11. Heather and I at a book launch at Barnsley Town Hall in the 1980s. Most of the women wore posh frocks, but Heather, as usual, fashioned her own outfit.

12. A proud dad, 1997; Billie with that smile.

13. The twins at the Cambridge Folk Festival during a set by Robert Plant. Billie said he was too loud.

14. At Whitby, a place we love and visit every year.

15. At Berne in Switzerland when the river was in flood. Billie thought it was one of the most wonderful sights she had ever seen, and stared at it for ages.

16. Billie on her way to All Saints Junior School – hummus and tomato sandwiches, and trusty violin at the ready.

17. Sunday lunchtime at the local pub. (*Paul Medlock*)

18. A painting Heather did for my birthday last year. She keeps saying that it's not finished, and takes it back every now and again to alter it.

dred people. We have given away a dozen instruments, bought with money from the fund, and at least two dozen more second-hand instruments have been put into schools – they were given to us in lieu of money. A working men's club in Sheffield gave us a set of drums after they found that the turns, these days, prefer backing tracks to live drum and organ. An old miner gave us a keyboard still in its box. He told me it had been waiting on top of his wardrobe for a home to go to since his wife had died. Violins have been pulled out of cupboards, dusted and restrung.

I had never written a song. When Geraldine asked me to write some words I just said, 'Yes,' because I daren't say, 'No,' to her. I only realized the consequences when I came to sit down and have a go. In the end I thought I'd reprise what I had said at the funeral and shape the song around things that Billie liked to do. Geraldine composed a piano accompaniment, then asked a musician called Graham Hall to play a violin introduction.

When Heather, Eddie and I went to the first performance of the song at a rehearsal for the concert we got a big shock. The piano parts are very beautiful and the singing was an absolute delight: around forty kids of all ages from all sorts of backgrounds stood in black T-shirts and sang like linnets. It was moving, as we'd thought it would be, but the shock was the violin intro. Graham Hall was the man whom Billie had talked to outside the Middle Earth Tavern in Whitby the year before, the man with the fiddle who had encouraged her to go to the Fishermen's Rowing Club on Sunday morning and watch the jigs and reels. We had never met him before that evening, didn't know him from Adam, and now here he was in an old school hall in Wakefield playing the introduction to 'Billie's Song', about a little girl who had longed to take her own fiddle to the festival but never got there.

She liked the sound of rain and the breeze,
The splashing of the drops that fall from trees,
Rays of sunshine making patterns on the leaves,
And she loved to chase the rainbows in the morning.

She liked the music of a single violin,
The way that voices come together just to sing,
Especially when everyone joined in,
And she loved to chase the rainbows in the sky.

So let's all get together to sing her song,
Join our hands and voices, we'll be strong.

She liked to run and jump and swim the butterfly,
Went walking in the mountains, touched clouds passing by,
Painted pictures of flowers as gentle as a sigh,
And she loved to chase the rainbows in the air.

She liked to think that everyone should share,
Told her many friends that she would always care,
Flashed a smile of simple beauty way beyond compare,
And she loved to chase the rainbows in the sky.

The first concert was a joy. In the weeks beforehand, we ran a competition in each of the four junior schools in Featherstone. The children had to tell a story or paint a picture about what music meant to them. I cried when I had to pick the winners. At All Saints a little girl called Lily had asked for a violin. I recognized her name because she had written a lovely letter to us the week before Billie's funeral. In her letter she had said, 'Billie, I will never forget you because you helped me when nobody wanted to be my friend and you were much bigger than me. You sat on the wall next to me.' At St Thomas's School we gave a classical guitar to a girl called Simran Sidhu, whose family had had to move on from the takeaway shop they ran on the estate where our Tony lives. We gave a flute to a lad called Conor who told us he needed to find an instrument other than his trumpet because he had a condition in his ears that meant he couldn't blow hard. A girl called Ellie May at North Featherstone School asked for a clarinet, as did Joseph Sutton, and at Streethouse School we gave a violin to a charming little lass called Chloe. We thought long and hard about who to choose. We wanted to be sure that we found kids who would really enjoy playing and whose parents would support them. There were one or two whispers about not giving instruments to certain kids because their dads would only sell them to buy drugs, but you'll always get that. Just like years ago you'd be told not to lend money to certain people because they would only go to the bookie's or the club and waste it on betting or ale.

The schools were brilliant in their response. North Featherstone School involved the entire register and displayed work on every available spare wall.

Just before the concert a mate of ours called Clare Jenkins, who works as a radio journalist, phoned up and asked if we might do a piece for *Woman's Hour*. We agreed and I went over to the BBC's Oxford Road Studios at Manchester to do a live interview with Jenni Murray. Jenni asked why I wanted to set up Billie's Violin Fund. I told her that I was always looking for ways of being creative and wanting to put things back into a town that had helped to shape me. She wanted to know how this would reflect on Billie.

'My Billie was a lover of life and living it. It was Billie's dream to play her violin at Whitby, at Cambridge. This won't happen for her now, but just suppose that somewhere in our home town there is a little girl who has a similar dream, and that all she needs is an instrument. It might be that the little girl's parents can't afford the instrument or the cost of the lessons. But if we can provide that, then a little lass might just go on and realize Billie's dream for her and that would make us proud.'

Jenni then played in the pre-recorded pieces that Clare had done with some children at school. Ellie May talked about writing a story called 'The Magic Trumpet' and how playing music soothes her and builds her up. Megan said she liked to play a tune called 'Twinkle Twinkle Satellite Dish' on her clarinet, and Joseph did his impression of the band of the Black Watch doing 'Scotland the Brave'.

When we came back live to the studio, Jenni wanted me to tell her about what had happened on the river that day. On the train on the way to the studios I had run this question through my mind. What would I say if she asked me about what happened? Should I just steer things back towards Billie's Violin Trust? I had decided along with Heather from day one that we should talk about what had happened in the belief that keeping it all in was not good for our spirits. That talking about it, even the horrifying parts, would help us and also other people understand what something like this does, not just to us but to the wider community.

I told Jenni that when you have twins it makes you feel very special. Especially if it is boy and girl twins. I was proud every time I took them out in the pram, and as they grew I was proud to hold their hands as I walked down a pavement. People look at twins – complete strangers are fascinated by them. I have even blurted out to people I don't know, 'They're twins, you know!' I've done it while I've been sitting on benches in parks, on walls at the seaside, in trains and on buses. Still to this day I hold Edward's hand – he doesn't want me to now he's twelve but I like to when we cross busy roads. Sometimes I feel myself stretching out my left hand into mid-air searching for Billie's. I had nine, nearly ten years of holding two little hands. Now I have just one.

'I didn't know which way to turn in that river, Jenni. Should I try to find Billie or get Edward out because I could see him?

Edward told me I should save his sister first. I think I already knew at that point that I'd lost her. I looked Edward in his eyes and he looked in mine. I told him that whatever happened in the future, nothing would be as hard for us as what we were suffering then – the water was still swirling round us at this point.'

Jenni Murray has a way with her that makes you feel as though you're just confiding in her. I suppose it's the skill of the veteran broadcaster.

'You've made a point, Ian, of not wanting to be seen as a grief-stricken dad. Why is that?'

'Because I think that sometimes you've got to stand in the middle of the fire and not shrink back. I've had my pain, and though it's painful still, I don't want to be a man who hides for fear of further pain. We're a robust family who love one another, and sometimes I think it's true that all you need is love. Nobody has suffered as much as our family over this, but our neighbours and our wider community have suffered too. I want to stand up to it because when I see somebody in the street I want them to know that they can still come up to me and talk about stuff.'

The pressures of live radio are peculiar. Even in the midst of this conversation I could feel that the programme's producers were wanting Jenni to wind up and introduce the next pre-recorded item. She had one last question.

'Was it true what you said to Edward in the river, that nothing could be worse than that moment?'

'I've had my nightmares. Sometimes I wake up and I'm still in the river. But nothing can be as bad as that day. I had to make a choice, an unbearable one.'

Jenni echoed my words: 'It's an unbearable thought.' And then she started to weep.

The next pre-recorded item played in and I sat for a few minutes trying to be brave. She told me about her battle with cancer, that she came originally from the Barnsley area, then wished me luck, composed herself and carried on.

I've thought a lot since about what I said on *Woman's Hour*. Up to that point I don't think I'd ever made it a story of a black-and-white choice as to which of my children I would save first, knowing that in rescuing one I might lose the other. The reality on the day wasn't like that. I just did what I could in the time and conditions I faced. It never occurred to me that I was choosing between my children, so why I should suggest that I don't know. Perhaps I was searching for ways of telling the story. I know I made a rod for my own back in doing so, because this way of telling it has stayed with me until now I almost believe it myself – that I made choices. If I have one regret about being so open with my feelings and the story of what happened to us, it is that I introduced the idea that I had to make a choice. I would come to regret it even more at the time of the inquest.

I hope that Billie's Violin Trust will be as solid as Les Young's dry-stone wall, as secure as the musical dynasty seeded by the young Watersons. The unknown yet to come is the same as the forgotten past, and I know that one day somebody will play the violin to which Billie once whispered.

10. The struggle itself was the victory

I'm sitting opposite Arthur Scargill in his office at the Miners' Headquarters on the corner of the Huddersfield Road out of Barnsley. It's a 1970s office if ever I saw one, with lots of brown and beige and piles of paper and index-card systems. The cushion on the chair I'm swivelling on keeps slipping forwards, and it's difficult to keep a sense of dignity and decorum when the main thought in my mind is how to keep still.

I'm making a programme for ITV Yorkshire that will celebrate Scargill's seventieth birthday. I don't want this programme to be just about politics and the struggles of the miners' union. A lot of my questions this morning have been about his mother and father: 'My father was a card-carrying member of the Communist Party and my mother was a deeply Christian lady who went to church on Sundays. She gathered sandstones when the grave diggers were working in the churchyard and sold them later out of a tin bucket for a penny apiece to ladies who wanted to scour their steps and windowsills.' I've asked about his friendships; he told me that he once shared a platform in Havana with Fidel, Joshua Nkomo, Yasser Arafat and Harry Belafonte. On the subject of music he told me he liked Irish folk, a nod towards Irish ancestry. He also told me that the Scargills were a noble family from Viking Norway, who once held sway from a castle in the northern Yorkshire Dales. 'The castle's still there – I'll show you it.' Some weeks later he does. On art, he tells me that his friends the Manic Street Preachers once invited him to the opening of an exhibition of the works of Picasso that they'd had something to do with.

I readjust the patterned cushion and gear myself up for a

question about the miners' strike. 'Does it still hurt that the miners' strike was lost?'

'We didn't lose that strike. The struggle itself was the victory!'

Twenty-two years before I came to be sitting on that awkward seat in Arthur Scargill's office, looking up at an oil painting of him jabbing a finger in mid speech, I was in the passenger seat of a rusty Hillman Avenger. My friend, Sean Tomlinson, was driving, and 'Deadly' Davison, a mate who worked at the Prince of Wales pit, was sitting between us in the back. We were travelling back from Lancashire after watching Feather-stone Rovers play at Oldham or somewhere. It was a Sunday teatime in the spring of 1985 and eleven months into the miners' strike. There had been a lull in the conversation while we stared at the rain and mist over Saddleworth Moor. Eventually Deadly cleared his throat and said, 'I've summat to tell yer, lads.' Sean and I looked at one another and a bubble appeared over both of our heads that contained the thought, Are you thinking what I'm thinking?

Deadly carried on: 'I'm thinking about going back to work in the morning.' Over the past few weeks the trickle back had become a bit more than that. 'Our kid's gone and he reckons everybody else is going. It's all over. We might as well all go back now. There's nowt left for us.'

Sean moved the car across to the inside lane and slowed down. I saw his eyes in the rear-view mirror. I spun round and looked at Deadly through the gap between the front two seats. 'Are you right in your bloody head?'

'Well, it's all ower bar t'shouting.'

'No, it's not, you daft twat. And, besides, tha'll be a fucking scab.'

'I might as well be a fucking scab – I've been every-fucking-thing else in this last year. There's fuck-all else for me to be.'

'Don't talk out of your arse!'

Sean joined in quietly to cut across the shouting; 'I can't see the point in going back. It'll be over in a week or two anyroad and you can go back with your head up.'

None of us spoke between Ainley Top and the turn-off for Leeds. We looked out of the window at streams of Black Marias with mesh at their windows going past us. This ritual was played out every Sunday evening: droves of police from all over the country descended on the coalfields, coppers on double time and more, drafted into villages and towns they'd never heard of to form uniformed barriers, break up pickets and stop people walking down streets they'd walked down all their lives. Those were the men who waved their overtime ten-pound notes at folk who hadn't seen a wage packet since last March. Those were the ones who arrested my mate Phil Paver under a medieval law called 'Following and Besetting' after he'd walked alongside somebody in his own home town and told him he ought to be ashamed of himself for black-legging. Those were the men who formed lines on the roads to pits to make sure that people who had decided to go back to work could get there unbruised.

Deadly didn't do much picketing after the first few months of the strike. I think he got hit on the back of the head with a brick thrown by somebody near the back line. Then he was roughed up by some coppers from the Met, who were up north for the fun of cracking faces that they'd never have to look into again once the strike was over. So Deadly had decided that picketing wasn't for him.

One of the big tensions in the strike was caused by the 'visits' of police units from well outside the coalfields. These were men who knew nothing of the local culture and motivations of the people who lived there. On the twentieth anniversary of the strike I presented three half-hour documentaries for York-shire TV called *Daddy, What Did You Do In the Strike?*. I inter-viewed John Nesbit, the policeman in charge of operations at the so-called Battle of Orgreave on 18 June 1984.

I asked him about the visits the Met lads made to the area and if it was true that some members of the armed forces had been drafted in and given police uniforms. John Nesbit said that the military were never involved in the strike in 'any way, shape or form'. He claimed that the rumour started when four hundred members of Thames Valley Police, who wore very distinctive light-blue jackets over the top of their uniforms, came to help with 'the push' at Orgreave. He said that on the day a fellow senior officer announced over a megaphone, 'Mr Nesbit, your reinforcements are here,' and that immediately miners at the front of the crush said, 'The army is here.'

On the subject of taunts made by police regarding how much money they were making in overtime payments, John Nesbit agreed that this did happen. He said that on two occasions some policemen from outside the coalfields were found to be waving five- and ten-pound notes out of the windows of Transit vans. 'I stood all these policemen in a line and told them that they were not to wave money and try to humiliate striking miners and that, more importantly, once this strike is over and these policemen have gone back to their own forces, it is the indigenous policemen of South Yorkshire who would have to police their community.' He also claimed that he rang the reporting centre in London and told them not to send any more officers from that particular support unit. John Nesbit had once been a miner and he was also the officer who assumed command at the Hillsborough Stadium disaster after the officer who was in charge panicked.

I suppose that anyone with even a bit of knowledge about the miners' strike will know that it started at a pit near Rotherham called Cortonwood. And that within days of the announcement of a strike the lads there had built a wooden shed out of pallet wood and christened it 'The Alamo'. Yet even though Sheffield, just down the road, lays a proud claim to being the place that manufactured his knives, Jim Bowie wouldn't be showing up. And Davy Crockett in the shape of John Wayne would never ride over those hills.

A man called Mick Carter was probably the first coal-miner to know that there would be a strike. He was the NUM branch delegate at Cortonwood. I met him at his council house. He still paid to rent his house – he had refused to buy it because he believed that selling off council houses deprived up-and-coming generations of somewhere to live. He told me that as he was coming up the pit lane after work, 'This car pulled up at the side of me. It was Arnie Young, an area agent, and he motioned me to go back. We went into the office. He said, "Can you sit down?" I thought, Bloody hell, what's up? I wondered if somebody had died. He said, "I'll give it to you blunt. I've just been to a review meeting and the area director made a speech and said Cortonwood ceases production on the sixth of April." I'd just spent that morning in the manager's office talking about a new face they were opening at our pit. I wouldn't know how much it was going to cost, but I should say top side of a million pounds. I couldn't believe it.'

Mick went on to tell me that he usually stopped off at Cortonwood Miners Welfare for a couple of jars before he went home for his tea. That day he passed on his pints and came home across the backs, over the fields, because he couldn't face anybody. He wouldn't have known what to do if he'd seen any of the men coming home. As he said, 'I took the bloody coward's way out, to be honest. When I got home I was in tears. My wife said, "What's up?" I told her. Her jaw hit the floor. She said, "What are you going to do?" I said, "First thing is to get on the phone and organize a meeting."'

Within thirty-six hours of the closure announcement on 1 March 1984, the lads at Cortonwood were on strike. I asked Mick if it was a unanimous decision. 'I didn't hear one dissenting voice!' In fact, he said it twice: 'I didn't hear one dissenting voice!' Arthur Scargill wasn't involved at that point, but within days the strike had spread. Mick told me, 'It was like an animal

– it had its own dynamism. It was like a greyhound coming out of a trap. Boof! And it had gone!'

Sean pulled his car up outside our flat in Station Lane. I got out and asked Deadly if he wanted to move out of the back and sit in my seat. He lived a couple of miles further on, a few streets away from Sean. He just looked at me without saying anything. He was like a man being taken to a police station or a courtroom with a coat over his head, like a man with nothing left. In the previous twelve months he'd gone without proper food. He'd sold all of his records – he sold his *Electric Ladyland* LP to me. He'd even sold the cassettes he'd made himself and the leather jacket that at one time he never had off his back. He'd shared my dinner more than once. He'd been paid into rugby matches and had pints bought for him. His mantra for twelve months had been 'Don't thee worry. As soon as this lot's all over, tha'll get back double what tha's given me.'

Before I close the car door, I said, 'Don't go back.' He averted his eyes. Sean put the car into gear and they drove off down Station Lane. They stopped at the traffic lights. I wanted to run after them, knock on the car window and say, 'Will you?' but I didn't, and as I came into our front door I knew that he would.

After that I didn't speak to Deadly for nearly twenty-two years. I heard he was badly beaten up in a pub in the town and when I see him from time to time he looks half the bloke that he was. Not long after Billie died I dropped on him in the veg- etable aisle at Tesco. He looked me in the face and said, 'Hello. How are you?' I said, 'All right, thank you,' and carried on with my shopping. I feel ashamed now to have let so many years go by without talking to a man who was my friend. This was a man I'd arm-wrestled with, supped pint for pint with, told jokes to, a man whose shoulder I've leaned on as we wove our way home from the pub. Now, as we look at each other uncomfortably in a supermarket aisle, our trolleys are not our only barriers.

I've said hello a few times since and I've seen him occasionally buying CDs in the second-hand-record shop, trying to replace all the precious vinyl he sold during the strike. It's taken that long.

In my late teens and early twenties I drank Tetley's bitter at a pub called the Blackmoor Head in the Cornmarket at Pontefract. Its small rooms had fireplaces that burned real coal, and the pub's layout and most of the décor hadn't altered since its last makeover in the 1920s. The clientele was an extravagant mix of old blokes in flat caps and overcoats who made out betting slips while licking blunt little pencils, hippies approaching middle age, who listened to Jefferson Airplane on the jukebox, and young punk rockers balancing cockatoo hairstyles. It was a real 'community' pub, presided over by an elderly matriarch called Ethel, who was the landlord's mother.

One day during the summer of the miners' strike some lads from Ackton Hall pit called in at the Blackmoor after picketing. They'd scraped up enough money between them to nurse a pint of bitter apiece. I knew one of them – my mate Phil Paver was a bit older than me, a big music fan, a great follower of the Rolling Stones. Another was a big lad whom everybody called 'Ebb'. Ebb played rugby league for the Jubilee Club in Featherstone. By way of making conversation I went up to them and asked if they were going to the Nostell Priory Festival. 'It's a right line-up,' I enthused. 'Jethro Tull, Lindisfarne, and the Band, who have just reformed.'

The pickets just stared at me. Then Ebb said, 'What with?'

I think I mumbled, 'Oh! Yes, I suppose you're skint.'

Phil Paver stared hard. 'Skint! Course we're fucking skint. We've been on strike for five months. Is tha simple?'

His words hit me like a house-brick. I felt stupid and embarrassed. To cover this up I suggested I might be able to lend them some money. I was working on a building site in Leeds during the strike and earning a good bonus, helping to build a shopping centre.

Ebb said, 'Lend us some money? And when does tha think we'll be able to pay thee back?'

I told them they might not have to pay me back. Phil put his head on my shoulder. 'Ian, it's good of thee to offer, but does tha really think that if tha gave us some of thi money we'd spend it on a fucking pop festival? We're eating tins of corned beef!'

Ebb added, 'Jethro Tull can kiss my ring.'

I offered to buy them all a pint. They declined, supped the pints they had and made for the door. I felt hopeless and daft. When Russ Campbell asked if I wanted to play him at pool for fifty pence, I told him to stick his cue up his arse and went home.

More than ten years later when I moved house, I saw Phil Paver walking in Station Lane. He told me that one of my new neighbours had been a scab during the strike. I told him I didn't know. He spat on the pavement and said, 'Well, I hope tha's not talking to him.'

I didn't know what to say, so I changed the subject. 'Do you still like the Rolling Stones?'

'A bit,' he said.

11. But you can't see the tears in my eyes

Jimmy Echo is on stage at the Willow Park Social Club as we arrive. He's singing 'Wonderful Tonight'. There's a fat old toothless lady in a floral-patterned dress near the stage looking straight into his eyes and singing along. Jimmy has been on the northern club circuit for above forty years. He once had a recording contract with EMI when the major labels were looking for a northern Tom Jones, but never made it big. It's a shame, really, because he's a powerful singer in the Tony Christie mould and he's also a great guitarist. Later he'll do his Shadows medley, 'Apache', 'Kon-Tiki' and 'FBI'. Tonight he's playing to a big crowd whose average age will be sixty odd, retired miners and their wives dressed up to the nines, all ready for a dance, a game of bingo, a pint of electric fizzy beer and a Malibu.

My mate Dennis Cliffe loves Jimmy Echo. 'One of the finest turns in clubland,' he'll tell you. Whenever he's playing locally Dennis phones me and wants me to go. I've spent a lot of my life avoiding working men's clubs. I've made many jokes about them, the horrible beer, the décor, the spartan furnishings and the bloody bingo, always the bloody bingo. But just lately I've become a bit of a fan. I've realized the part they play in community life, the meeting place they offer to neighbours, the structure they offer through committees and trips away, and the chance they give people to converse, debate and enjoy themselves.

Dennis loves the club. He doesn't work, these days, so he sits in the club making out his betting slips, reading his *Daily Mirror* and telling jokes to a motley gathering of old ladies, old blokes with carriers full of stuff from the allotments and younger lads without jobs to go to. Dennis has a gold sovereign ring on nearly every finger and gold chains round his neck. He likes to wear the money he wins at the bookie's. Dennis smells of Lynx deodorant and aftershave and always keeps his shoes well polished.

'What a bloody singer that man is!' he says, as he comes back to the table with a pint apiece. 'Does tha want any nuts?' He doesn't wait for an answer, sits down and starts playing drums on his thighs. 'What a bloody singer! Do you know, you could go to London and not find anybody better. What a bloody singer. He's a proper belter.'

Jimmy finishes his song, and there's loud applause. The lady in the floral dress stands up and tries to whistle, discovers she can't and blows him a kiss.

'Ladies and gentlemen, you're a lovely audience. Better than the other day. I played a lunchtime show in an old folks' home. An old lass got that excited she started dancing on the table and then she pulled her frock above her head and shouted, "Super Fanny!" An old lad in the corner woke up with all the commotion and said, "I think I'll just have the soup, please!"'

A collective guffaw erupts from a hundred beer bellies, pots slammed on to Formica tables and Dennis says, 'He's a bloody case, y'know.'

'Now then, ladies and gentlemen, if you want to get up and have a dance, now's your time, cos we're going to do "La Vida Loca"!'

Some younger women get up and dance together, twirling each other round as Jimmy cranks up the volume. Their menfolk are not ready yet, preferring to sit and sup and tell each other the jokes that Jimmy has just told them.

Another song finishes. 'Right, thank you, that's the end of this spot. I'll be back right after the bingo.' Jimmy Echo takes his bow and unstraps his guitar, then walks to the little back-stage dressing room to change his shirt.

The lights are already up and dazzlingly bright and the concert secretary announces eyes down for your first house. Dennis has his pen poised at the ready. He has a special felt pen for bingo that leaves a big green blob over the numbers.

'All the threes ... thirty-three ... Maggie's den ... number ten ... Heinz ... fifty-seven ... two little ducks ...' There are shouts of 'Quack' from some enthusiasts at the back of the room.

'House!'

'Bloody hell!' says Dennis. 'She wins it every time I come in. I only wanted them two an' all.'

I ask Dennis if he wants another pint. He looks over his glasses. 'Bloody hell, old lad, has thee had a kipper for thi tea? I've only just nicely taken the froth off this.' A woman on the next table tells us to shush. The concert secretary says, 'Come on, now, give the best of order please.'

When Jimmy Echo comes back on he goes straight into 'Suspicious Minds' and most of the audience join in.

> We're caught in a trap
> I can't walk out
> Because I love you too much baby

The woman who told us to shush sings her words straight at the bloke next to her.

> Here we go again, asking where I've been
> But you can't see the tears in my eyes ...

More applause. Jimmy cues up his next song and tells his next joke. 'There's this little lad at his grandad's house. He says to his grandad, "Were you in the war, Grandad?" His grandad says yes. Little lad says, "Have you got any medals?"

'"Yes, I have."

'"Chuffing hell, Grandad! Will you show us 'em?"

'"Yes, I will, but only if you stop swearing."

'"Right, Grandad."

'His grandad goes upstairs and brings down a box. He opens it up and takes out medals that he won in the desert fighting Rommel. "Bloody hell, Grandad! What else have you got in your box?"

'"Look, lad, I'll show you, but you've got to stop swearing."

'"Righto, Grandad."

'"Well, I've got a German sergeant's cap badge here, look."

'"Bugger me, Grandad, what else yer got?"

'"I've told you to stop swearing or I won't show you owt else."

'"All right, Grandad, I'm sorry, carry on."

'"Now, I've got a German Luger pistol in here. Do you want to see it?"

'"Oooh, yes, Grandad."

'"Do you promise not to swear?"

'"I do."

'"Right, here, look."

'"Chuff me, is it real?"

'"Right, that's it! You said you wouldn't swear, I'm not showing you owt else."

'"Aww! Grandad, go on. I won't do it again."

'"Right, last chance. Upstairs I've got a German officer's coat, shall I show you it? Mabel! Do you know where my German coat is?"

'"Yes, love. I was tidying the wardrobe the other day and it smelt a bit foisty so I put it on the tank to air."

'Little lad says, "Fucking hell, Grandad! As tha got a tank as well?"'

The laughter erupts again, along with one or two tuts. The lady next to us turns round and says to Dennis, 'There's no need for that talk in here, y'know.' Dennis puts his sovereign fingers on her shoulder and says, 'Close your ears, love,' then turns to me and says, 'I knew what was coming – I've heard him tell it before at Top Club. It's a good 'un, though. "Fucking hell, Grandad! As tha got a tank an' all?"'

Jimmy is already into 'Spanish Harlem' before the laughter subsides.

By ten to eleven the floor at the front of the stage is full of women doing that dance where you step from one foot to the other and move your arms as though you're rinsing out a shirt in the sink. Some half-drunk blokes have made it to the floor and, believing themselves to be Elvis Presley, are thrusting their pelvises.

'Now, ladies and gents, I'm coming to my last few numbers, so I'd like to do a medley of songs by Dire Straits and Chris Rea. I call it the "Dire Rea Medley".' There's the slightest pause while the penny drops and more laughs.

Jimmy launches into:

This ain't no technological breakdown
Oh, no! This is the road to hell . . .

It's been a great night of fun, the second time this year I've enjoyed the club. A few months ago, it was generous enough to put on a fundraiser for Billie's Violin Fund. The concert was organized by ESP, who were golden-hearted to us and put on a great show that raised nearly eight hundred pounds through waived fees, bingo and raffles.

The working men's clubs that survive round Featherstone are peculiar places. They usually have beautifully maintained snooker tables. They put on some dire turns, some that didn't even get shown failing their audition on *The X Factor*. They do glorious suppers, known colloquially as 'old men's treats', and they host a motley collection of renegades, the workless, the mobility-benefit seekers and the bookmaker-addicted in the afternoons, but I have a lot of time for them. I just wish they served proper beer.

12. Bring me my cello

In May 1992 a man called Vedran Smailovic, a cellist in the Sarajevo Opera, was holed up in his apartment while the city was besieged. He avoided snipers in the street when he went to the market and dampened his ears to the sound of falling shells.

One Saturday morning a queue of people from his community were waiting to buy bread at one of the city's last working bakeries when a shell exploded right next to them and killed twenty-two. The day after the massacre Vedran took his cello to the ruins of a library, sat on a scorched chair in full evening dress, tailcoat and white dickie bow, and played Albinoni's *Adagio in G minor*. Then, at various times over the next twenty-two days, he repeated his performance. After the first week he was asked by a journalist, 'Are you crazy?' He replied, 'My city is being bombed and innocent people are dying and you ask me if I am crazy for playing my cello?' The following year Vedran left the horrors of the war in Bosnia and came to Britain.

In the autumn of 1994 I met him in a large downstairs workshop room at London's Royal Festival Hall. We were to work together on a project that became known as 'Bring Me My Cello', one of the craziest music-education projects I've ever been involved in. Since 1989 I have been working as a storyteller with several big musical institutions. I helped write and opera for Opera North's education department alongside the well-known director Stephen Langridge. He became a close friend and I continued to work with him on projects organized by the London Sinfonietta, the Britten-Pears School at Aldeburgh and the Festival Hall. On this occasion the South Bank's Education Department brought together a group of more than thirty people to create a performance and souvenir book, taking as its influence the opera *Sarajevo*, which had been composed by Nigel Osborne. A team comprised of home-less people who were part of a *Big Issue* sellers creative-writing group, plus one from St Botolph's, a charity that helps the homeless, were being led by a very wide-ranging group of artists in education. John Pawson, who had studied central Javanese gamelan at York and at the Academy of Performing Arts in Java, sat quietly behind his gamelan orchestra instruments. The game-lan is an ancient Indonesian ensemble of xylophones, drums and gongs, tuned to be played together. Once the instruments of the gods, they were now being whacked with gusto by a gang of blokes in the stale clothes of the street-dweller. The brilliant young English cellist Matthew Barley, who in more recent times has been described as 'the world's most adventurous cellist', was leaping about full of energy and enthusiasm. I met him again a few years later, and when I reminded him about the 'Bring Me My Cello' job, he said, 'That was a pretty wild one, eh?'

I was called towards the end of four days of workshops to lead storytelling exercises along with my mate Ian Daley who had been asked to put a book together about the whole thing. We left my house at five o'clock in the morning and drove to London in a hire car, arriving at the workshop just after the morning session had commenced. Nigel Osborne was putting the finishing touches to the music for the song 'Bring Me My Cello', while Vedran Smailovic was sitting in the middle of the room on a chair with his cello resting on his knee, swig-ging a can of Carlsberg Special Brew. I overheard one of the Festival Hall assistants say, 'He's asking for his money in cash.' Apparently Vedran liked to be paid for each day's work on the morning of that day in banknotes.

In a corner of the room some of the *Big Issue* sellers were practising a piece they were to perform. They were chanting:

People, what are they worth?
People, they're only dirt
People, don't call my name
People, find someone else to blame

Nigel Osborne introduced me to the group and invited me to do something. I launched straight into a storytelling exercise. 'Shall we tell about where we've been and where the road is leading us?'

A handsome young Chilean lad with long, wavy black hair told a story about the aftermath of the murder of Allende, which he later wrote up into a tiny story. A young woman told a story that she called 'The Secret Nightingale', about a bird singing its song of hope across the meadows from its perch in a tree. I looked across at Ian. He hunched his shoulders and held out the palms of his hands as if to say, 'What the hell is going on?' I did that expression that says, 'I haven't the foggiest!'

Vedran stood up and lurched over to me like a circus bear. He put his arms round me and lifted me six inches off the floor. 'I like these stories, my friend. Come . . . now we will make music!' The gathering launched into the cello song:

Bring me my cello,
I just have to play,
Why is it the innocent
Who always have to pay?

Rockets in the distance,
I see shimmering light,
Snipers all round me
But who gives a shite?

At the end Vedran laughed loudly and said, 'It's good, no?' Then he propped up his instrument by the wall and announced, 'Fuck cello! Bring me my beer!'

Nigel Osborne pioneered the use of music as a therapy for children who are victims of conflict. He has unstinting belief in its power to heal, both mentally and physically. He had been to Bosnia during the bombings but had first fallen in love with the country's music when, as a teenager in the sixties, he had gone hitchhiking on the hippie trail to Asia. How he pulled the cello project together I'll never know, but somehow he did and a lot of people took a lot out of it. Me for one. I learned that there is a creative expression to be had at every opportunity, that friendship, however transient, is something we can all do easily, and that something sweet can come out of absolute chaos.

I still recall an image planted in me by one of the homeless women on that project. In another of the storytelling exercises I wanted to find metaphors for life on the edges using articles of clothing to spark off a tale. The woman wrote:

> It is a dress, torn, worn and spoiled.
> Shame! it shouts from its folds.
> It is a shoe left out on the street,
> A left shoe. That once was a right shoe.

Later that evening I walked along the side of the Festival Hall near to the sculpture of Nelson Mandela's head. A man with his legs in a sleeping-bag asked me if I had any spare change. I recognized him as one of the people from the workshop. He looked up at me and said, 'It's you!' It was a strange and surreal moment at the end of a strange and surreal day.

When I dropped into our comfy bed in the early hours of the morning I was full of stories that I wanted to tell to Heather. I finished with the encounter near the Nelson Mandela sculpture. In a sleepy voice she said, 'That once happened to me.' She reminded me of the time when she had volunteered to serve soup to rough sleepers in London when she was on a 'practical' as part of her social-care course. 'The first man who came up to the soup van said to me, "Did your dad used to be called 'Wrassler'?" I told him he did. He said his name was Flanagan and years ago he used to drink with my dad in a working men's club on Halfpenny Lane in Pontefract.'

It was the *Times* journalist Robert Crampton who asked me the question I'd asked myself many times. 'Do you feel as though you're being punished?' What he actually said was, 'Do you feel you're being punished for your success?' This was in response to me telling him that I'd travelled a long way in my life from where I started. I'd developed a sense that to an extent I could control things that happened to me. I write books, I broadcast, I travel a world far beyond the one my family knew. It's given me a sense that I can cope and measure things. Then this massive jolt came and it made me realize how tiny I was. In that river I knew how small and powerless I was. In response to Robert's question, I said, 'No, it doesn't work like that, does it?'

'No, it's random, heartless chance,' he replied.

'It's what happened, Robert. It wasn't bound to happen, it might not have happened, but if my dad hadn't met my mam on the waltzers at Bridlington it wouldn't have happened either.'

He nodded.

'But knowing that doesn't make it easier, because nothing can make it easier.'

13. The carapace of the northern working-class male

Since Billie died I've struggled with the media. My friend Christine Talbot did a lovely interview with me just before the funeral that went out on *Calendar*, ITV's regional news programme. When I set up Billie's Violin Trust I did a similar piece with the BBC's *Look North* news programme. I did *Woman's Hour* because I trusted Clare Jenkins and Jenni Murray. Robert Crampton wrote a thoughtful piece for *The Times*. I worried when I saw it that I came over as a hard, unemotional man, avoiding grief by toughing it out – Robert wrote about 'the carapace of the northern working-class male'. When Heather read it, she said, 'That's you! It's true – you are a northern working-class male who says things like "You've got to be tough." What's a carapace?'

'It's the protective shell on a lobster or a tortoise – it stops them getting hurt.'

'That's you as well. Working-class tough guy who knows a lot of big words.'

Edward sits opposite me at breakfast. We like to eat breakfast together every day. It's become a ritual, so much of a ritual that most nights when I give him his kiss goodnight he asks me what we're having for breakfast tomorrow morning. We could almost put a menu up on the kitchen door. Saturday: bacon and tomato sandwich; Sunday: kippers; Monday: porridge; Tuesday: boiled egg and Marmite soldiers. Edward will finish his boiled egg, dab the corner of his mouth with the tablecloth and say, 'Mmm! Bloody lovely.' Then he takes his teaspoon to the empty shell and knocks a hole in it so that a witch can't use it as a boat.

It reminds me every time of Billie. I never tell him not to do it. But it's the little things like this that bring her back to my mind, and after he leaves for school I sometimes cry. On Saturday teatime she comes strongly into my mind. We have another mealtime ritual of lasagne for tea on Saturday. When Billie was alive I had to cook two separate dishes: meat lasagne for Heather, me and Edward, and vegetable for Billie. She loved lasagne with red peppers, courgettes and mushrooms. They often helped me with freshly washed hands and cooks' striped aprons that were far too big. Edward stood at my right hand with a frying-pan full of mince and onion and Billie with the left-hand pan of simmering vegetables that she had helped to chop. Sometimes I still begin to take a second pan down from the hook above the cooker.

I've encouraged Edward to keep a journal and write down some of his feelings. He tried it for a couple of weeks and then the European football tournament he's set up on his PlayStation took precedence. Newcastle United – he's found allegiance with the Magpies, a good, solid, northern working-class club, I suppose – are doing very well against AC Milan and Barcelona. He's got his journal tucked away, though, and in it he describes Billie as 'the spark of the school'.

He once asked me if I thought he ought to write about New Year's Eve just before the Millennium. The story that Edward likes above any other about him and Billie took place on the stroke of midnight that day. Heather had to work nights at the children's home. I put the twins to bed, then got into bed myself to watch Jools Holland's *Hootenanny*. The fireworks were exploding all over our town and rattling the windows. I climbed out of bed and parted the curtains to watch the display. Then I heard a little giggle and looked round. Edward and Billie were standing at my bedroom door holding hands.

In the sleepiest of voices Edward said, 'We were woken up by some loud noises and lights flashing.'

And Billie, in an even sleepier voice, said, 'And then all we could see was a big white arse between the curtains.' They ran off back to the room they still shared and laughed. I laughed too.

Edward still laughs when he reminds us of the story. He says he wants to write a limerick and asks me what I think the best rhyme is for 'fat arse'.

Heather writes her own poetry about Billie. She rarely shows it to me, but on the odd occasion she has left her book open at a certain page on her desk. The imagery is startling, all twisted branches, tangled hair and water swirling around stones. There are tears in every current, eddy and flow.

There are moments in most days when nothing else seems to matter apart from who has the strongest opinion, the loudest voice, the right way of doing things. Anything we want we want now; everything we say becomes a rule or a marker. There is no logic, no rationale: we want our own road and that's final. Edward will interrupt any conversation we might be having to tell us that he has found dried mud on the stair and will then conduct an investigation to find out who has been going to the upstairs rooms wearing muddy shoes. He will do it at the drop of a hat, in the middle of homework, in between forkfuls of dinner, with a towel wrapped round him dripping from the shower. Heather will suddenly decide, apropos nothing, that she doesn't like her job at the children's home any more. That thought can push any other out of her mind. She will suddenly decide that I am too fat, too whiskery, that my breath smells, that I only love her because I've got nobody else to love. And I, stinking of beer from the night before, will tell them both that there will be no drinking for me today and in the same breath think about the twenty-to-twelve bus that will take me to the tap room at the Shoulder of Mutton.

I get the monk on if I'm tired, even when the tiredness is down to the fact that I've spent half the night reading books about once-famous music-hall comedians like Hylda Baker and Frank Randle, or I've spent hours sitting with a mouse under my right index finger waiting to do one-click buying on Amazon. I've amassed all these books I might not read on everything from W. C. Fields to the green man in English folk-lore, misericords, and obscure shifts in the recorded history of delta blues music. There are piles of DVDs still sealed in plastic that if I watched end to end I'd still be watching in six months' time. I have collected the Czech new wave, the entire works of Chaplin, Buster Keaton, Louis Malle, Fassbinder, Jean-Luc Godard, the Belgian feminist film-maker Chantal Akerman, and the American independent director John Sayles. Our house is gathering DVDs, books, records and dust, more and more dust. Billie liked to wipe off the static and dust from our television screen. Sometimes I do it now with the backs of my fingers and this little thing reminds me of her.

If there is a gap in conversation someone's voice fills it. If there's a small job wants doing, too many hands reach out to do it. When Edward slowly and laboriously polishes his shoes, I grab the brush from him because I can do it faster. When I clear the dishes, Heather wants to know why I'm interfering again. When she burns her hand taking things from the oven, I throw an oven cloth on to the kitchen floor and shout, 'Don't you know what that's for?'

14. You want to get back to Russia

Arthur Scargill wants to take me to Orgreave to show me the spot where he was arrested and beaten by the police during the strike. I think that, approaching his seventieth birthday, he's looking back on his life and wondering how it might have been different.

'Shall I wear the cap I wore that day?' Arthur has a great sense of fun, an appreciation of the absurd, and a wonderful rogue's eye for the theatre of it all.

Orgreave is just a wasteland now. Lorries and earth-movers run up and down contouring the landscape. Arthur stands by a steel gate topped with barbed wire. He has a twinkle in his eye. 'You know, lad, when they finally decided to close this works down I phoned the police and told them to get somebody down here quick. The police wanted to know what on earth that was to do with them. I told them it had plenty to do with them. When my union tried to close it for a few days in the strike, they sent thousands of bobbies.'

He laughs. Arthur loves to tell darkly funny stories. We walk up to a railway bridge near to where he was arrested. Arthur believes that the police wanted to set an example on that day at Orgreave, that they had planned to arrest him come what may. And he *was* arrested, for obstructing the public highway. I tell Arthur that I once made a programme featuring Chief Superintendent John Nesbit, the man who arrested him. 'He told me that some of his constables were talking about a bounty on the head of Arthur Scargill. He said he put his foot down and announced, "If Arthur Scargill wants to come here and picket in a peaceful manner, then he's perfectly entitled to do it, but the minute he transgresses I shall arrest him."'

Arthur winks at me. 'Yes, I saw that programme. But what you've got to remember is that at the same time as the chief superintendent was stopping me his troops were charging up the hill like a Roman army, with shields, batons, dogs and horses, hitting people on the back of the head as they tried to move away.'

When we sit down later to talk about what has shaped and powered Arthur Scargill, he talks about his family and the community he was brought up in. 'All my mother ever wanted, and she was a good Christian woman, was for me to have a good job with decent money and not to come to any harm. My father was a superb teacher. He taught me in my environment. He showed me rabbits, hares and badgers, he knew how to identify various birds. He was a tremendous reader, a master of words. He told me that mastering words enabled you to understand the world in which you live and, more than that, to try then to put it right.'

He told me he had developed his sense of justice and fairness almost from his first day at work. He reported to a man called Lomas, who was wearing a pork-pie hat and a brown suit stained with oil. He followed this man across the pit yard and down some steps, then down some more steps. 'I thought I was going to hell. When I got to where I was to work, I knew that I was in hell, in Dante's inferno. This was the screening plant where coal was sorted. This was where the ill, the disabled, the men with one arm or the half-crippled worked. They were picking stone out of the coal on five conveyor belts. I nearly turned and ran, but I didn't. And it was there that I started to learn the meaning of comradeship, the need to stick together and not buckle under, and that was important.'

I tell Arthur that after we lost Billie I didn't know where to turn, where I would find comfort. I am not a religious man, I can't turn to God. I'm not a nervous man, I don't lack confidence, so I didn't want tablets or counselling. The one thing that comforts me more than anything is the community that has shaped me. I enjoy the comradeship and sense of knowing where I'm from and the pride that gives me. That has been the biggest help.

Arthur tells me that to have a sense of belonging and to be proud of where you're from and what you do is the best thing anyone can aspire to. 'When the history books are written properly, the true stories will be about those who fought back, those who stood up for their fellow man and woman. When my father was still down the pit, a group of miners were discussing their children. One said he wanted his lad to train as an accountant, another said he wanted his son to be a lawyer. They turned to my dad and said, "What about you, Harold, what do you want for your son?" My dad said, "Arthur is going to be president of the Yorkshire miners one day." And they all laughed. In 1973 I became president with the biggest majority ever known. I went to see my dad that night and I told him the victory was his.'

The Central Working Men's Club in Featherstone was where my grandad got regularly skint playing cards and dominoes for money. It's the club where I saw the greatest rallying call and most defiant stand of my life. At the beginning of 1985, when some strikers had started to drift back to work, Arthur Scargill made a tour of clubs and institutes and miners' welfares to rally the troops. At the Central Club he made one of the greatest speeches ever heard in this town. It was probably one of the best of his life. He said that the government had stockpiled coal, but not as much as they were claiming; he said the piles were like his hairstyle, plenty round the side but not much in the middle. On the way out, I heard the club treasurer say, 'He's t'best turn we've had on here for years.'

At Orgreave now, Arthur stands peering through a chain-link fence at the barren wasteland. He has a croak in his voice. 'You know, communities are jobs. Where there are jobs there's lawfulness and stability. Without jobs, there's helplessness and no hope. The villages have gone, the people have gone, because the jobs have gone, and that's why we're left with a crime culture and a drug culture.'

I recall a conversation I had with a young woman called Joanne in a former pit village called Thurnscoe. She told me that to keep her job with Marks & Spencer her best friend had moved to Morocco. 'Imagine that, love, flitting from Barnsley to Morocco!'

I ask Arthur if there had been a point during that big strike when he'd felt like giving in.

'Not once!' he says. 'Not once!' And then he said it again. 'Not once! In fact I was disappointed when they called the strike off. We were that close to bashing them into the ground. The fight was a right one.'

The fight became a bloody and violent one at the back end of May in 1984. If I had to pick out just one image from the millions in my memory of that strike, it would be the few seconds of news footage from ITN that showed a policeman repeatedly hitting a picket and his mate over the head with a truncheon. I met Wayne Linguard and his mate Russell Broomhead twenty years after the day they were set upon. Wayne told me, 'When they're in a corner, them in power will do everything they can to wriggle out of it. In court they said that Russell had to be hit because he might have had a knife on him. Russell was wearing a T-shirt and shorts! They just tried to blacken our characters.'

Russell told me that the horses came charging through, and he and Wayne were isolated in the middle of a field from the rest of the pickets. The policeman hit Wayne first, then collared Russell. He rained truncheon blows on his head and neck and later admitted in court that his truncheon broke during the attack. He continued hitting with the broken truncheon. Wayne said, 'I was dragged back through the police line and they were queuing up to have a kick at me – they were just frenzied.' It was at that point that Wayne managed to look up with a bloodied face and noticed the TV cameras. He said, 'You want to get your bloody cameras in there and see what they're doing!' Russell told me that by the time he was dragged back to the Black Maria the police had resorted to taunting. 'They were saying things like "We know all you miners are Communists. You want to get back to Russia." It was ridiculous.'

A woman called Jean Marsh, who worked in the soup kitchens during the strike, told me, 'There are people from outside of these areas who don't seem to understand the way we live in our villages.' She thought the miners' strike was a great tragedy, but a revival of community spirit came out of it, an understanding of the struggle we were all in and a pride in where we were from. 'An old lady up the road from us baked scones for the soup kitchen every Monday morning. She knew what it was all about. And another old lady, she's a hundred and one now, she brought fifty pence for the strike fund every week. She insisted on climbing the steps to hand it over personally. She said it was her chapel collection, but the chapel could wait when coal-miners were hungry.'

I love these stories – they could only exist in a coal-mining community. All my stories exist here too. Every story needs a neighbourhood to inhabit and mine come from here.

Near the chain-link fence at Orgreave Arthur Scargill told me that you should always fight for your community and never cross a picket line, and I'm sure he brushed away a tear.

15. Bringing at all back home

I could cry.

It doesn't work like that, though.

I could lie down on the settee and cry for ever. I could sit on the edge of a causy – a footpath – sometimes and cry as the traffic goes by me.

When Billie and Edward were just a year old I worked in America for two months straight. I missed them so much. One night in Nashville, in a famous honky-tonk bar called Tootsie's Orchid Lounge, I paid some dollars to a washed-up old country singer to sing me a sad song. He sang 'I'm So Lonesome I Could Cry', the old Hank Williams number. I cried that night and spent a fortune on a transatlantic phone call just so I could say goodnight to Heather and listen to the kids breathing.

Ten years after that my friend the musician Richard Hawley appeared with Jools Holland on some country sessions and he chose to sing that song. He did the most lonely version of it I'd ever heard. That made me cry. He once said to me, 'I'll come over to your house soon and we'll play some sad songs and have a good cry.'

It doesn't work like that, though.

I won't be a victim.

I won't cry when I don't want to.

I'll tell all my friends and neighbours about it.

I'll talk to people I hardly know on buses about what happened if I feel like it.

We've lost our Billie, but everybody else has too.

A friend of mine called Dr Arnold Kellett told me that a French poet, whose name he couldn't remember, mourned the death of his girlfriend in a lake. He mused that this was not just his loss. His girlfriend had drowned in a lake and this was a loss for the whole world. I will rely on my friends and neighbours, on my community, my home town to pull us through. My home town knows how to deal with loss and grieving. The graveyard in my town is full of men and children killed in coal-mining accidents. Too many lie there who died young of respiratory illnesses caused by inhaling dust. The two lads who were shot by their own military while picketing at the pit gates. More recently, lads and lasses in their teens and twenties died too soon because they got hooked on the drugs that washed through the pit villages in the hard times after the miners' strike. My home town knows how to deal with death. I will rely on it to pull us through.

Featherstone is a long, thin town, built, like all Victorian pit towns, on a linear plan. Houses were thrown up along the sides of roads that linked one place to another. There is one main street, called Station Lane, and the old Lancashire–Yorkshire railway line that once carried the town's coal away still runs on a level crossing straight across our main street. At the top of Station Lane is the Featherstone Hotel, a big, once bustling, straight-up-and-down boozing palace. Everybody calls it the Top House. It has had only seven or eight landlords in its near hundred-and-twenty-year history. It was here in 1893 that some people climbed the scaffold the builders were using to erect the upper floors to watch the military fire on locked-out miners. The Top House stands on the corner of Station Lane and Green Lane. Green Lane, Featherstone, was the site of the last killing of English workers by their own military.

Head south down Station Lane and on your left you'll see James Duggan Avenue and James Gibbs Close. Almost a hundred years to the day after they were shot, the local council named these two streets in their honour.

The former pit, Ackton Hall colliery, is on the right, or what's left of it is. The pit was levelled with indecent haste right after the miners' strike in 1985. When they knocked the three winding gears down, local folk said it was like 'knocking the crown off the king's head'. These days, it's an 'enterprise zone', a home to various small businesses making everything from first-aid kits to plastic fabrications. In the years immediately after the strike a lot of ex-miners turned their hobbies and redundancy money into little businesses. One I knew made jodhpurs for girls with ponies and rugby shirts for local teams. In other towns nearby tropical fish suppliers sprang up, parakeet and parrot shops, leather belts and saddle bags for western re-enactment events. For a while in Station Lane we had a shop that sold iguanas and other lizards.

Business advisers and financial consultants rushed to the area to set up little offices to help redundant mineworkers spend their money on daydreams and half-baked whims. I remember a council officer from the local economic-development unit telling me, 'You can always tell these so-called financial advisers. They have sharks' fins in their trilby hats.' For a while in Featherstone there were more building societies and financial-advice agencies than there were bakeries.

When the redundancy money ran out so did the financial advisers, and Station Lane ended up with a lot of empty shops, some of which were turned into flats for young people who couldn't get a council house. Others became takeaways and fast-food outlets. The older end will tell you that at one time you didn't have to go out of Station Lane to buy anything. 'You could buy owt from a three-piece suit to a ferrule for your walking stick.' There was even a shop that sold flat caps, just flat caps – they called it Charlie Smith's Cap Corner. There was a good tailor's called Burras Peake, a household-goods store called Maxwell's and a lovely toy shop where I bought Airfix models as a boy.

If I walk down Station Lane now I can count four beauty and nail-enhancement shops, four hairdressers, two tanning parlours, one called E Z Tan and the other Brown Envy. There are three Chinese takeaways, one called 'Ming House', two Indian curry shops and three pizza places. There's a café called Café Amuesments, with 'amusement' spelled incorrectly, a bargain booze shop and a tattoo parlour called X Treme. The Central Working Men's Club, where Arthur Scargill gave his rousing speech during the last weeks of the miners' strike, has long since closed down and its premises now sell disco and karaoke equipment. We still have two good butchers, a hardware store where you can buy anything from a handful of screws to a dog kennel, and a fishing-tackle shop. There's a very good greengrocer and an excellent newsagent that also sells toys. For many years the newsagent was owned by the Dransfield family. My gran bought her papers there for half a century and had a little tick book that she used to buy our Christmas toys. Not long before she died, she discovered that the shop's owner had sponsored the Tory candidate at an election and was beside herself when she realized that some of her money might have gone to help the Conservatives. When Blair and the New Labourites came to power in 1997 my gran put on her red coat, red skirt and shoes and went to pay for her papers. She took the money out of a red handbag and offered her best red-lipsticked smile.

Now, at the bottom of Station Lane, a Union Jack flies from a flagpole erected on the site of an old chapel. The flag of St George flies from canes and poles fastened to various walls and window frames. My ancestors would not recognize the Featherstone they walked to more than a century ago to find work in the mines.

My great-great-grandfather, John Fletcher, or Staffordshire Jack as he became known, came here from Netherton, near Dudley, searching for work. Almost every family in this town traces its roots back to the Black Country. They spoke a peculiar dialect, which mixed with the local Yorkshire language to form a distinctive accent. It seems to be spoken mainly by those who live above the coal seams that run between

Barnsley and Castleford. It's notable for the use of the glottal pause, as in 'I'm going t'shop', and the two forms of you. As in other languages, there is the familiar and unfamiliar form of address. In Germany, for example, they say '*du*' and '*Sie*'; in Featherstone and round about they still use 'thee' and 'you'. Though these days 'thee', 'tha', 'thy' and 'thine' are seen as old-fashioned and wrong, you still hear them in the school playgrounds.

Jack Fletcher's forefathers had made nails, chains and anchors. They were firmly rooted in what they did and regularly struck whenever things altered. He came to Featherstone as a young man in the 1880s to find work in the big new pits that were opening in Yorkshire. My own grandad could remember him and told me he was a right character. Jack married a local lass and had four children, all born in the 1890s. There was Lillian, Oliver, Edward (my grandad's dad) and Charlotte. I remember Great Aunt Charlotte: she lived on Albert Street off Station Lane and was still there when I was a teenager. Oliver lost his leg in the pit; a man with enormous strength and courage, he remained conscious while they recovered him from the fall of stone and asked that his rescuers bring out his leg with him 'just in case the doctor can fasten it back on'.

Jack spent his life digging coal, betting on horses, fighting and avoiding hire-purchase agents. On rent day he would leave his money and the book on the inside windowsill, then retrieve it after the rent man had knocked on the door and gone. When I was a boy my grandad sat with me on a stool at our back door to tell me all these stories about his grandfather. 'I've heard the rent man many a time say, "That Jack Fletcher is a good man, he's gone to work, but I can see he's left the rent money." What he didn't know was that part of the rent money was spent on ale, even before he'd left the street.'

Once when Jack was coming home covered with black muck from the pit, in the days before pit-head baths, he paused to take off his cap to acknowledge a passing funeral hearse. A door-to-door salesman, who sold pots and pans on the never-never, approached him and, without recognizing him because of the muck, said, 'Who are they burying, mister?'

Quick as a flash, Jack said, 'It's poor old Jack Fletcher.'

And the salesman replied, 'Oooh dear! And he still owes me money!'

My grandad loved to tell that story and I loved to hear it. This was when I was growing up in the 1960s. Girls were running about London in mini-skirts from one psychedelic happening to another, boys were growing their hair long and joining rock bands, but at home old miners like my grandad were spinning bizarre yarns about their ancestors who still pawned suits and pocket watches on a Monday morning, only to retrieve them on Friday so that they could go out to the club.

My grandad's dad, Edward, married a woman called Edna Bull, one of two sisters who sold cotton and buttons in a little shop. She died of peritonitis in her twenties when my grandad and his siblings were babies. The other sister, Ethel, stepped in to help raise them, because Edward only knew how to dig coal and sup ale. My grandad told me that his two mothers were both bonny women. 'Ethel only had one dress. When she wanted to go anywhere she tacked coloured sleeves on to it to make it look different.'

One day she scalded him very badly. As a fifteen-year-old my grandad had come home from the pit and had fallen asleep on the hearth rug. His aunt Ethel reached over to take a pan of water off the fire, tripped over him and the water went all over his back and shoulders. He was left scarred for life. I remember as a little boy watching my grandad wash at a big white pot sink in our kitchen: the scars on his back stood out stark against his muscles. His back was blue and white: white from the scalding, blue flecks from scarring caused by cuts that had healed over coal dust. He worked in a twenty-two-inch seam of coal with a pick, and he cut his back and sides every day.

My grandad was a boxer, a sprinter and a rugby player. He

had biceps like Popeye's. From when I was about twelve I used to arm-wrestle him. He used to pretend I was beating him, then laugh and wrench my arm down. He never let me win.

He told me that in the 1930s some Blackshirts started to come to Featherstone and hold meetings in a little marketplace at the back of the Central Working Men's Club. 'We were cruel to them, really. They were all simple buggers who, if you promised them jam today and tomorrow, would join owt. We used to give them a good hiding whenever we saw them. I've cracked many a Blackshirt with a pick shaft.' My grandad's pick shaft was still in our coal house when I was a lad.

My grandad taught me that I must never vote for anybody who didn't come from a working-class background. Having said that, he also told me that this country would always need coal, that it was Winston Churchill who shot the miners at Featherstone and that Margaret Thatcher would never be prime minister as long as she had a hole in her arse. 'Never tolerate Conservatives, lad!' was another of his maxims. When I told him he had once advised me to be tolerant, he said, 'Yes, lad, but whenever did you hear a song about the Conservative struggle?'

My grandad blamed Winston Churchill for everything that had gone wrong in his life. Somehow it was Churchill's fault that Featherstone Main Colliery shut down in the 1930s. It was his fault that they'd had to drink their tea out of jam-jars. When Featherstone Rovers lost their first Challenge Cup Final to Workington Town in 1952, Churchill was somehow to blame. And the fact that I had to join the queue at George Street Junior Mixed for free school dinners could also be attributed to Churchill.

When I told my grandad that I'd been doing some research at the library and discovered that Churchill hadn't had anything to do with the shooting of coal-miners in Featherstone, he didn't bat an eyelid. He just tapped his pipe on the mantelpiece, told me not to believe everything I read in books, and announced, 'Well, he would have done if he'd been there.'

My home town is full of mythology. It relies on stories to tell its history and superstition to bind it. I love this about it. I feel special when I walk the streets where my ancestors once trod. It feels solid and reliable. My home town has no fear of hard work and comradeship. It likes to celebrate, and put its arm round you when you're feeling down. My home town is proud of its own history and of the men and women who come from it. Just to say the words, 'I'm from Featherstone,' makes me swell with pride. Everything here was hard got.

The aristocratic Scottish adventurer and politician Cunninghame Graham came here on horseback in 1893 to speak after the funerals of the miners who were shot while picketing at the gates of the pit. He wrote a short story called 'A Yorkshire Tragedy', and even more than a hundred years later I recognize in it the Featherstone he describes.

It was an idle day; in every street men stood about and talked in whispers, or squatted on heels as miners do accustomed to a narrow seam. A pall of coal-dust almost obscured the sky, and on the grass and leaves of trees, on slates and window panes and on tops of posts it formed a sort of frost, but black and hideous as of a world decayed . . . the women stayed at home, working or gossiping across low walls and fed their children, of whom they had not quivers but whole arsenals well stocked, on canned milk, tinned meats and biscuits to save cookery – an art in which they were so little skilled that they wasted what would have kept two families in any other land.

A sordid class distinction, scarcely apparent at first sight, but yet intense, kept the sport-loving colliers and their employees separate; but yet bound to each other, as marriage binds man and wife, for the protection of their child's prosperity.

This was the Featherstone that my great-great-grandad Jack Fletcher came to. A town so unsanitary that the infant-mortality rate was the worst in the kingdom. A place where mothers used laudanum and other opiates to quell their children's cries. This is a town that in microcosm tells the history of the British Labour movement. And my own family's story too.

When I first started drinking with my grandad at the Girnhill Lane Working Men's Club, a huge fat man would stand at the corner of the bar and growl every time I went near him. He frightened me. Every time I told my grandad, he went strange on me. If it had been any other man, he would have been straight up on his feet to challenge him to come outside or 'put them up'. With this man he would shake his head, mutter something under his breath or just say, 'Take no gorm of him.'

As time went by I found out that this man frightened most people. He had been a Featherstone Rovers front-row forward in the 1950s and 1960s, and even the Drake Twins, two fearsome rugby-playing brothers from Hull with terrible reputations for hard play, would only play against him if they were both fit. 'We bite him, kick him and punch him,' they once told Terry Clawson, another hard man of the game, 'but we can never best him.'

Later still, I found out that the big fat man had been involved in a terrible accident. At the pit bottom in the Haigh Moor seam one Sunday morning a rush of sludge and water had trapped four men in a little office. They stood for ages up to their necks in the filthy, freezing water, breathing in a space somewhere up near the girders that supported the roof. The big man tried to hold up one of his comrades, but was forced to let him go. The man was later found drowned. After hours of thinking they were about to die, the other three were brought out by a rescue team. One could never face going underground again and took a job on the pit top. The other two, including the man who growled a lot, were scarred for the rest of their lives.

Whenever I saw the big man after that I heeded my grandad's advice and 'took no gorm of him', even when he once threatened to eat me and wash me down with a gallon of beer.

After the pit shut, the local pubs and clubs were full of redundancy money. A mate of mine I'll call Johnny went on more holidays to Spain in four years than he'd had in the rest of his life. Once he even set off on holiday on the same day that he got back from one. He was picked up at Manchester airport only to learn the taxi driver was taking another gang of mates to the airport that evening. Johnny got home, unpacked his case, refilled it with fresh clothes, booked himself on their flight and was back in the taxi just four hours after he'd got home.

Johnny started to drink every day, afternoon and night. He started with twenty-seven thousand pounds, but it didn't last long – people who drink heavily tend to pick up drinking partners, afternoon and night. After a while Johnny started to turn a peculiar shade of yellow. The doctor told him he was ruining his liver. Johnny carried on drinking – he couldn't stop. I'd always associated him before with the smell of wintergreen and liniment, the smell of the rugby-league player; Johnny had been a great rugby player in his youth. Now he smelled of stale booze. Whatever time of day you saw him he'd have a can in his hand. 'I'm all reet,' he'd tell you. 'I'm bloody enjoying myself. I've worked hard all them years, so it's party time now.' Johnny died with a liver twice its natural size before he reached fifty.

Another man, who I'll call Ron, became more and more eccentric after the pit shut. He'd ride up to you on a bike painted pink and green and tell you he'd seen wolves in the pit houses, or that Engelbert Humperdinck had come to him in a dream and sung 'Please Release Me' from behind a wardrobe door in his bedroom. One day at the bottom of Station Lane, Ron started directing the traffic like an Italian policeman, waving his arms and spinning round with a referee's whistle in his mouth. Another time he took me to one side and said, 'I think I've mastered the art of flying, tha knows!' Ron died on the pavement below the balconies of a block of flats after he launched himself into the air.

Dick, another lad who'd worked at the pit and whom I'd played rugby alongside, told me that his lad was a 'smackhead', and that he couldn't do anything with him. It was a shock. He told me you could buy a wrap of heroin in Station Lane as easy as an ice cream. After the redundancies and the financial advisers, the hard-drugs dealers had ridden into town. I heard it said that some of the former coal towns had worse problems with heroin than some inner cities. And now the sons of lads I'd known and grown up with had started on it.

My town has had a lot of the stuffing knocked out of it. Yet somehow it comes off the ropes for more. Nobody in Featherstone digs coal and takes pride in powering the nation – very little coal is dug round here, these days. I always liked to see the photographs in the *Evening Post* of miners waving their helmets next to banners that proclaimed a new record for tonnage mined at a local colliery. Now the old miners will tell you there's more coal mined in the tap rooms of the local boozers. Mining from memory and stories.

Our Tony travels a thirty-mile round trip to a freezing warehouse where, alongside immigrant workers, he puts vegetables into boxes for supermarkets. He takes little pride in his job, but has pride in providing for his family, keeping a nice house and garden. He still follows the Rovers and, like me and everybody else who was born and shaped in Featherstone, he won't hear a bad word said about his community, still wants to tell people that he's 'from Feath'.

A few years ago the Rovers played their big-city rivals from Leeds in the Challenge Cup semi-final. We were beaten easily that day. As I came out of the ground with Heather and our friends to walk back to Leeds railway station, we were behind some lads with the blue-and-amber scarves of Leeds round their necks. A police horse had shit on the roadside and one of these lads stopped and hovered his foot over the pile. 'Oooh!

I nearly stood in some Featherstone,' he announced, and his mates laughed.

Heather saw that I was furious and held my arm. 'Please don't say owt, Ian.'

I loosened my arm from her grip, walked up to the lad who had mocked and tapped his shoulder. 'That's my home town tha's talking about.'

The lad and his mates looked at me. Then one of them said, 'It was a joke about a rugby team, it's not personal.'

There was a bit of a stand-off. I said, 'I don't find it funny and I want you to apologize.'

'Or what?' said one of the Leeds gang.

'Or I'll shove your face straight into that pile of shit and rub it in!'

The lad who had been mocking said, 'All right, I'm sorry, but honestly, some people . . .'

'Good job!' I said.

Heather took my arm again and said, 'Let it be now!' and we walked on to the station.

I'm attached to this place for all sorts of reasons, many of them sentimental and nostalgic. I think about the lovely flowerbeds and fountain in the Purston Park of my childhood, the football I played against the gable ends at the top of our street. They're stored, intangible collections, in the filing cabinets of my head. I dream a lot about my dad's allotment, my granny's Sunday dinner, and the way she could fashion a dinner from a dish clout, as they say round here. Even my Edward reminisces about 'old Granny's shin beef and mashed potato', the loveliest meal, he says, he ever tasted. Most of all I'm attached to this community because of the kindness it showed us in our grief over Billie. The best letters and cards of condolence were pushed through our letterbox by hand without stamps on. These cards said things like, 'We're with you, old cock' and 'If ever you want a shoulder mine are broad enough'. Among all the litter and greasy pizza boxes that blow up Station Lane, there's something, too, that restores me, the great intangible mystery that plays out in towns like mine – call it community spirit, call it the invisible hand of kindness passed on through generations. This town pulls you through because it knows how to pull together.

I have an elderly friend called Geoffrey Lofthouse. He was a rugby player, a coal-miner, an MP and now he's a lord. He was deputy speaker in both Houses of Parliament, the first person to do so. Geoff was brought up in Featherstone's Stewpot Row, one of the most poverty-stricken streets in our town. I sat on his settee one Sunday morning and he told me some stories about his life. He told me how he had come to Stewpot Row as a child in the 1920s. 'My dad was virtually sold into hard labour on the farms when he was a young man. Land-owners would feel the muscles of labourers, hire them and give them a tied cottage to live in.'

His dad collapsed and died while working in the fields when Geoff was a little boy. The landowner evicted his mam from the tied cottage even before the funeral took place. Geoff came to Stewpot Row to live with some relatives, then went to the pit while he was still a boy. He developed an interest in injustice and exploitation through the unions and the Labour Party, and in his later life worked tirelessly as an MP and then as a peer to ensure that miners received compensation for industrial illnesses. When he chose his coat of arms he didn't go with the usual Latin motto. He picked a saying that his comrades in the mines often used: 'Stick and Lift'.

My town embraces; it sticks and lifts. It continues to lift me. My grandad had it right more often than not: 'Never let owt get you down.'

16. Washed-up pebbles

We were unsure about going on holidays. We didn't even go for weekends to York, the Dales and moors for a long time. Lack of confidence, perhaps, or just that we felt secure in our own home in our home town.

The school where Edward goes every Saturday morning for his piano lessons organized a trip for their musicians to northern Italy. Three concerts were set up, one in San Remo, another in Savona and one up in the mountains in a beautiful medieval village with a monastery called Dolceacqua. We were invited, and Edward was asked to play the piano in an ensemble doing 'Brown Eyed Girl' and 'Everlasting Love'. We thought it would be a good opportunity for a break and we'd be with good friends. Eileen and Darryl, who own the music shop and school, have been especially kind to us since Billie died, and they love our Edward.

The first gig was in the village in the mountains. The band played in the square in front of the town hall and it seemed that all the women in the place had baked cakes and pizza. One woman told me she was English but had lived in Italy most of her life, working as a housekeeper. She was currently employed by an English musician who, she said, I might have heard of: 'His name is Jack Bruce.'

'Really!'

'Yes, and he's been at this concert tonight. He said he enjoyed it very much.'

I told Edward on the bus going back to the hotel that a famous musician called Jack Bruce had been to see him play. It was near midnight and he was falling asleep. He said, 'That's good,' and followed it with 'I had nine pieces of pizza off them ladies.'

Edward keeps me sane. Whenever I did anything amusing, or offered a dry observation on something, my gran used to say, 'Hey, lad, tha's a bloody cough drop.' I never knew what she meant by a cough drop, but now I know that Edward is my cough drop.

We walk to piano lessons on Saturdays. One winter morning we came across a dead fox. Someone had run it over, then dragged it on to the grass verge at the side of the road.

Edward said, 'There's a dead fox there, Dad!'

'Yes, I've seen it.'

'What will happen to it now?'

'Well, I should think that its body will rot down into the earth and then its spirit will go to another place.'

'I didn't know they had a heaven for foxes!'

'Well, I'm not sure they do. But its spirit might go on to nature. Into the fields and trees and up into the sky.'

'Will its fur go up?'

'I don't know.'

'Will its teeth go up?'

'I don't know.'

'What about its eyes? Will they go up?'

'I don't know.'

'Will its ears go up?'

'I don't know!' I was becoming exasperated – we were late for his piano lesson and he just stood there asking question after question.

'Will its paws go up?'

'Edward! For crying out loud! I don't know.' I marched off.

Edward stayed where he was by the fox. I carried on walking, but after thirty yards or so I stopped because I was worried about leaving him at the side of a busy road. He stubbornly refused to budge. Every time I looked back at him, he turned his face and pretended he hadn't seen me, like little lads do with their dads when they're angry with them.

I put out my arms and said, 'Come on, son, I'm a silly old father and I'm sorry for snapping at you like that.' He quizzed me with his eyes for a bit, then came trotting up to me. He jumped straight into my arms and I cuddled him close up to my whiskers and rubbed them on his cheek like my grandad did with me. He called it 'chin pie'. 'I'm sorry, son. Sometimes dads get a bit impatient when they get asked a lot of questions.'

'Dad!'

'Yes, son, what?'

'Will its bushy tail go up?'

A world-champion cough drop.

Before the concert in Savona, we had a day off to explore Genoa. I'd heard that the best pesto in the world was served in its restaurants and we weren't disappointed when we found a place with outside tables. Heather and I tucked into a delicious bowlful apiece. The menu was Italian and Edward asked the waiter to translate something that caught his eye. He was told that the dish he was pointing to on the list was a traditional peasant dish eaten after the weekend and made from leftovers. It comprised pieces of beef in a tuna sauce.

'That'll do for me.' He devoured it with relish and insists now on making his own version at home, substituting mayonnaise for the tuna sauce.

After lunch we walked down to the quayside through a higgledy-piggledy maze of narrow, cobbled snickets and ginnels. We passed a lot of tiny sewing shops that seemed to be run by young women in their twenties. They displayed one or two frocks and perhaps a coat. Heather started looking in one that had a small rack with a dozen or so coats. Each had a pebble sewn to the designer's label.

'Does that mean each coat is as unique as a pebble?' I asked the young woman behind a counter made of packing cases.

'Yes. And I have been open for two years and you are the first person to notice that.'

I remembered the story that Geraldine Underwell had told me about Barbara Hepworth. I told it to the girl in the shop and she was thrilled to hear it. 'I like stories.' She told us that she waited for the new season of fashion to start and then bought last year's materials from the people who supply the big fashion houses for a knock-down price. I bought Heather a lovely mauvy-pink coat, and the girl knocked a few euros off in exchange for the Barbara Hepworth pebble story. 'I shall tell the story now to my customers.'

On the quayside at Genoa harbour rows and rows of African men were trying to sell shoddy copies of designer handbags and pirate DVDs. They were on the very edges and margins of Europe with their backs to the sea. They didn't smile. Edward asked what they were doing. I told him they were trying to make a living. Edward said, 'It's obviously not a good living because they all look sad.'

I said to Heather, 'I feel like them.'

'What do you mean?'

'A refugee. Even when I'm at home I feel like I've gone to a country I don't know and I'm standing with my back to the water. I feel as though I don't belong.'

Heather looked at me. 'We're all refugees, aren't we? We're lost and I know exactly what you mean.'

As Edward passed the last man in the line, he whispered, 'He looks like that Congolese man who sells bubble guns at Pontefract market.'

Sometimes on Wednesdays the young man comes with an old ladies' shopping trolley full of plastic guns that blow out big bubbles when you press a trigger. I've never seen anybody buy one, but he stands there for hours blowing bubbles. He has a little pitch near Argos, just up from the Windmill pub – it's always one of the first to open and by eleven o'clock a gathering of likely lads are standing at the front door smoking around a steel ashtray fastened to the wall.

I walked past them one morning and one shouted across, 'As tha seen him up there with his bubbles?' I said I had. 'Illegal immigrant him, tha knows. He wants arresting.'

'How do you know he's illegal?'

'He looks it!'

My temper got the better of me. 'At least he's bloody working! He's not stood outside a pub at eleven o'clock on a morning with a pint and a cig and claiming mobility allowance!'

'Get thi face felt!'

'Why do I want my face feeling?'

'Cos tha's too soft!'

I looked at the line of African men in Genoa. I wondered who they were. Who were their families? How had they come to be there? Had they come on boats, clinging on for dear life? I felt as washed up as a pebble. I thought about Billie for the rest of the afternoon. I thought about the man selling bubble guns in Pontefract market and how, these days, I felt like a refugee in another land. I thought about a bully outside a pub who told me I ought to get my face felt.

We cheered up in the evening. Edward took part in a wonderful open-air concert in Savona's main square. The local brass band led a procession of young English musicians on a march around the town and played with gusto all the way. When the concert was over, we went to the band's rooms in a building just behind the piazza. Photos of the bands from the 1920s onwards looked down from the walls in fading frames. I felt as I'd felt once in the brass band's headquarters in the Working Men's Club and Institute at Grimethorpe: I felt strangely at home. We ate slices of pizza instead of pork pie and peas, and drank sparkling wine instead of Tetley's bitter, but the room smelt the same and the welcome was just as warm.

★

Fifteen years ago I worked at a rough council estate near Mixenden on the edge of Halifax. The estate was one of those built in the 1960s when local authorities were pushing their council housing out to the fringes of their towns. There was a mixture of half-empty tower blocks that looked incongruously over cow fields and semi-detached houses separated by mainly broken wooden fences. Most of the gardens were overgrown or full of old carpets, broken kitchen units and cars on breeze blocks that were being mended. One stood out. It was framed by a freshly painted fence with a gate that clicked shut properly. There were flowers and a little path made from broken flags. The woman who lived in the house was sitting on her doorstep sipping a beaker of tea. I smiled as I walked past and remarked that she kept a lovely garden.

'That's my little haven!' she said. 'This house and all that's in it is my harbour. This garden up to that gate is my haven. And where you're standing is the open sea. Everybody should have a haven and a harbour because you can be tossed about in all sorts of storms once you go beyond your front gate ... especially round here.'

I hold on to that. Like I hold on to the pebble from Heather's unique coat.

17. Send a gleam across the wave

When I walk Billie's dog John in the fields I sing. I sing Dion and the Belmonts' 'A Teenager in Love', I sing Jimmy Reed's 'Bright Lights, Big City' and 'Baby, What You Want Me To Do?'. And I sing an ancient Methodist hymn called 'Let The Lower Lights Be Burning'. It's a hymn I first heard when I worked up on the Moray Firth in a fishing town called Buckie and then I learned it from some old men in a fishermen's choir at Filey. It was written by a man born in Pennsylvania called Philip Bliss. He was the son of a Methodist minister who converted to Presbyterianism when he married his wife, Lucy. Bliss made his living as an itinerant music teacher, travelling from place to place on horseback. He was inspired to write the hymn after he had heard the story of a shipwreck near the harbour at Cleveland. All the lights of the town were turned off and the ship's pilot steered his vessel on to some rocks. The popular Christian reaction at the time was that, though God would send out his guiding light to all, like the beam from a lighthouse, it was up to us, the community, to keep the other lights, the lower ones, burning.

> Brightly beams our Father's mercy from His lighthouse
>   evermore,
> But to us He gives the keeping of His lights along the shore.
> Let the lower lights be burning, send a gleam across the wave,
> Some poor struggling, sinking sailor, you may rescue you may
>   save.

Just after Christmas in 1876, Philip Bliss and his wife Lucy embarked on a train journey on the Pacific Express out of

Buffalo, New York. A blinding snowstorm was blowing. The train made its way to the Ashtabula river crossing in Ohio, but as it trundled over, the trestle bridge collapsed and the engine and every carriage plunged into the icy river in the ravine below. Two-thirds of the passengers were killed, either by drowning, cold or in fires that burned through the carriages when the kerosene lamps overturned. Philip Bliss initially escaped and made it to the riverbank, but when he couldn't find his wife he went back to the wreckage to look for her and they drowned together. The bridge designer fell into a deep depression and committed suicide in the weeks after the disaster. An inquiry blamed poor maintenance and corrosion on wrought- and cast-iron supports and trusses on the bridge, which had been hailed as experimental when it was built.

Bliss left us his beautiful hymn. I sing it most days. Not long ago some contractors were knocking rust off an electricity pylon, before painting it, in a barley field near where I walk the dog. I stood for five minutes to watch them clambering like monkeys high in the sky. I was singing 'Lower Lights' and jumped with surprise when a contractor appeared from behind a hawthorn hedge and told me he knew the hymn I was singing. He was a Welshman and had heard it in chapel as a boy. On the way back up the path I sang one of Billie's favourites 'You Are My Sunshine'.

I tell my hurt feelings to this farmer's track that runs on a ridge of land from Richard Copley's farm down to where the M62 cuts across the last bit of green-belt land in our area. Three magpies wait for me most mornings near to what Billie called 'the yonder tree'. I had once said to her when we were out walking John, 'Shall we have a race to yonder tree?' Ever after, that was what she called it.

To the north and west I can see Leeds, twelve miles away as the crows fly. To the east, about five miles away, the skyline is dominated by the cooling towers at Ferrybridge. There is an old trailer at the bottom of the track. On one side of the trailer it says, 'Believe in Jesus and you will be saved. motorwaysigns.com'. The trailer once stood at the edge of the field facing the traffic on the motorway travelling east to Hull.

Families of partridges, sometimes twelve or fifteen in number, fly low across the fields. I see hares in the springtime, wood-pigeons descend in the summer to eat the shoots of oil-seed rape and the odd fox burrows into the sandstone banks. I watch the seasons changing when I walk Billie's dog.

Billie loved this walk. It was on this walk that she told me she wanted to be a farmer. It was here, too, that I saw her pick up the worm after the rainstorm and drop it gently into the grass so that it could crawl back to be with its family. We picked blackberries to make bramble jelly here. Billie always got the most scratches because she would plunge her arms into the hedgerow to find the biggest berries.

I showed Billie and Edward their first hedge sparrow's nest on this path. The delight on their faces as they looked into the nest when I held them up to see four turquoise eggs stays lodged in my memory.

Edward joins me on my walk down here, but only on Sundays. He's created a little ritual around his Sunday morning. 'Spend-some-time-with-me-dad morning', he calls it. When the farmer brings sheep to the bottom field around Christmas time, we have to be careful with Billie's dog. We also get the chance to leap over a gate that is pulled across. This year I told Edward I thought I might be getting too old to leap over the gate.

'Go on, Dad! You've got to do it. You do it every year.'

I lined myself up, pawed the ground like a bull about to charge and off I went. I cleared the gate by a few inches, caught my knee as I went over and bit my tongue when I landed. I swallowed the blood and hoped Edward wouldn't notice.

'See, Dad! You're not bad for an old 'un!'

On the Monday, when I was on my own, I tried it again.

I slipped on the ice, hit the bar hard and fell flat on my arse. I didn't dare tell him.

I sometimes feel Billie on this path. I talk out loud to her. Odd, fragmented phrases, like 'me lovely daughter, me cup and saucer'. Then I look round to make sure nobody has been listening, like dads do when they're leaping gates they shouldn't be leaping.

Edward is a hero. I worry constantly about the psychological effect Billie's death has had on him. I probably needn't. He seems tougher in spirit than either Heather or me, and handles any conversation about Billie with great dignity and sometimes humour. He remembers the funny things she said and did. He gets embarrassed when I remind him that she once made him sing James Blunt's song 'You're Beautiful' to her when they were playing in his bedroom.

There was one time in particular when I worried about him. He was taking a bath while I did some work on the computer. I wasn't listening for it, but ten or maybe fifteen minutes went by and I heard no sound of moving water or washing. Curiosity got the better of me and I sneaked a peek around the bathroom door. He didn't see me, so I watched him for a few seconds. We have three rubber ducks that sit on a rack that spans the edges of the tub, a large one and two more that are the same size and smaller than the first. Edward whispered something softly to himself as he manipulated the ducks. The big duck carried one of the smaller ducks to the rack and then went back for the smaller duck that was being held under the bath water. He must have felt me watching him because he looked up. He just said, 'What?' I felt as though I shouldn't be there – I *shouldn't* have been there – so I just said, 'Don't forget to wash your hair, will you?' He smiled and said, 'I washed it on Wednesday when I had a shower.'

I don't think I told Heather about the ducks that night. I might have mentioned it some weeks after when we were having one of our Billie talks in bed. Heather always says, 'Let's not get too planned about what happens. Let's just deal with things as we go along.'

I hold on to a beautiful image of Billie playing with new-found friends at the Cambridge Folk Festival. We're all in a big marquee at Coldhams Common campsite. The Northumberland singer Rachel Unthank has agreed to lead a children's instrument-making and singing workshop. Of course, Edward and Billie always want to join in with these things as soon as they see other kids having fun. Rachel Unthank, who in recent times has recorded the most beautiful traditional folk album with her band the Winterset, lines all the kids up for a song called 'Here Comes Sally':

> Here comes Sally,
> Walking down the alley,
> Here comes Sally,
> Just like that.
> Here comes another one,
> Just like the other one,
> Here comes another one,
> Just like that.
>
> I look down the alley and what do I see?
> I see a great big man from Tennessee,
> I betcha five dollars I can beat that man,
> I betcha five dollars I can beat that man.

The kids are lined up in two parallel rows to form an alley and the song begins. The two at the top of the row strut down the middle of the line as each chorus comes round. As the song continues, the strutting becomes more and more eccentric. Now it's Edward and Billie's turn. Edward comes down the line, half shyly pretending to be a strutting elephant, waving one arm in front of him like a trunk. Billie is glorious: she sways her hips like a Hawaiian with a beaming smile that would light up the waves on a stormy night at sea. Later in the day I see Billie lining up some children at the Magic Corner to teach them the song that Rachel Unthank has taught her.

Billie loved teaching on very quickly what she had just learned. She often filled our music room with up to thirty teddies and dolls, sat them down like a classroom and went through her register. 'Anastasia, I hear that you have a cough today. Make sure your mummy gives you a spoonful of Buttercup Syrup when you get home. And, Edwin, please clean your shoes if you get them muddy when you play football ... Now, children, on to today's lesson, which is called Golden Time.'

When Great Aunt Alice was ninety, we took her out for lunch at the Chequers in Ledsham. It's a posh little country pub with log fires, real ale from local breweries and good homemade food. Auntie Alice's ears are completely shot now and she embarrasses us all by saying, 'Hey?' or 'What?' very loudly to everything she can't hear properly. Billie was the only one who didn't lose her patience that day, even when Auntie Alice complained very loudly about the undercooked vegetables in front of the lady who brought our food.

'The chef likes to do the veg *al dente*,' said the lady.

'Hey?'

'I said the chef cooks *al dente*.'

'Well, he wants to learn how to boil his carrots a bit better than that, love. Nine pounds seventy-five for meat pie, a bit of gravy and carrots as hard as a threshold? It doesn't stand looking at.'

We all reddened up. Billie laughed. She thought Auntie Alice was hilarious.

Auntie Alice is ninety-four now. She can barely hear even when you shout. Her memory has faded and she repeats herself constantly. She keeps saying, 'I wish the Lord would take me.'

When I go to see her at Brentwood sheltered housing, she always asks me to tell her about Billie and Edward. I have to remind her that Billie has died. Auntie Alice looks at me and shakes her head. 'How did she die?' I try to tell her, but I know she can't hear me. I started once at the top of my voice, 'It was in a river!'

Auntie Alice said, 'Was it her liver?'

Sometimes she's lucid and remembers, and then she picks up a coaster that Billie made for her to stand her tea mug on. She turns it over and over in her ancient fingers and cries. 'Why didn't the Lord take me instead? I'm sat here all day waiting to go and she was just a little girl.'

I tell her it doesn't work like that.

'Hey?'

'It doesn't work like that!'

But Auntie Alice has closed her eyes now and leaned back in her chair.

I pick up her *Daily Mirror* and read the sports news. After five minutes she opens her eyes and says, 'Have you been working?'

'Yes, I'm writing a new book.'

'Can you write me a blank cheque?' Then she smiles and her false teeth drop down. She takes them out and places them in a beaker by the side of her chair arm. 'I shall never get used to them teeth.' She's been saying that for nearly fifty years.

Auntie Alice is the toughest woman I've known. She has never married, worked in munitions during the war and was blown up by a faulty shell on her first day. For most of the rest of her life she worked in the liquorice factory in Pontefract stamping Pontefract Cakes. Once on her way home from work in the 1960s she was knocked down by a motorbike that didn't stop. She hurt her neck quite badly, but got herself better by lying on the couch for a few days.

'Can you remember my neighbour, Annie White?'

'Yes, I can, Auntie Alice. Is she still living?'

'No, she's dead now.'
'And what about Miss Ponds who lived on the other side?'
'She's dead as well. They're all dead except me.'

18. The sad songs of Sarajevo

When Miki Salkic phoned me from the asylum-seekers detention centre before he was flown back to Bosnia, he said, 'I hope that one day we will be together again, my friend.' I couldn't see that happening, but of course I said, 'I hope so too.'

That was in the autumn of 2006. By the spring of 2008, after a few emails and phone calls, Heather, Edward and I found ourselves sleeping on the departure-lounge seats at Gatwick, waiting for an early-morning flight to Sarajevo. It didn't feel real, especially when I woke up in the middle of the night. I was completely disoriented and couldn't remember where I was. I opened my eyes slightly and saw a woman a few yards away with ballet slippers on, going up and down on points. I heard loud snoring, too, and glanced round to see a massive fat man on a bench nearby with his sandals clutched between his knees. He snored and growled almost in time to the ballet dancer's moves. Edward brought me round. 'That man's been farting all night, Dad!'

Miki was waiting at Sarajevo for us with his cousin Baya, a private detective who had a big four-by-four. We took the road north-east out of Sarajevo towards Tuzla. During the civil war this had been one of the most dangerous roads in the world, and burned-out farmhouses every few hundred yards along it still bore testament to this. Edward had been sick in Sarajevo airport, right in front of the Customs desk. Baya, in very broken English, insisted that he ought to eat some soup. We stopped at a wooden chalet by the roadside, a traditional Bosnian place, and while Baya and Miki lit their Turkish cigarettes from a burning ember in the open fire, Edward tucked into a steaming bowl of veal and pearl-barley soup. He said after that it was the best soup ever and that he didn't feel sick any more. When he got back into the car he slept all the way to Lukavac, Miki's home town. He didn't even wake up when we stopped for slivovitz and cheesecake. Baya tested the homemade slivovitz by rubbing a small amount between the palms of his hands and smelling it.

Miki said, 'Baya is the best maker of slivovitz in the whole of Bosnia.'

Baya shrugged and decided this offering was reasonable, good enough to drink, and we had two glasses apiece. We'd stopped high in the mountains at a kind of fish farm, and Baya chose three types of fish from some stone tanks fed by mountain streams. The translation of fish names was difficult, but I think we had perch, catfish and pike.

'Baya is also the best maker of fish soup in the Balkans and tomorrow you will try it,' Miki announced, and lit another cig from a smouldering stick.

Baya had been acting as a sort of unofficial bodyguard for his cousin since Miki returned to Bosnia. There were people who still resented Miki's pacifist stance during the war and some committed crimes that Miki knows about.

Miki's wife Alma and daughter Tina met us at the front door to their apartment block. Before the war Miki and Alma had had a house by a lake up in the mountains, but now they're left with a small flat in a 1960s Communist-designed block on the edge of town, rather like the kind I saw on the Mixenden estate near Halifax. Alma has a bunch of lovely flowers for Heather, and Tina says, 'Hey up, you three,' in a perfect Yorkshire accent. When Tina arrived in Yorkshire she couldn't speak a word of English, but by the time she was sent back to Bosnia she spoke it like a native of Pontefract.

Edward is delighted to find a telly in the apartment and over-joyed when he flicks through the channels with the remote to discover the Cartoon Network. 'Just think, Dad, all my mates are about to start a geography lesson and here I am watching cartoons in the Bosnian language, sitting on a couch in Lukavac.'

I remind him that we haven't brought him to Bosnia outside of school holidays to watch the telly.

'Man United are playing Roma tonight, Dad. Will they play that in the Bosnian language as well?'

Tina cuddles up to Edward on the sofa and says, 'Yes, they will, or they might do it in German, because a lot of our satellite TV comes from Germany.'

'I'd like to hear about Rooney in German!'

Tina laughs and says, 'Well, little Rooney, you can even buy a copy of his shirt in Tuzla market and it'll be a lot cheaper than it is in the market at Pontefract.'

Edward likes it when Tina calls him Little Rooney and the name sticks for the time we spend there.

Miki, Alma, Heather and I sat on the balcony overlooking the grounds of a Catholic church. Miki offered cigarettes and slivovitz, and showed us an ashtray he had designed. It had curved sides to stop the wind blowing ash all over the place. 'I thought of this design when I was in Pontefract. When I knew that the government would ban smoking in pubs I thought that everybody would smoke outside so I designed this prototype.' Outside the Horse Vaults pub in Pontefract they throw their tab ends into a steel bucket or straight on to the pavement.

We looked across at the church. Miki said, 'All religions are in Lukavac: Orthodox, Catholic, Muslim. I know this Catholic priest, he is a good man, I will ask if we can have a look in the church tomorrow and then I will see the imam and ask for a look in the mosque.'

We talked about friends Miki and Alma had made in Yorkshire and what they were doing now. Miki said he missed his walks round the grounds at Pontefract Castle and Alma said she missed her neighbours on the Willow Park estate. She cried when she remembered the elderly coal-miner who had been her next-door neighbour. He had died not long after they were sent back to Bosnia.

Miki talked about the war. 'All peoples here were friends before the war. Orthodox, Muslin, Catholic, all friends. Everyone was welcome in my café and then the shells started to fall. Do you know the first Serbian shells to fall on Lukavac were fired from the mountains near the lake where I swam as a boy? The first Serbian shells killed a Serbian man and two horses. What is point? Fire shells and kill own people and horses. That is stupidity of civil war.'

Alma pointed. 'Look at these windows. During the shelling I came out to clean these windows. I clean my windows on Tuesday morning, every Tuesday morning. If shells fall on Tuesday morning, I still clean my windows. Windows still need cleaning even in war. I joke with other women in this apartments that shells will not kill us when we clean our windows.'

Miki added his favourite maxim: 'What does not kill you makes you stronger.'

I'd woken up that morning to a ballet dancer in Gatwick airport, now I was listening to a Bosnian housewife talk about window-cleaning during the Balkan war.

'Did I ever tell you why I am called Muhammed? My father was a good Communist, a supporter of Tito. He was a friend to imam but didn't go to mosque. My mother was not really religious either, but was superstitious. They wanted to have children for eight years, but no children came. My mother went to see a fortune-teller and the fortune-teller told her that soon she would become pregnant with a boy child, but only if she promised to call the child Muhammed. And that is why I became Muhammed.'

The next morning we went to visit the Muslim cemetery to see the graves of Miki's parents. It is on the edge of town overlooking the houses, just like the one where Billie is buried in Featherstone. On Billie's stone a carving of a dove flies skyward. Miki's dad's stone has a star and a sickle moon.

'He was a very civilized man who taught me good way to live,' Miki said.

We had lunch in a Robinson Crusoe themed bar by the lake where Miki spent much of his childhood. Hotels, bars and apartments lined the water; they had all sprung up in the few years since the end of the war. Miki told us that many were built by men who had profiteered from the misery of the war.

In the afternoon he showed us buildings in the town that still bore shell holes and shrapnel scars, and the place where he had rescued the little girl whose house was being bombed.

Later in the day we met the imam at the mosque. I think it was the first time he had seen Miki since he had come home. Alma, Tina and Heather covered their heads with an assortment of scarves. Little Rooney was very excited to visit his first mosque and rolled around on the deep carpets. When I told him off, the imam touched my arm, smiled and said, 'Let him.'

I told the imam I was slightly surprised that he was clean-shaven. He laughed and said, 'Muhammad had a long beard and hair. I don't want to. It's what's inside that is important.' He gave Edward a Bosnian Toblerone and told us to be careful with the raki.

Miki wanted to show us the marketplace in Tuzla. We arrived there in the rain and Miki led us to a rough street-corner café where he had arranged to meet a young wedding photographer. We found him drinking plum juice. He had come equipped with a little hand-held video camera. 'This boy will make a souvenir of your visit to Tuzla,' Miki announced.

The young man shrugged his shoulders. 'Shall I just follow you around?'

Miki said, 'Yes, just follow, make a good film.'

Our first stop was at a war memorial. Miki asked Tina to read the words on the stone. She read them out loud while the wedding photographer dodged about with his little video-cam. Tina read first in Serbo-Croat, then translated into English.

HERE WE DON'T LIVE JUST TO LIVE
HERE WE DON'T LIVE JUST TO DIE
HERE WE DIE JUST TO LIVE
MAK DIZDAR

HERE ON 25 MAY 1995 THE SERBIAN FASCIST AGGRESSOR
DROPPED A GRENADE AND KILLED 71 PEOPLE.

SAY A PRAYER AND REMEMBER IN YOUR
MIND THE YOUNG PEOPLE OF TUZLA.

The wedding photographer panned his camera up and down the list of names of those who were killed. We stood under shared umbrellas to pay our respects. Nearby there was a clothes shop called Trendy, a bar selling Tuzlanski Pilsner beer and an old man in a Russian fur hat selling hot cashew nuts. Just like there was on that Saturday morning, 25 May 1995.

In the market we bought Edward a Bosnia–Herzegovina football shirt. He could have had a counterfeit Rooney one, a del Piero one, an Adebayor one, but he wanted a real Bosnian one. We called him 'Roonikovic'. Heather bought Bosnian mint tea from an old granny who sold herbs, and I bought a beret. I didn't take it off for ages. We bought a ring for Tina and a brooch for Alma when we thought they weren't looking and later on, in a lovely Bosnian restaurant overlooking Miki's lake, we gave them their presents.

Bosnian manners are very similar to working-class northern-English manners. These manners involve a lot of wringing of hands, a protestation that says, 'No, no, no, you shouldn't have,' and finally an acceptance of the gift: 'Oh, it's beautiful, thank you, but it's not necessary to give a present.'

Miki said, 'My friend, I am sorry, but I didn't buy you a present. I give you my heart and some raki.'

We ate soup and a huge selection of meats that included chicken, fillet steak and the neck glands of veal, something I'd never eaten before that I thought it good manners to try.

Miki talked about the importance of manners and said that since the war good manners had faded away. 'Before the war, my friend, everybody waited until the other person finished talking before they said something. Now all people try to talk at the same time. This is not good manners, but they do it because they worry that it will be their last chance.'

I couldn't help wondering why Miki had wanted to seek asylum in England when he was obviously proud to be Bosnian. I told him that the food here was fresh and delicious, that I thought the people were kindly and tolerant, and the scenery was beautiful.

'My friend, we need to find better life. Government must change. I saw so many bad things here. Fighting, corruption, cheating. Ordinary people is good, but the people who have power do not show respect. I am Muslim, but I have Jewish friends, Orthodox friends. We need to find the humanity once more. This is the Balkans, and because of war, the Balkans have lost humanity.'

I told him I couldn't imagine what it would be like to have the army and police rounding people up in their own towns because they came from a certain religious or ethnic background. Then I remembered that in Pontefract, one morning at dawn, policemen from West Yorkshire in body armour had knocked down the door of Miki's council house with the kind of hammer used on drug raids. 'How did you feel that morning, Miki?' It was the sort of question that cub reporters ask people whose home has burned down. The sort of question the newspaper people asked me after we lost Billie.

'My dreams of the new life were broken that day. The kettle was filled with water ready to make tea for policeman when he came. Many policemens came and they didn't want to drink tea. Only to take me and my Alma and Tina to detention centre. At Bosnian Embassy in London the official smiled straight at me and said, "You should be happy now, Mr Salkic. Soon you will be going home." I wanted Pontefract to be my home. No one should have right to tell what is your home. My family were coal-miners in Tuzla and Lukavac. I wanted to make my home with coal-miners in Pontefract.'

I could see what Miki meant. I, too, felt more at home with the ordinary people I met in Tuzla than I did with some of the people I met at home in Yorkshire. My home town has more in common with towns in Bosnia than it does with others in Yorkshire.

In the evening Alma's mother, brothers and their children came round to visit. The best china was set out with more cake than anybody could eat. Alma's brother, a coal-miner, told us his son was a ballroom dancer and embarrassed him by requesting that he perform a cha-cha-cha for us. The little lad obliged. He danced beautifully around the small living room, stepping between plates of cake and cups of tea. When he finished we all clapped. Then his dad told him to go off with the older children while the adults talked. It took me back to my gran's front room when I was seven or eight. They would get me to dance around the sofa and then sing a Beatles song. Afterwards relatives and neighbours would press pennies into my hand. Then my grandad would say, 'That's enough now. Tha's a good turn, but tha can be on too long.' My grandad liked his entertainment in small doses, preferring conversation and stories about life. Once, when he was asked if he liked the comedian at the Girnhill Lane Working Men's Club, his reply was 'He's all right if you like laughing.'

I sat with Miki on the balcony and told him about the time I had spent in Belarus making a documentary film about the plight of children in its orphanages. I mentioned that while I was there I had befriended a man called Vadim, who reminded me a lot of Miki. One day Vadim and I had sat drinking vodka and smoking bootleg cigarettes. I asked him if he ever thought of moving out of Belarus and trying for an easier life in England where he had friends. Vadim told me that Belarus was an impoverished country with a poor record in human rights. The nuclear explosion at Chernobyl had devastated the southern half of the country and poisoned the earth, wages even for university graduates like himself were terrible, and the president behaved like an old-style Stalinist dictator.

'Well, just move, then!' I said, full of naïve nonsense.

Vadim drew long on his cigarette and swigged a half-glass of spirit. 'Someone has to stay, Ian. Gandhi said, "If you want to change the world, you have to be the change you talk about."'

On his balcony, Miki sipped his raki and looked out across Lukavac. 'I told you, Ian. Before the war people had the good manners to wait before they started a story. Now everyone has extreme moods. There is madness here. Too much drinking, rushing, exploiting. We should be building roads, running railways, but we can't even wait for the old story to end.'

I knew exactly what he meant. How do you know what happens next, when the story you're currently in hasn't yet finished?

We wanted to see Sarajevo so Miki hired a car from one of his mates. The journey is only sixty miles or so through the mountains, but there are no fast roads in Bosnia and it can take three hours. Edward got car sick on the way and we stopped by the roadside above a town called Olovo, with blocks of apartments that still had shell holes in their sides. Edward and I walked up a grassy bank so that he could be sick away from the road. He bent over and I rubbed his back. Nailed to a tree I saw an enamelled sign with a skull and crossbones on it and a warning that this was a minefield. I panicked and told Edward not to move. Less than two years after we had struggled out of rapids we had come to stand by a roadside minefield in the middle of Bosnia. I looked behind me, all the time holding Edward's arm. Miki, Alma and Heather sat in the hire car talking. I turned back to the skull and crossbones. I wanted to be sick too.

'I think I'm all right now, Dad,' Edward said. 'You can let go of my arm – you're holding me too tight.'

We made our way back to the car. About a mile or so on Edward, who had waited for a lull in the conversation, said, 'Who put that sign up with the skull and crossbones on it?'

Miki looked at me and raised his eyebrows. He told me later that a lot of minefields were still waiting to be cleared.

In Manchester, many months later, I went to a meeting with a charity called MAG; Princess Diana had been involved with it. At their offices they have a glass-fronted cabinet full of different landmines. I winced when the director of the charity, a former sapper called Lou, handed one to me to examine. 'Have a look at this, Ian. We call it the Versace (VS50) because it's Italian. It's designed not to kill but to maim. It will blow off your foot and send muck and stones up into the bleeding stump. The idea is that gangrene will set in and the wounded person will tie up valuable human resources. You deprive your enemy of manpower if you wound rather than kill.' John Greaves, one of the charity's trustees, told me that they had worked in Bosnia alongside Cambodian mine-clearance specialists. The Cambodian liked Bosnia and Kosovo because they found lots of snakes while they were detecting. In the evenings after work they roasted them over open fires.

In Sarajevo we looked at some of the ancient mosques and toured the marketplace. I did my usual thing of trying to sniff out a record shop. I claim that I can be dropped in any town in the world and within ten minutes I'll find a good one. Alma and Heather wanted to drink Turkish coffee and eat chocolate cake, so I seized my opportunity and told them, 'Wait here and I'll be back in a quarter of an hour.'

I wandered through some narrow passages near the edge of the market that were filled with stalls selling rugs, coffee sets and fezes until I found my record shop. It was a tiny cupboard of a place run by a young man who told me he was Bosnia's biggest fan of Joe Strummer. I flicked through the boxes. Most of the stuff was pirated Western rock music, but in one box I found Sarajevo music, the *sevdalinka* stuff. My fingers rested on a CD called *The Mother of Gypsy Soul* by Ljiljana Buttler. It cost me six convertible German marks, the strange emergency currency of Bosnia that you can only spend in markets there.

Before we drove the three hours back to Lukavac, Miki took us to parkland below the mountains that surround the city. 'I want to show you where the river Bosna is born.' We walked through the parkland next to fast-flowing and crystal-clear water. We came to a part where it bubbled up from underneath some boulders. 'This is where she is born,' Miki said. 'Please, walk to the edge and I will take a photograph.'

Edward and I held each other and gingerly walked down some slippy stones until we came to the water. I felt Edward tense, and I did too, which I'm sure he noticed. The river swirled two yards from our feet. We looked at it momentarily, then lifted our heads to look at Miki's camera. Alma and Heather stood watching, arms linked. Heather waited and waved, and as soon as she heard the shutter click, she said, 'Come on now, you two, and go steady – them stones look slippy.'

Edward and I held each other's hands and climbed up from the river.

Miki said, 'My father brought me here when I was a boy to see the river that gives our country its name being born from these mountains.'

I smiled at his colourful broken English.

'This river. She is born new every day.'

On the road through the mountains back to Lukavac I asked Miki to put my Ljiljana Buttler CD on the car's player. It's a beautiful, sad and poignant record. Ljiljana, the mother of Gypsy soul, has an almost baritone voice. She is backed by the

Mostar Sevdah Reunion band and they sing of loss, of grief and of trying to find a way home. By the third song Miki was singing softly and beating time with his fingers on the steering-wheel. There is a song on there called '*Ja k'o ostala deca*'. It is incredibly sad and has on it a clarinet solo that cuts you in two. 'This song, Ian, is about a poor Gypsy child who is lost in the world and tries to find parents to love.' Every time the song finished Miki pressed the skip-back button and it came round again. His singing got louder and louder. Two streams of tears were running out of his eyes and down his cheeks to drip off his chin. He sang:

Ja k'o ostala deca
I'm like any other child,
Anybody who knows me knows my song,
No one knows my destiny, no one knows my pain . . .

He slapped the top of my thigh with his right hand. 'Ian, my friend, you have helped me to sing again. Since the war I never sang properly. Today I sing with my heart. I am happy with my river of tears.'

Later in the evening, after Edward had gone to bed, I sat again on Miki's balcony. He told me he had talked with Alma about going to the river Bosna. 'I hope, my friend, that you could see the beauty in the river and that you were not offended.'

I told him the river was beautiful and that from now I would think of rivers as feminine. And that listening to him sing had been a real highlight of the time we had spent in his homeland.

A few days after we got back from Bosnia, Edward and I went to get our hair cut in a little barbershop on Gillygate in Pontefract. It's run by another Ljiljana, a lovely lady whose husband Dragan works in the cartridge-refill shop. They, too, escaped the civil war in the former Yugoslavia to live in

Pontefract and were friends with Miki, Alma and Tina before they were sent back. Lily asked what I had liked most about the trip to Bosnia. I told her I'd been surprised by the quality of the food, the friendliness of the people, but most of all I'd enjoyed the music I'd listened to in Sarajevo. I told her about driving through the mountains and minefields back to Tuzla and Lukavac to a soundtrack provided by Ljiljana Buttler and the Mostar Sevdah Reunion Band and their record *Mother of Gypsy Soul*. Lily stopped clipping my hair and looked at me in the mirror. 'Dragan's brother helped to produce that record!'

Some of the millions of fragments I often feel I'm in began to piece themselves back together.

19. A procession of images from history

For two years people would stop me in the street to ask when the inquest into Billie's death would take place. I could never give them a date because I didn't have one to give.

In the weeks after Billie drowned I dealt with visits from the Welsh police. I made a statement in our front room that was filmed by Detective Colin Fish and another detective called Ian, who told me he had twin boys. The two men also attempted to interview Edward. It was a harrowing experience for everybody. Edward, just short of his tenth birthday, sat on the settee with Heather's arm round him. The policemen asked if I might go to another room. I went to sit at the kitchen table, but could hear them trying ever so gently to coax out Edward's story. Edward remembered the canoe tipping over and holding on to the branch in the river until I got to him, but couldn't remember much else. According to Heather, he just stared into space. Later, Colin told me he hoped he would never have to do that again. Colin was deeply affected by our case – I believe he became emotionally involved. Whenever he sat at our kitchen table I watched him gaze from time to time at a beautiful picture of Billie on the wall above a radiator. He told me that on a recent holiday to Center Parcs he had forbidden his own children to go on a pedalo.

Edward doesn't talk much about what happened to us. If I try to bring it up when we're out walking, he changes the subject by pretending he's got a stone in his shoe or draws my attention to a bird he can't identify: 'Is that a pied wagtail, Dad?'

Only once has he opened up. Out of the blue one day he said, 'I think I saw Billie when I was under water, Dad.'

I wasn't expecting it – we were trying to coax the dog out of a field where he had been chasing some partridges. 'Oh, right. And was she close to you?'

'She had her eyes shut.'

'Was I there, then?'

'No, we were on our own, together in the water, and then I came up.'

Two thoughts haunt me constantly. One is about how close I might have been to touching Billie when I put my arms under the water to search, and the other is, what were Billie's last thoughts? Was she thinking, Why hasn't my daddy come for me?

In the two years we waited for the inquest to take place, I had set a lot of store by having some of these things explained to me. Did the rescuers who came know things about that day that I didn't? Was Billie still alive when they finally pulled her from the water? The waiting was torture.

Colin Fish visited us from Wales a few times. He told us that although Brecon Police had arrested the two canoe-company owners in connection with Billie's death, the Crown Prosecution Service thought there wasn't enough strong evidence to proceed with a corporate-manslaughter case. After the first year of waiting he kept us up to date with occasional phone calls. He told us that a lot of witness statements needed to be gathered, then that the old coroner had retired and a replacement had to be found. The last time I talked with him Colin told me we had been waiting far too long and perhaps it was time for me to write a firm letter to the coroner's office asking for an explanation. I took his advice and sent my letter. By ten o'clock in the morning of the day after I had sent my letter I had an email response from the coroner's assistant. He said that they agreed the whole thing had taken too long and that they were looking for a date within the next six weeks.

It was finally set for 16–18 June 2008 at Welshpool Old Crown Court.

In the stark black and white of the photocopied letters sent to me by the coroner, Peter Maddox, it all seemed very matter-of-fact: 'In the Powys Coroner's Court (sitting at Welshpool) and in the matter of an inquest touching upon the death of Billie Holiday Clayton.' A note attached said,

I enclose herewith statements of the witnesses to be called to give oral evidence. Copy statements I propose to adduce pursuant to Rule 37 of the Coroners Rules 1984. Provisional timetable for the calling of witnesses. Please note I have not included the post-mortem report although a copy will be available at court for inspection. I am sure that much if not all of the above will bring back very difficult memories. You should not feel obliged to read the documents in advance of Monday, but I am anxious that you should have the information should you need it. Yours sincerely, Peter Maddox, HM Coroner

I had no idea how to prepare for an inquest or what to expect. I said to Heather that we should book into the best room in the finest hotel in town and try to be gentle on ourselves. I didn't even know if Welshpool had a railway station. Jane Hickson telephoned, like an angel again, and said that she would drive us to Welshpool and pick us up when it was over. Ever since the day when she arrived to collect us from the Rest for the Weary Traveller in Hay, she has shown friendship and compassion beyond the call of any duty. She phones every week and just listens. She listens to me missing Billie, listens to my outbursts of anger with the world, listens to me trying not to cry.

I don't remember much about our journey back from Hay, just trying to hold Heather's hand too tight, and one more thing: I wanted a cigarette and a pee. I walked barefoot to a gap in a hedgerow at the side of the road. I peed behind the hedge while standing on some mossy stones. When I got back to the car I looked at everybody's faces and tried to smile. Heather was white and looked so vulnerable, and Edward said, 'You've been a long time.' Jane couldn't look at me for more than seconds without lowering her eyelids. I said, 'That was the softest moss I've ever trodden on.' We all got back into the car without saying anything more. I closed my eyes and thought that it was exactly the sort of thing my barefoot little Billie would have said.

Jane arrived at our house on Sunday lunchtime the day before the inquest. She told us she'd spent the morning with her son William at an under-nines rugby match, then dropped her daughter Ellie off at her mother's house. We ate ham sandwiches and drank tea, and then we set off, without Edward: he was staying at his friend Jason's home. I told Heather and Jane to get into the car while I locked up. I came back inside, went up to Billie's bedroom and took down from the wall her last school photo. I kissed her nose, then put the photo into my briefcase.

By four in the afternoon we were checking in at the Royal Oak Hotel in Welshpool. The young woman behind the reception desk told us she hoped we would enjoy our stay and said the bar was still open if we wanted a drink. Welshpool felt like the solid old market town that it is. Built on marshy land by the river Severn, just four miles inside the Welsh border, it was one of the first towns to be sacked by Owain Glyndŵr when he mounted his rebellion against Henry IV in 1400. It still boasts the biggest sheep market in Europe. Heather and I had a walk round in the early evening drizzle and found the courthouse.

'This is where we'll be in the morning, then,' I said.

Heather said, 'There's a fish shop up there that says it was voted the best in Wales. Shall we have some?'

We sat on a street bench and ate fish and chips out of newspaper with vinegary fingers. After that we held hands like teenage lovers and walked to a pub near the start of a heritage railway line. Some young men were conducting a sweep on the

European Football Championships. One was very pleased because he had drawn Croatia. Strange, the loyalties football fans form when their own nation isn't involved.

Heather wondered what to wear on the first morning of the inquest. She decided on a trouser suit, and then we stretched our legs by an old canal and looked at ourselves in the water from a lock bridge.

Outside the courthouse some press people had already gathered. BBC Wales had a cameraman there, and ITV Yorkshire had sent a news team from *Calendar*, our local news programme. The team were workmates of mine. Chris Kiddey was the reporter. I'd known him for nearly twenty years, ever since we did a funny feature about an arts renaissance in Castleford. He had laughed when I'd suggested that there was nothing to stop Castleford becoming the Montmartre of the north and that people in the future might talk about the 'left bank of the river Aire'.

There was a shower as we approached the courthouse door and Heather and I were obscured beneath a big umbrella. Later the press people asked us if we wouldn't mind walking into the courthouse again without the umbrella because they hadn't been able to see our faces. We went along with the game.

The courtroom was laid out as it had been since Victorian times. The coroner sat behind a large desk on a raised dais. We were shown to seats on his right, while the three lawyers – one called Mr Howells representing Wayne Sheppard, one called Miss Jones speaking for Derek Lloyd Price, the two canoe-company owners, and another woman acting on behalf of an insurance company – sat opposite the coroner. Behind them were witnesses and the press. Wayne Sheppard and Derek Price were opposite Heather and me. I hadn't seen either of them since the day they'd asked us to smile for a photograph as we paddled away under the bridge at Glasbury. I had been wondering all night about looking at them. Heather and I had spent two years telling people, including press and police officers, that we didn't blame them for what had happened, and we knew that they and their families would have suffered for Billie's loss too.

I took out a pen and writing pad and put them on the table in front of me, then asked Heather if she was all right. She didn't say anything: she was looking straight at Wayne Sheppard and Derek Price. I looked across at them too. They sat with their heads bowed, their fingers laced together resting on their thighs.

I lifted my head and surveyed the walls. Paint was peeling where the water had leaked in. A dusty portrait of Queen Victoria hung over us all. For some reason I started to think about the Victorian verses on the blackened sandstone grave-stones at Featherstone cemetery. The ones about God and his chast'ning rod.

The coroner entered and everybody stood up. He sat down and so did we.

'I propose to start by laying out the purpose and scope of this inquest. It is not in the form of a trial. There is no prosecution or defence. Our work over the next three days is to find facts. With some limitations, there has to be a robustness to the process. We are here to find out how Billie Holiday Clayton died and by what means. I will inform you of what witnesses are to be called and when I will call them. My verdict will be returned as either a short-form or a narrative verdict, or a combination of the two.'

I felt terribly nervous. As I had never been to an inquest before, I knew nothing of the procedures. The only inquest I'd ever read about in any detail was the one that took place after the shootings in Featherstone in 1893.

I looked at Heather again. She was still staring at Wayne Sheppard and Derek Price.

The first witness was Marcus Bailie, head of inspection for the Adventures Activities Licensing Authority. He told us in very measured tones that he was answerable to the Health and Safety Executive, which was part funded by central government and part by licensing fees. He said that the principal function of the organization was to inspect certain providers of adventure activities as, under an Act passed in 1995, it was a legal requirement for providers to undergo inspection of their safety-management systems. He added that the law refers to those under eighteen, but not those accompanied by parents, and that canoe-hire companies were exempt from such inspections. All of this was definitively laid out in the licensing regulations.

The coroner suggested that the requirements for licensing seemed quite complex. In response Marcus Bailie said that the licensing scheme only applied to those who offer certain adventure activities and who operate in a commercial manner. The incident in this case involved the use of a hired canoe without instruction and therefore fell outside the remit of the licensing scheme.

The coroner said, 'Let's be clear. The canoe that Mr Clayton hired is exempt from any licensing?'

'If there is no leadership or guiding it is exempt. Where a young person is accompanied by a parent it is also exempt. The only stipulation in this case would be that the equipment hired must be fit for purpose.'

The coroner made some notes, then looked up and said, 'It is entirely probable, then, that there are some businesses operating on the river Wye about which you know entirely nothing?'

Marcus Bailie hesitated to answer, then said, 'Yes,' and added, 'Although there are whistleblowers and competitors who would say something to us.'

In his witness statement to the court, Bailie wrote, 'The British Canoe Union estimate that some 250,000 people descend the Glasbury to Hay section of the river Wye each year, making it one of the busiest, if not the busiest, sections of river in the UK for canoe hire activity. There would however seem to be a need for clearer guidelines for those who provide a canoe service without an instructor or a guide.'

The coroner said he had no further questions, then turned to me. 'Would you like to ask anything, Mr Clayton?' I don't know whether it was through naïvety or simply because I had no knowledge of court procedures, but up to this point I hadn't thought about speaking. I'd assumed I had come to listen. I decided to go for it.

'Yes. Mr Bailie, you mentioned that a quarter of a million people canoe on the stretch of river I went on with my children. How many of them are licensed?'

Bailie hesitated again. 'I don't know.'

'Would you like to have a guess?'

'Perhaps ten per cent are licensed.'

'So that means that two hundred and twenty-five thousand people are on that river without any protection from the Adventures Activities Licensing Authority.'

The coroner made a note, then called the next witness, Howard Jeffs, a safety inspector. He told the court that he had inspected the equipment we had used. He said that all the helmets seemed like new, as did the buoyancy aids. He had tested the paddles and the canoe, and found them to be fit for purpose.

I was invited to ask questions again. I told Jeffs that I was interested to know his opinions on the way canoeing trips were sold to people. I'd thought I was being sold a family pleasure trip down a gentle beginner's river. I asked him, 'Are there any health and safety rules about the wording on advertise-ments and brochures that offer these trips?' He told me that the obligation and responsibility was on the people who take out the canoe. If the equipment was fit for its purpose, then the hire company had no responsibility beyond that.

I was the third witness to be called. I went to the stand with my briefcase. The coroner looked me in the eye and said, 'Mr Clayton, I realize that this will be very difficult for you. Would you now tell the court your version of what happened on that day?'

I told him I would, but first I would like to say a few words about Billie. He smiled now and said, 'Yes, please go ahead, tell us some things about Billie.'

'I don't want people to think that this case is simply one about health and safety, about rules and the implementation of regulations. Our little Billie was a living and breathing human being who had a lot of life to live. Whatever we talk about in these days at this court, I hope we can put Billie at the centre of it.' As I was saying this I reached into my briefcase and took out the school photograph of Billie. 'This is Billie – she's just nine here. She was in Mrs Sherman's class at All Saints School. You can see that she had a lovely smile and those beautiful eyes. She's got her hair fastened up because she seemed to be susceptible to head lice. We had tried everything – tea-tree oil, fine-tooth combs, braids.' I realized I was making it up as I went along, but everybody seemed to be listening so I carried on.

'Heather and me waited for nearly eighteen years before we decided to start a family. At first we never seemed to have enough money. We were a couple of working-class kids coming up in a town where the pits had shut and the job prospects were bleak. We both went away to find work, first in Devon in the hotel trade and then for me on building sites and for Heather in the clothing factories. Heather then decided to take a couple of O levels at night school and went on eventually to university at Leeds and got her degree in Social Policy. I started writing and in the first couple of years barely made enough to pay income tax. We lived in a poky little flat above a shop. We had to walk around one another to turn the television on to another channel. My gran, who was coming towards her eighties, was always on to us about starting a family – "I want to have some great-grandchildren while I'm still fit enough to nurse them," she'd say.

'After Heather graduated and I started making a bit of money from a job I got broadcasting at Yorkshire Television, we decided to try for kids. Heather became pregnant in the autumn of 1995 and on the thirteen-week scan she was told she was having twins. We were overjoyed. I ran to my gran's council flat and had told her the news before I even got both feet over the threshold. She laughed and said, "Bloody hell, old lad, bullseye straight up!"

'Billie and Edward were born on the ninth of May 1996. We didn't sleep for three nights, constantly checking that they were breathing.'

I angled the photograph towards Wayne Sheppard and Derek Price. I wanted them to look at Billie. They continued to hold their heads down.

'Billie grew to be a strong, athletic girl. She had a very caring nature. She hated the images of the Iraq war on the television news and wanted to know who had decided that there must be fighting there. Billie could kick a football as hard as a boy, and throw a javelin. She was a strong swimmer and runner. She played the violin and loved our annual visit to the Cambridge Folk Festival. When we were at Cambridge, Billie liked to visit the various colleges. We have at home a lovely photo of Billie in a yellow summer dress standing in front of the entrance to King's College, another photo of her sitting on the lawn at Jesus College. She once said to me, "Daddy, one day I will come to one of these colleges and be a student." I told her it was quite difficult for working-class girls to do that. She said, "But not for me, Daddy." And I'm sure she would have been right. She was optimistic, full of ideas, funny and given to strange and surreal malapropisms. She once told me that she liked the story of "Snow White and the Seven Wharves", she called treacle "cheekcurl" and when we played cricket she liked to stand behind the wicket and called herself "the innkeeper" in a pair of smelly old gardener's gloves that Peter, our neighbour, once gave her.

'People will tell you that time is the great healer, and that memories are a wonderful thing to hold on to. Time is not healing Heather and me. We feel the hurt now as much as we felt it on that day in April two years ago. We are not getting better. There is nothing that you can do about the missing and we miss her so much.'

I looked across at the two lawyers acting on behalf of Wayne Sheppard and Derek Price. The man, who looked like an ex-public-schoolboy type in pinstripes, had his head bowed. The woman, quite stocky in a tight-fitting two-piece, was wiping her eyes with her handkerchief.

I went on to tell the court about the day in question. How the kids had been excited about canoeing. How we'd been having a lovely time up to the part where we came to the fast water. I paused, lost my thread. Something came into my mind, an image from a writing workshop I had been running about ten years before. I was encouraging a group of budding writers with an exercise: a character comes to a fork in the road. What does she or he do? What happens if they take the left path and what happens on the right one? We had a discussion. Then one of the group, a lad who had a master's degree in creative writing from a university in Wales, said, 'What if he took neither of the ways? What if he just stopped and waited?' He went on to write a story about a man who came to a crossroads and just sat and waited.

I was trying to explain to the court my decision to turn into the part of the river with the fast water. It occurred to me now that I might have tried to stop and not continue the journey. What would have happened if I had done that? It seems ridiculous now to think that this thought only occurred to me while I was standing in the witness box giving evidence about our tragedy. I gathered my thoughts and started to cry when I described trying to turn into the fast water and how when we hit the tree I became disoriented, then frantic in my efforts to rescue Billie and Edward.

★

About four months after the inquest was over I found myself standing in the corridor of a train next to a National Union of Journalists' delegate called Granville. As often happens, the story of Billie's drowning came up. Granville pondered on what it is that brings people to a certain catastrophic point. He told me a story of how in 1964 he was hitch-hiking in Switzerland with a girlfriend. They jumped into a Citroën 2CV with a kindly man who told them he was driving to Paris. They were delighted. They were heading back to England with a few pennies in their pockets and were thrilled to bits by their good fortune in getting one lift all the way from Switzerland to Paris. They talked and laughed and shared food. 'The next thing I knew I was lying in a field. I saw someone kick the driver's legs and heard him say, "*Il est mort.*"' They had crashed into a lorry.

I told him I often wondered why we had had to be at that bend in the river on that day. Granville nodded, and I knew he must have had that kind of thought.

He asked what sustained me in my grief. 'The way my neighbours and community have rallied round. It might be Gail, our Tony's wife, bringing a box of Typhoo tea bags on the day after we got back home because she knew we'd be making lots of tea. Or Featherstone Rovers players having a two-minute silence before the match against Keighley. So many good things restored us in the two years before we came to the inquest.'

I finished my evidence. The coroner thanked me, then asked the lawyers if they had any questions for me. They shook their heads. He said, 'I propose to adjourn for lunch now.' Everybody stood up.

In the corridor outside the courtroom a gaggle of press people surrounded Heather and me. Colin Fish ushered us into a little anteroom to wait until they had gone. One of the journalists asked, 'Can I have a copy of the photograph you held up?' I told her, no, we had already released three or four pictures of Billie and I didn't want to release any more.

We walked from the courthouse the few hundred yards to the lounge at the Royal Oak. Marcus Bailie and Howard Jeffs, the health and safety experts, were standing at the bar drinking coffee. They came over to me, shook my hand and said how sorry they were about what had happened. I said I thought I should have been advised not to go anywhere near the fast water on that bend in the river. They looked uneasy, as though they were still in the witness box rather than the public bar of a hotel. Jeffs said, 'To do the manoeuvre you were trying to do, you would have had to make a much wider arc. A professional canoeist would have been able to do it.'

I was about to say, 'And a beginner?' when Colin Fish came and told me our coffee was waiting on a table outside. I think the answer to the question I didn't get to ask was implied in the first, so I decided not to push it. It was an uncomfortable minute anyhow.

After lunch the coroner introduced a statement from Detective Jonathan Griffiths, who said that he had interviewed Wayne Sheppard at around five o'clock teatime by the side of the river Wye on Wednesday, 12 April 2006. Sheppard had told him that he was the proprietor of Hay-on-Wye Canoes and that this was his first day in business. He had no previous experience in this field of work and no expertise in canoeing. Before lunchtime on that day he had hired out his first canoe to a male and his two children and provided them with three buoyancy aids, two helmets, three paddles, a canoe and a waterproof barrel. He had charged them thirty-five pounds for half a day's hire. He said he had given a safety brief, which was that they should stay away from the side of the river, keep their heads away from overhanging branches and keep to the clear side of any rapids. Colin Fish had told me two years earlier that, when questioned later at the police station, Sheppard had answered, 'No comment,' to any other questions beyond that statement.

A procession of witnesses who owned canoe companies on the Wye were then called. Alfred Wright said he would not have hired a canoe to an adult and two children in the conditions as they were on that day. Jane Hughes, the owner of Wye Valley Canoes, said she had turned away inexperienced canoeists on that day. James Gamon, who hired canoes downstream from a landing point at Hay-on-Wye, told the court that around five o'clock on that day a lady had approached him to say she was waiting for her husband and two children. He said he had phoned Jane Hughes at Wye Valley Canoes to see if the lady's family were her clients. 'She asked if the lady was in earshot and I moved away. She then told me that there had been an accident possibly involving the lady's family.'

Heather had gone to meet us at the landing point in Hay. She told me that she instinctively knew that something had gone wrong. She said that everything seemed so grey and the river looked so much bigger than she had imagined it. A police officer drove over the gravel up to her. He asked a few questions to establish who she was. Heather dropped the shopping that she had brought with her. In one of the bags she had a birthday present she'd bought for Billie. It was a book called *It Was a Dark and Silly Night*. The policeman told Heather that Edward and I were fine and being treated for hypothermia in hospital, but they were concerned about Billie. He drove her to the hospital with her shopping.

The coroner called more witnesses from canoe-hire companies. Carl Durham, a director of Black Mountain Activities, told the court he had been canoeing on the river Wye since he was eight years old and had never encountered a problem. He said he had hired canoes to families with babies as young as eighteen months. Another witness said that you didn't necessarily need any experience to take out a canoe; he'd had a few problems some time before with drunken stag parties, but basically if you looked capable enough and weren't drunk, you could pay to hire a canoe.

It had been a very hard day. Our heads were spinning with the vast amount of information we'd been expected to take in. We went back down the road to the hotel, followed by a growing band of people from the press. Some were staying in the same hotel, as was the coroner, and I think the lawyers were too. At dinner it was like playing musical chairs.

In our room Heather soaked off the day in a bubble bath, then sat wrapped in a towel on the bed to read through the court papers. She looked up. 'Have you been watching Wayne and Derek?'

I told her I'd glanced at them from time to time.

'Do you think it was their fault?'

We'd been through this a thousand times over the years. Every time we came to the conclusion that they were not to blame, though we felt angry that they had allowed us on to the river.

I said, 'I don't feel bitter towards them. I never have. I just think that they didn't really know what they were doing, but they wanted us to have a good adventure.'

'I'm the same,' said Heather. 'And to tell you the truth I feel as though I want to tell them I feel sorry for them.'

Put it down to a weird sense of working-class solidarity, but I agreed. Perhaps it was the alien atmosphere of the coroner's courtroom, with Queen Victoria's portrait looking down on a gathering of lawyers, policemen, members of the press and officials from the world of health and safety. If it had been any other meeting place I think the two that Heather and I would have gravitated towards would have been Wayne and Derek.

Before I put my head down for the night I thought about this complex notion of friendship, solidarity and who you stand by when push comes to shove. I thought about Deadly Davison and how I'd blanked him for twenty-odd years for black-legging in the strike, about Arthur Scargill who had told me that struggles were the real victory, about how I had always felt uncomfortable as a working-class lad whenever I'd rubbed up against officialdom, the police and middle-class mores. I remembered something I'd overheard Rachel van Riel once say to Brian Lewis. Rachel and Brian were the visionaries behind the Yorkshire Art Circus, the community arts organization I worked for that had given me my big leg-up in the world of writing and broadcasting. The subject of class had come up as it often did, and always came down to two questions, which we never seemed to answer. First, are arts organizations middle class by their very nature? Second, when arts companies work alongside working-class communities, who really leads the project? Brian said that class didn't really come into it because friendship and camaraderie cut across all of that. Rachel said she thought that Ian, given the chance to go to a party full of artists and academics or to the pub with his mates, would always go to the pub with his mates. I wasn't hurt by what I'd overheard but I wondered why she thought she knew me. That night in the hotel room I realized she did know me, in many ways better than I knew myself.

Of course, I have friends across a wide spectrum of people, these days. If you work in the arts business for over twenty years you are bound to. But whose birthdays do I know, who are the ones whose sisters and cousins I know, the ones whose secrets I share? I have friends whose doors I knock and wait at when I visit. I have others whose door I feel happy just to push open and walk straight in. That must be a class thing. I thought about Wayne Sheppard and Derek Price sitting in the court with their heads down and fingers laced. I thought about the lawyers representing them. Which ones would I trust to be honest with me? Which ones could I rely on?

I hardly slept that first night in the Royal Oak at Welshpool. All sorts of waking dreams shot through my head. I thought about Billie and how close I might have been to pulling her out of the water. I thought about Edward and had a thought that has often recurred – that instead of pulling Edward up, I found Billie and it is Billie who is alive and Edward who is lost. And then I thought that somehow we'd missed the tree and continued our journey downstream, and the end of the story had changed.

At breakfast Heather told me she wanted to say in court that she forgave Wayne Sheppard and Derek Price for any part they might have played in Billie's drowning. I agreed with her.

Before the court started that morning we went to the little anteroom, guided by one of the court officials. I think they had arranged this so that we wouldn't have to bump into Wayne Sheppard and Derek Price in the corridor or on the stairs. When Colin Fish arrived we told him we were planning to accept any apology they might make that day and also tell them that we didn't blame them. Colin advised us that this might not be the most appropriate time to do so. We had learned over time to listen carefully to him, and had come to respect his opinions, but when he went out of the room Heather said, 'It will make us better people if we can see it from their point of view.'

The first witnesses on the second day were a man and his wife who had been involved in an accident on the river just a week before us. Christopher and his wife Diane had hired a canoe to celebrate Diane's fiftieth birthday. It had tipped over in fast water after they'd hit a tree just a few yards lower down the river than we were. Like us they were inexperienced canoeists, although Christopher caused a few smiles in the courtroom when he remembered having a go in a kayak when he'd been in the Sea Scouts. I looked at him and thought, If ever a man was a Scout, it's you. The male lawyer asked Christopher what had made him come forward as a witness.

Christopher told the court that he had seen the pictures of our accident on the evening news and recognized the stretch of river. As a public-spirited person he had decided to come forward.

The next witness was a firefighter called Richard Wildee. He told us he was a selfemployed timber merchant and retained firefighter who was a trained rescue-boat operator. On Wednesday, 12 April 2006, he had been out with his family on a picnic near the river Wye. It was his day off, but he had taken his pager with him. At about five to four that afternoon it had bleeped and he had jumped on to his bicycle to go to the fire station. I'd read Richard Wildee's witness statement the day before we'd come to Welshpool for the inquest. In it he described how he found Billie.

We travelled into the main body of the river and could see the Police air observer pointing towards the left hand side of the river junction. As we entered the river several Talgarth firefighters who were stood on the bank to our left were shouting and pointing towards a clump of bushes in the river which was surrounded by fast flowing water, they were telling us that they could see a paddle in the water, tangled in the bushes.

As we approached the bushes I could see the paddle and tried reaching for it. My colleague, Firefighter Turner, then reached into the water and pulled something to the surface. I could see he had pulled on a buoyancy aid and a girl's body had come into sight. I noticed the girl's body appeared to be laying on her left hand side facing the flow of the water, feet pointing towards the bank and her head pointing towards the centre of the river. The body was being pushed against the bushes. I assisted Firefighter Turner in lifting the girl's body into the boat.

The girl was wearing light brown cotton trousers, a T-shirt, a red helmet and a buoyancy aid.

I began CPR, the casualty appeared lifeless on removal from the water. Limbs and face were bluey grey even ivory with her pupils fixed and unresponsive. I saw water bubbling from her nose when we turned her on her side to clear her airway. I would say that the girl was aged between twelve and fourteen.

Firefighter Turner began compressions and I started mouth to mouth at a rate of 15 to 2. We continued with CPR whilst en route to the launch site. On arriving back at the launch site the girl's skin appeared to have changed colour, it was now pink and blotchy but her body was still lifeless and limp. I remember I had difficulty raising the chest.

The girl was placed into the air ambulance helicopter and I believe taken to Hereford Hospital. We then removed our boat from the river and travelled back to Hay-on-Wye fire station where we were debriefed by our Assistant Divisional Officer.

Richard Wildee cried as he gave his evidence, his voice choked with emotion. The coroner asked if I had any questions for him. I said I hadn't but would like to thank him. I thanked him for his local knowledge and for working on his day off. I thanked him for finding Billie. I told him I had fought for a long time in that river trying to find my Billie, but that it was he who had found her.

There was a lunch break after Richard left the witness box. We went back to the anteroom and Colin asked Heather and me if we would like to meet the firefighters. We said that we would like to shake their hands and give them our personal thanks. Colin showed Richard Wildee and his colleague in.

We shook hands. I burst out, 'You thought Billie might have been fourteen?'

'Yes,' Richard said quietly.

'She was a grand strong lass.'

Richard and his mate smiled. There was an uncomfortable silence. We looked at one another and smiled again. Colin put his hand on the door knob.

'Can I ask a question, Richard?'

'Of course.'

'I've never known if Billie was alive or dead when she was pulled from the water. Was she dead?'

Richard looked at Colin, at his colleague, then at Heather and finally me. He just nodded. Then he said, 'Can I tell you something?'

Heather said, 'Yes, please.'

'Billie looked very beautiful. She had the most serene look on her face.' He started to choke back tears again.

We walked back to the hotel lounge and I took out my court papers. I found a photocopy of Wayne Sheppard's handwritten statement that he had made to the police a month after Billie drowned. I read it to try to make some sense of what I was preparing to ask him when he entered the witness box after lunch:

I hire canoes. I am not an instructor. I don't claim to be an instructor. I simply hire canoes. Mr Clayton was asked if he had been canoeing before. He said no, but he had been in boats before. I told Mr Clayton to watch out for overhanging branches, dangerous objects in the water, and to stay to the right-hand side of the fork, and follow the flow of the water which would take him to Hay, and to get off on the right just after the bridge. I told Mr Clayton if he wanted to practise in the slack that was fine. He seemed confident, intelligent and an able man. He was the master of his vessel and in charge of it. I am extremely upset at what has happened. And I cannot be held responsible for it. I have no further comment at the moment.

When we came back to the court we walked into the anteroom and accidentally interrupted a briefing from the male lawyer to Derek Price, whose face reddened when he saw us. He looked frightened.

The coroner asked Wayne Sheppard to take the witness stand. He picked up the Bible in his right hand and swore by

Almighty God to tell the truth. He continued to hold the Bible when the coroner asked his first question.

'Is your business still operating?'

'No.'

'Have you been on canoe trips in the past?'

'Yes. I have taken my children and their friends down the river on several occasions, and my dog sat on the back of the canoe and we thought it was a lot of fun.'

'Would you like to tell us how you came to set up your business?'

'I spoke to the relevant licensing authorities before I started up. They told me I needed no licence as long as I didn't instruct. I'm not a canoeing instructor, not an expert.'

He then looked directly at Heather and me. 'I was too frightened to say anything to the police. I didn't see any dangers that day. I promise I wouldn't have let you go out on the water. The boy who did my website printed off the disclaimer ... I didn't know the river was dangerous – I wouldn't have put you on the river.'

The coroner asked him if he thought the oxbow part of the river was potentially difficult to negotiate.

He shook his head but clearly wasn't sure what to say. He glanced across at his lawyer who continued looking down at his papers.

The coroner said, 'I suppose it's difficult to say since this was your first hiring experience.'

Sheppard said, 'I go fishing a lot. We didn't intend to put anyone on in bad weather. I wish I'd never seen them damn canoes.' Then he looked straight at Heather and me again. 'Please believe me. It's been very difficult for me, and my family as well. When I go to the chapel I light a candle for Billie every time.' Then, with a bit of anger in his voice, he turned on some of the witnesses we'd heard the day before. 'It's a free-for-all – they're all trying to get business. It's not true what they were saying yesterday. They said they wouldn't have let you go out with two children, but they would have done. They're only saying it now to protect theirselves.'

The coroner invited me to ask Sheppard some questions. I had been making notes as he spoke so I used these to form my questions.

'You told the court that it was probably in the autumn of 2004 when you last went canoeing. The oxbow part of the river hadn't formed then, so you weren't aware of the possible dangers at that bend. Is that true?'

'I've been fishing on the river since then, so I knew about the oxbow.'

'Did you know how fast the water was running on the bend that day?'

'No, I didn't know it was running so fast.'

'If you had done would you have let us go?'

Sheppard's lawyer stood up and addressed the coroner. He said he thought his client should not answer that question. In his introduction to this part of the inquest the coroner had told me that some questions might not be answered. He turned to Sheppard. 'You do not have to answer that question if you prefer not to.'

Sheppard looked across at me and said, 'I'm sorry, I can't answer that question.'

I tried another: 'Were you surprised when you came to offer help with the rescue at the speed of the water on the bend?'

Sheppard looked at his lawyer again. The lawyer looked at his papers. Sheppard hesitated and then said, 'Yes.'

I carried on: 'I've heard a lot in this court about the criteria by which hire companies judge potential customers. What criteria do you use?'

'It's common sense, really. I tell people to watch out for branches and shallows. I check that the river isn't running too high by looking at the shingle near the bridge at Glasbury and how much of it is visible.'

I wanted to ask more, but I couldn't bring myself to do so.

I could see that he was floundering, and it seemed unfair to keep bombarding him with questions that he was ill-equipped to answer. I knew at this moment that I couldn't blame Wayne Sheppard for what had happened. He was just a working lad who had wanted a piece of the local economy. He wasn't the best-prepared canoe-hire businessman, but this could have happened to anybody. That it had happened to him on his first day of business, with his first ever customers, was just cruel random chance.

His face told a thousand stories. He hunched his shoulders inside a suit that he was obviously uncomfortable in. He rested his hands on the table in front of him. On the knuckles of his right hand I noticed again his tattoo – 'LOVE'.

I thanked him for coming to the court. Colin Fish had told me weeks before the inquest that he didn't have to appear if he didn't want to, didn't have to go into the witness box or answer questions. I'm sure his lawyers would have reminded him of that too, but he did. I think I know why. He wanted to tell me that he wished he could turn the clock back, and that he lit a candle for Billie when he went to the local chapel. Heather and I admire that. Out of all the words we heard at that inquest and all the legal jargon, it's sentiments like that you remember.

Derek Price, Sheppard's business partner, came to the stand. It was to be the first time I would have spoken to him since he had let go of the bow rope that held our canoe near the river-bank. He had a prepared statement read out on his behalf. It mentioned that we were the company's first paying customers, and that Sheppard and he had been offered second-hand equipment but had preferred to buy brand-new, up-to-date, kite-marked stuff. He reiterated that neither he nor Sheppard were qualified canoe instructors and didn't claim to be. His final paragraph read that he deeply regretted the death of Billie and that his deepest and sincere sympathies remained with her family and twin brother Edward. I found myself wondering if he had twins in his family.

The coroner asked Price if he had undertaken any specific risk assessments. He didn't seem to know what to say. I asked him if he had been canoeing on the river recently. He said he had, but when I asked him when exactly, he said he didn't know, then seemed to have a panic attack and blurted out, 'I'm all mixed up.'

Heather indicated that she wanted to say something. The coroner said she could go ahead.

'There's a lot of situations where you can't always account for things that might happen unawares. We can see that you're both sorry for what happened.' After that I decided not to ask any more questions.

The coroner told the court that he now proposed to read out statements from the pilot of the police helicopter and from the two constables who came to help me try to rescue Billie. I was sorry that Geraint Skyrme and John Whiles were not attending court. I had last seen them at Billie's funeral and thanked them for what they had tried to do, but I wanted to say it publicly.

At the end of the second day the coroner said that tomorrow morning he would listen to representations from the lawyers and from me. There was a bizarre few minutes as the coroner and the lawyers ping-ponged a conversation back and forth in a kind of legal formal language that was quite odd.

'Am I to understand that you are staying locally?' the coroner asked one of the lawyers.

'That would be correct. And I am to understand that you, too, are staying locally?'

'That, too, is correct. We should then be able to exchange documents without too much difficulty.'

They were staying in the same hotel. When I got back there, an envelope full of legal papers was waiting at the reception desk. They could have shoved them under my door.

I bought a cup of coffee for Heather and me and we sat at a table outside the hotel front door smoking roll-ups and watching the world go home for its tea. Wayne Sheppard came running full pelt down the footpath, swerved between cars setting off at the traffic lights to cross the road and shouted to a man driving a taxi to stop. In hot pursuit was the cameraman from BBC Wales. He sprinted across the road with his camera on his shoulder and nearly got run over by a white van. Sheppard jumped into the back seat of the taxi and leaned over to tell the driver to drive away. The driver couldn't because the light he had pulled up at was on red. Sheppard pulled the jacket of his dark suit over his head. He looked like a man running the gauntlet of a mill of pickets outside a power station during the miners' strike. The cameraman focused his lens and poked it up to the window of the taxi. The taxi shot off as soon as the lights turned amber. Heather licked the paper on another cig and said, 'Poor bugger, they shouldn't do that.'

I finished my coffee and walked back up the street towards the courthouse. It started to rain heavily and I sheltered inside the Yorkshire Television news van. The reporter Chris Kiddey told me they had tried to interview Price and Sheppard as they came out of the courthouse. He said that Price had shot off like a rocket as soon as he saw the cameras and that Sheppard had put his coat over his head.

Chris's counterpart from BBC Wales came up and said, 'Can I shake your hand?' We moved to the doorway of a little bakery and chewed the fat, trying to make some sense of the day.

I tried to tune the hotel-room telly into the local news, but couldn't get a picture. I wanted to know what the press were saying. The lady at Reception told me that a big tree was in the way of news programmes from BBC Wales, so they got news from the English Midlands.

Later I met Chris Kiddey for a pint in the hotel bar. He told me he thought Sheppard and Price had made themselves look guilty by running away. I told him I felt sorry for them, and Heather said she did as well. We talked about what the coroner's verdict might be. There seemed to be three options open to him. He could say it was an accident, that it was a misadventure or an unlawful killing. I said to Chris, 'You can forget the last one.' He agreed, and thought from his experience of these things that it had misadventure written all over it. I remembered what Peter, our neighbour, had said to me more than two Christmases before. I'd shared a bottle of Bunnahabhain malt whisky with him and he'd said, 'Put out of thi mind anything about bringing anybody to task for what happened to Billie. It was a misadventure and as soon as they have an inquest into it they'll tell thee exactly the same as I'm telling thee.' Featherstone wisdom.

I sat up most of that night. I thought about my home town. About Peter, our neighbour, leaning on the gate to watch Edward and Billie playing. About George, Peter's mate, who had helped to build an extension to our house and about how he had left a ladder, which Billie had climbed almost to the chimney pot when she was just three. I thought about Featherstone Rovers having a two-minute silence for Billie, and the male voice choir singing 'Comrades In Arms' in her honour. Then I thought about the only other inquest and inquiry I knew anything about.

In the summer of 1893 the coal-miners at Ackton Hall colliery were locked out after refusing the owner's demand for a wage cut in the face of reduced coal prices. At first there was almost a holiday atmosphere. Ponies were brought to the surface and ran kicking their heels into the fields. The miners sat about smoking clay pipes on street corners and forecasting that it wouldn't be long before their representatives negotiated a settlement and then it would be back to work before winter set in with some dignity intact.

As the weeks rolled by and no settlement seemed to be forthcoming the miners looked to other strategies to move the process on. At some pits scab labour was prevented from working and at a pit near Barnsley some windows in out-buildings were broken. At Featherstone some blackleg labour had been employed to load coal on to railway wagons bound for Manningham Mill – Lord Masham, who owned the pit at Featherstone, also owned the mill at Manningham near Bradford. The scabs were jeered by a gang of women at first, then set on by some striking miners who stopped them loading and overturned the wagons.

Alfred Holiday, Lord Masham's agent, dashed to Wakefield police station to request police protection and arrived at the same time as Lord St Oswald, another colliery owner who was on the same mission. The chief constable had no spare men and told them he would need a magistrate's permission to request military back-up – at which point Lord St Oswald put on his other hat, reminded the policeman that he was a magistrate as well and demanded that he receive military protection.

As my mate Brian Lewis once said, 'The involvement of a peer of the realm in any aspect of English life can alter the situation dramatically.' Brian likes to retell the anecdote about Bertrand Russell who was once demonstrating in Leeds. The police charged him with a truncheon at the ready. 'Stop!' shouted a bystander. 'He's an eminent philosopher.' The copper took no notice, the bystander tried again: 'Stop! He's the country's greatest mathematician.' The policeman raised his truncheon again. 'Stop! His brother's in the House of Lords!' At that the policeman helped Russell to his feet.

Lord St Oswald's intervention at Wakefield police station ensured that the local coal owners would have protection both in their homes and at their properties. In the middle of the after-noon of 7 September 1893, the soldiers, under a Captain Digby Barker, arrived at Featherstone station. They were carrying the then new Lee–Enfield rifle, a weapon that could kill at a range of two miles. The *Yorkshire Post* later reported on the use of this rifle at Featherstone and said, 'Under very trying circumstances, the incident at Featherstone proved a very good scientific test for the new Lee–Enfield.' Presumably they meant it proved that a Lee–Enfield bullet would enter the front of the body through a hole no bigger than a shilling piece, blow out the flesh and bone and leave a hole the size of a dinner plate in the back.

The soldiers marched from the station to the colliery, followed by a jeering gathering who wanted to know, 'Who has asked for redcoats to come here?' The crowd grew in size over the next hours while Barker and his men sat and waited in an old engine house to ponder what they might do. The local bobby, Sergeant Sparrow, who boasted that while he was in charge Featherstone was the sort of place where you could hang your watch on a farmer's gate and expect it to be there next day, tried to negotiate an agreement between the soldiers and the ever-growing crowd that had gathered at the pit gates. He was worried that the situation might get out of hand if the soldiers did not withdraw.

After assurances from picket leaders and Sparrow that there would be no trouble or destruction of property, Barker decided to march his men back to the railway station. He was met there by a magistrate called Bernard Hartley, who had been disturbed at his dinner in his house at Pontefract. Unlike Featherstone, where the population was almost entirely working class and predominantly coal-miners, Pontefract was an ancient borough and market town where architects, doctors, lawyers, bankers and magistrates lived. Hartley, who not long after the shootings at Featherstone had a pair of terraced streets named after him, ordered that the soldiers return to the colliery. It appears that he wanted to teach the protesters a lesson.

The soldiers lined up just inside the pit gates, fixed bayonets, and faced a now angry gathering of locals, numbering nearly a thousand. My great-great-grandfather, Staffordshire Jack, was probably in that crowd. At nine o'clock Bernard Hartley, with the power invested in him as a magistrate, came forward and, by the light of a lantern held up by his page, read out the Riot Act:

Our sovereign lady the Queen, chargeth and commandeth all persons, being assembled, immediately to disperse themselves, and peaceably depart to their habitations, or to their lawful businesses, upon the pains contained in the act made in the first year of King George the First, for preventing tumults and riotous assemblies. God save the Queen.

The crowd continued jeering and the soldiers opened fire. A man called Joseph Blaydon pulled down his trousers and showed where he had been shot. Another produced a white rag and waved it from the front of the crowd. Later it was found that a man called Gabriel Oakley, walking near All Saints Church at North Featherstone nearly a mile away, had been hit in the neck. By the pit gates James Duggan and James Gibbs lay close to death. Duggan was put on a cart and carried the six miles on bumpy roads to a hospital at Wakefield where he was found to have bled to death from a wound in his knee. James Gibbs was a Sunday-school teacher who had walked across the fields after he had seen 'fire in the heavens'; some pit buildings burning. He'd only just got to the pit gates when a bullet went straight through him and then through his brother's shoulder. Gibbs was carried by comrades to a Dr Thomas's surgery but died just after midnight.

Within a week of the tragedy a mass meeting was called at Barnsley to condemn the deployment of troops. The magistrates acted quickly and brought the troops out again. In Parliament, John Burns made a speech condemning the actions of the government. 'The authorities think less of the community and maintenance of law and order than using soldiers for morally intimidating men whom they, as masters, are fighting.' The press were also accused of giving the impression that 'The death of a collier here and there, amongst a surplus population, was of no great moment in England.' These sentiments echoed down the years to resonate at Orgreave during the big strike of 1984–5.

The inquest into James Duggan's death took place at Wakefield where he had died. Some witnesses who had accompanied him to hospital said that he had been an innocent bystander who had taken no part in any trouble. The doctor's report suggested that the bullet that killed him had entered the back of his leg, and that therefore he might have been trying to run away. The coroner, directing the jury, which was made up of people who hadn't been there, said, 'He was at the Green Lane entrance to the pit where most of the trouble was,' and therefore the verdict should be justifiable homicide. This is the verdict that was returned.

Gibbs's inquest was held at the Railway Hotel in Station Lane, Featherstone, just a few hundred yards from where the shootings occurred. Captain Barker casually informed those present that the new bullets the soldiers used could pierce three to five inches of solid elm. A juror asked, 'Who told you to bring such bullets?' The coroner intervened to stop any answer to the question by joking, 'They don't make bullets for pop guns, you know.' Later the coroner, Mr Arundel, was to state, 'The troopers were in Featherstone at the behest of the government, and the government can do no wrong.' Later still, a little street off Station Lane was named after Arundel. There was a clash between him and the solicitor representing James Gibbs's family. The solicitor, Mr Lodge, suggested that Arundel was only calling witnesses who told one side of the story. Arundel replied, 'There is only one side to the story. We have to ascertain the cause of a man's death, but if you must, I shall hear your witnesses.'

Four Featherstone coal-miners were called. John Flynn said that he had heard booing and jeering from youngsters in the crowd but not much more. Samuel Fox said he hadn't believed the soldiers would fire. Reuben Johnson said he had been there a long time and had seen no stones thrown, and Charles Philpott agreed with this.

The jury, which had been called 'a queer one' by the press,

took two hours to reach a verdict. It was not the one the coroner wanted to hear and he pressed them to return a verdict of justifiable homicide. They refused and issued a statement:

The jury find that James Gibbs was killed by a bullet wound inflicted by soldiers firing into a crowd from Ackton Hall Colliery. James Gibbs was a peaceable man and took no part in any riotous proceedings. The jury regret that such extreme measures were adopted by the authorities.

The coroner declared, 'That is scarcely a sufficient verdict to return,' then continued to press the jury to say a riot had been taking place. The jury refused. The coroner then asked if the jury thought it was a justifiable homicide. The jury foreman replied, 'We are not prepared to say.' At this the coroner decided the verdict would be 'open'.

The verdict caused an outcry in Parliament, and the Home Secretary, H. H. Asquith, who became known among many working people as 'the Featherstone murderer', appointed a parliamentary commission 'to inquire into the circumstances connected with the disturbances at Featherstone'. The three men he chose to sit on the commission were Lord Bowen, Richard Haldane and Sir Albert K. Rollit. Rollit was the Conservative MP for South Islington, Bowen was a principal in the law firm at which Asquith had worked after Oxford, and Haldane had been the best man at his wedding. They took evidence from the police, the military, local business people and magistrates, and from the adjutant general, Sir Redvers Buller. Buller, who had been at the Charge of the Light Brigade, was asked if a revised regulation might be put in place whereby a bugle or drum might be sounded before shots were fired. He replied that this might be too complicated and that the better option was to shoot first, ask questions later.

Much of the evidence of the coal-miners who came forward was disregarded. The feeling of the committee was that it was imprudent of people not to move away in the face of soldiers firing bullets. The families of the men who were killed were begrudgingly awarded compensation of a hundred pounds. Asquith said he would not recognize this award as a precedent, or that the government were in any way responsible for the deaths.

The fallout from what had happened at Featherstone resonated down the years. Keir Hardie came to speak in support of the miners and their families a year after he had been elected to Parliament as the first Labour MP. He showed the community that there could be an alternative politics. The town was a Labour stronghold for almost a century until Tony Blair's policies started folk grumbling. Streets were named after those magistrates and coroners. And in almost perfect symmetry with Margaret Thatcher's speech about 'the enemy within' the Eton Debating Society recorded its own verdict. A boy wrote in the school magazine:

I am entirely on the side of the owners and can find no serious argument in support of the miners. The latter are a very rough set of men and in receipt of wages much too high for their class. The money they receive is for the most part spent on gambling and any increase of it could only lead to mischief. The action of the military was not severe enough, had they shot down 100 or more strikers they would have taught them a very good lesson.

On the final day of the inquest into Billie's death, Peter Maddox, the coroner, invited the lawyers acting on behalf of Wayne Sheppard and Derek Price to make their representations. The coroner suggested that I might struggle to understand a lot of what they were about to say but reminded me that he was there to help if I had any questions about it. I did struggle to understand a lot of the legal language, but that was mainly through boredom rather than lack of understanding. It was like being in a lesson at school and staring out of a window at other people having fun on the playing fields. The public-school tones of Mr Howell, the pinstriped lawyer, grated. He droned on about previous cases in which people had been injured or killed while indulging in adventure activities. The gist of his argument was that if the equipment provided for these activities was sound then the onus was on the person taking part to ensure their own safety. Miss Jones reiterated this: 'There is no duty of care where there is no faulty equipment or assumption of responsibility.' She then suggested that hiring a canoe was much the same as hiring a car: once the vehicle was hired it was not the responsibility of the hirer to inform the customer about dangerous bends on the road; dangerous bends on roads are the same as those on rivers.

When it came to my turn I asked Miss Jones if she really thought that a bend on a road was the same as one on a river. She said, 'Do you want me to answer a question?' The coroner interrupted to remind me that the time for more questions was over, but I might make an observation. I said, 'Right. It is my observation that a bend on a road is constant, but one on a river is changing all the time with the weather and conditions.' I was flailing really, desperate to make a point to show that we were victims of circumstance on the day rather than unaware of our own responsibilities. I wanted to show that I had been sensible, careful and responsible towards myself and my children, and that what had happened to us was not through any fault of mine. I still bore no malice towards Wayne Sheppard and Derek Price, but I was getting more and more agitated with the proceedings and the legal jargon.

When I'd talked to Heather the night before we'd found that we were of the same mind. We accepted that Sheppard and Price were in no way responsible for what had happened to us. We felt for them and knew that they and their families had also suffered terribly. We knew that a collision of circumstances had caused Billie's death: the fact that they were in their first day of business and were perhaps inexperienced in their knowledge of what the river was like at that bend; the fact that I was trying to make a turn into a current without realizing a tree was in the way; that the water was running far faster than anybody had anticipated; that we were in Wales on a canoe because Billie and Edward had wanted some adventure after becoming bored in bookshops. All these things had conspired to kill Billie.

In my head I knew all of this. But my heart and emotions got the better of me and, for the first time in those three days, I became angry. I was angry with the legal process, angry with the formality of it all, angry with the lawyers for no other reason than that they were lawyers, angry because I'd seen TV cameras pursuing Wayne Sheppard down the street with his coat over his face. I was angry with some press people who came into court late. And I was angry because I had lost my little girl, and now my little girl and the story of what had happened to her seemed to be everybody's property. Thoughts of my dad punching my mam came into my mind, followed by a whole surreal parade of images from my history: sitting on a frozen outside lavatory and being frightened by a rat that poked its nose under the door; my grandad threatening to punch my lights out because I'd told my gran to 'piss off' when I was a stupidly drunken teenager; my mother singing beautifully at the back of the ironing board while watching *Opportunity Knocks*; me calling my brother 'Apache' after he had a large plaster put over his eye to correct a lazy eye; listening to men singing in the street on the way home from the working men's club.

I squeezed Heather's arm. She looked unbearably sad, but smiled and patted my leg. The coroner tapped the papers containing his verdict and findings, seven pages in total. He said, 'Throughout this hearing I have been mindful of the fact that we have been dealing with the circumstances leading up to the tragic death of a young child. Billie Clayton was not just a name. She was a real person – a much-loved daughter and sister. I am certain that no one could have been unmoved by the evidence we heard from Billie's father, Ian, on Monday. In what must have been dreadfully difficult circumstances, he spoke with great dignity about his daughter and her love of life and family.'

He went on to summarize the evidence he had heard from the various witnesses. He made plenty of reference to the fact that the licensing system for canoeing was potentially confusing and said he proposed to write to the Adventures Activities Licensing Service and the Health and Safety Executive to suggest a review of practice. He then laid out twelve findings of fact. The last of these said, 'At the point of the river where this incident occurred the river was extremely deep and fast flowing. I heard graphic evidence about this from Mr Clayton and from PCs Whiles and Skyrme. On the basis of the river at Glasbury and what he had been told before commencing his journey, nothing could have prepared Mr Clayton for the speed and ferocity of the water just past the oxbow lake. I do not think Mr Clayton could have done any more to try and save Billie in what must have been terrifying circumstances. The actions of the two police officers showed incredible bravery.' He then applied the law to his findings of fact and returned his narrative verdict. It read:

At approximately 2 p.m. on 12th April 2006 Billie Holiday Clayton in company with her father Ian and twin brother Edward commenced a river journey by canoe along the River Wye from Glasbury to Hay-on-Wye. The canoe in which she was travelling had been hired to her father by a business operating close to the river. The business was not licensed or regulated by the Adventures Activities Licensing Authority or any other body. The fact that the business hired out canoes without instruction meant that it was exempt from any licensing requirement. Billie and her family were not experienced canoeists and had no personal knowledge of the river. They were provided with a short and rudimentary safety briefing, but this did not make specific reference to a section of the river in the vicinity of the oxbow lake that was known by others to be a potential hazard. At this section of the river the water became extremely fast flowing and the canoe in which Billie was travelling collided with a tree and capsized. Billie was thrown into the water where she became submerged and drowned. Billie Holiday Clayton died by reason of misadventure.

Heather and I were shown to the little anteroom. Colin Fish said something about the verdict being what was expected. I'd once asked him two years before to tell me who he and the police in Wales thought were responsible for what happened. It was at a time when I believed that it was all my fault and that I was to blame for what had happened to Billie. He told me that the police believed Wayne Sheppard and Derek Price may have been responsible and that was why they had been arrested. I looked at Colin now and wondered what he really made of the verdict. Colin put his arm round a tearful Heather and told her that she was a remarkable woman. For two years he had shown nothing but kindness and understanding towards us. I thanked him for everything he had done to help us. He asked me if I felt ready to make a statement to the press who were waiting in the street outside the courthouse door. I said I was, took a lungful of air and picked some papers out of my briefcase. I had scribbled some notes the night before and completed them as the coroner was summing up just twenty minutes before.

We walked to the stairs leading down to the door. Halfway down the flight a woman who said she was a journalist from the *Daily Mirror* came alongside me. She told me that her editor had asked her to make an exclusive offer for our story. Colin told her to go away. I said I was about to make a statement and that she should join the rest of the press.

When I saw the size of the crowd waiting I panicked, lost my confidence. I asked one of the ladies from witness protection if there was a back door. She obviously thought I was going to run away, so I told her I needed to have a cigarette before I did anything else. She showed me the way to the back door. We came out into a little side street and I rolled one. The pinstriped lawyer was already on his way to his next job, pulling an overnight case behind him with one hand, briefcase in the other. He came over to where I was standing and said, 'You handled yourself very well in there, Mr Clayton ... Perhaps you would make a good lawyer.'

I muttered something about that not being my line and that playing with words to prove a legal point was not something I was interested in.

He looked at me and my roll-up and said, 'Yes, I think you've realized that sometimes it does come down to semantics.' Then he wished me luck, said goodbye and went off down the street pulling his case. I made my way back to the front door thinking, Have I poured my heart out for three days for it to come down to wordplay?

When I reached the front of the press crowd, a woman with a microphone thrust out asked me if I wouldn't mind standing just in front of her handbag. I put my arm round Heather and told the press I would read my statement and that would be it, no questions. It came out in an angry stream of emotion. I jabbed my finger in the air and almost shouted my words: 'Every parent should teach their children that as a community we ought to look after one another. My children were more sensible by the age of nine than most adults. At the heart of everything we have talked about over the last three days has been our beautiful daughter Billie Holiday Clayton. A little girl with her whole life in front of her, who fell through a hole in the health and safety laws and drowned.'

I said that the canoe-hire business was a shambolic mess, a stupidly unregulated thing, that any Tom, Dick or Harry could take money for hiring out canoes without any regulation. I talked about how in these days of increased awareness of health and safety we ought to be able to balance risk, adventure and safety, have real-time information about potential hazards in rivers.

Jane Hickson, who had come back to Wales to take us home, was standing inside the courthouse door. She said that the coroner was also standing there and listening, and that from time to time as I read my statement he was nodding. After I'd made my statement, Wayne Sheppard and Derek Price came outside with their lawyer. They stood behind her while she read their statement. She said they were both relieved at the verdict.

The day after we got home the postman pushed nearly a dozen envelopes through our letterbox. Most were from news agencies and magazines. The commissioning editor of *best* magazine told me she appreciated that it must be a difficult time for us but wondered if at some point I might feel up to talking to *best*. 'I promise the matter will be sensitively dealt with,' she said, and left me her phone number. A representative of *Bella* magazine said she felt 'compelled' to write and offer her deepest sympathy and if I chose to speak to them they would pay me a generous fee for my time and trouble. The assistant features editor of the *Daily Mirror* sent a young woman from Manchester to hand deliver her letter. I was sitting at the kitchen table with our Tony when she knocked on the door. She handed me her letter and wrote down a mobile-phone number, then said, 'I realize you might not feel up to talking at the moment, but if you do, give me a call.' I read the letter on the doorstep: 'I hope you don't mind me contacting you in this way. I'm sure you have been pestered by countless newspapers and broadcasters and I'd hate to add to this.'

I said to the young reporter, 'Have you come all the way over from Manchester this morning?' She said she had and that someone down the road had told her where I lived. 'Do you want to come in for a cup of tea before you go back?' She looked surprised to be asked and declined.

After she had shut our gate, Tony said to me, 'Why didn't tha just tell her to fuck off?'

'She looked like a nice person.'

'Arseholes, Ian.'

20. Fate is not a mystical thing

The musician Robert Wyatt was the first person to phone us after the inquest. He had watched the television news and seen me angry and Heather hurting on the steps of Welshpool courthouse. I started to tell him what had made me angry. 'Forget that stuff now. You have to look after your lady and your boy.'

Robert had also been one of the first to phone when he had read the *Guardian* the day after Billie died. 'You're going to have to help me with this one, man!' He has a knack of making you think by saying the slightest of things. 'I've lost good mates in John Peel and Ivor Cutler and now little Billie.' I told him it was good to hear his voice – it was always reassuring and gentle. 'Billie drew me the most beautiful robin on her Christmas card last year, it was the best one I ever had.'

I asked him why these things happened – why would this happen to an innocent little girl?

'I don't know if you believe in religion or anything, but perhaps it's fate. And, you know, fate isn't a mystical thing, fate is just what happens.'

Robert has been really kind to us. He sends lovely quirky letters to Heather and CDs to Edward, a James Booker record, another by Lambert, Hendriks & Ross with Count Basie, and Thelonious Monk doing 'Misterioso'.

I met Robert more than ten years ago when I did a little film about his chalet at The Fitties. The Fitties is a beautifully ramshackle holiday place near Cleethorpes. He said he liked to spend time there because he could melt into his surroundings, like getting into a warm bath when the water is at the same temperature as your blood. I've wanted to do that, melt into my community and feel part of who I am, where I'm from. My neighbours have helped me to get somewhere near to that. Others further away have too. A man called David Suff who runs a record company called Fledg'ling sends me his new releases. I have never met David, have spoken to him only once on the phone, but he sends me lovely records of traditional English folk singers like Shirley Collins and Sandy Denny. He had read about Billie and just wanted to show kindness. I love the stuff he sends. They say a nation turns to its folk tradition in times of crisis. I'm listening to lots of old folk songs at the moment; perhaps that's what grieving dads do.

Some things are hard to deal with. After the inquest some people who didn't know the first thing about us put blogs and responses on to the web criticizing my decision to take out my kids on a dangerous river. Others blamed me for not taking responsibility, or even suggested I was entirely responsible for Billie's drowning. That hurt. I don't know why I read that stuff.

It hurts, too, when cold callers ring our house at teatime to ask if anybody has had an accident in our family recently because we could be due compensation. It has never entered our heads to ask for compensation. Sometimes I want to shout that down the phone, but I never do. I just say, 'No, we don't have accidents in our house.'

The coroner never read out the results of Billie's post-mortem at the inquest, but responded to a letter I wrote him by sending me a copy. As soon as I opened the envelope I thought, Do I really want to read this? I remembered what my gran had told Dr Islam when he suggested a post-mortem on my grandad: she didn't want anybody messing about with his body even in death. I forced myself to read the pathologist's report.

The body was that of a white-skinned girl of height 1.39m and weight 43kg. Pubertal changes were just beginning. She had shoulder-length wavy brown hair. There was drying of the lips which were indented with the outline of her front teeth. There were scattered petechial haemorrhages over the eyelids and within the conjunctivae but none were seen in the mouth, to the skin of the face or behind the ears. There were no marks to the front of the neck. There was no froth within the nose and mouth. There was no genital/anal injury/abnormality.

There were marks of medical intervention: an endotracheal tube; pressure marks to the front of the face in keeping with ties holding that tube in place; puncture wounds to the crook of each elbow, to the back of the right hand, to the right collarbone area and the base of the left side of the neck; an intraosseous line in the upper left shin bone and pressure marks to the left side of the chest in keeping with defibrillation/electrode marks.

There were a few trivial grazes and bruises such as can occur when a body is submerged in water and moved by the current against the riverbed and banks. There is some difficulty now in being certain of the cause of death (from the pathology alone) since findings specific to drowning are not present (resuscitation masks the signs of drowning). There is nothing to suggest any natural disease or assault. Samples have been retained for diatom analysis should that be necessary but given the history of having been pulled out of the water after 45 minutes submersion, were that history to be confirmed in statement/evidence my opinion would be that the pathological findings were in keeping with that history and that the cause of death should be regarded as

1a Drowning.

The document was signed by Dr D. S. James.

I don't want these to be the last words about Billie. I want people to know about her grubby fingernails, her beautiful blue pyjamas. That she was scruffy and laughed in baritone. I want to see her polishing her violin and running her duster through the static on the TV screen. To smell her hair when she's had it washed with my ginger shampoo. I want her to listen to bedtime stories and tell me it's not fair when she hears about injustice.

The folk singer and storyteller Bob Pegg gave me a story that he likes to tell. It's an old Scottish folk tale about the queen of the seals. When I think about Billie drowning in that river, lying on that hospital operating-theatre bed or alone in the cold mortuary I bring this story to mind. And in my dreams I dance with my Billie.

There was once a man who killed seals for a living. Every day of the week, except Sunday, he would climb down the steep path to the beach, push out his boat, row out into the middle of the bay and wait for the seals to come to him. With him he took a little silver whistle which he had from his father, who had it from his father before him, and so on, back through the generations. And with the whistle came a tune, which was a seal-calling tune. When he played the tune, the seals would gather round the boat to listen.

One day, when the seal killer was playing the silver whistle, a huge seal broke the surface of the sea, just by the boat. The seal killer put down the flute and picked up his bone-handled knife. He plunged it deep into the back of the seal. The seal was so large and powerful it sank down beneath the waves, taking the knife with it. The seal killer couldn't believe what had happened. The knife had come down to him with the whistle. It was old and knew how to do its job. Without it he couldn't carry on his trade. He rowed back to the shore, climbed up the path and opened the door of his little cottage. He sat down at the kitchen table with his head in his hands and wondered how he could get another knife.

All day the seal killer sat at the table. When evening came a storm arose, thunder and lightning. The seal killer drifted in and out of sleep. Then, some time after midnight, there was a knock at the door. He went to it and opened it. There stood a tall man, a stranger, with a black coat wrapped round him and a wide-brimmed black hat pulled down over his eyes.

'Are you the man who kills seals for a living?'

'Yes, I am. What do you want with me?'

'I've a job for you. You must come with me now.'

There was a flash of lightning and the seal killer saw a big black stallion waiting patiently at the cliff edge. The tall stranger mounted the stallion and pulled the seal killer up behind him and they rode off into the mouth of the night. They rode through the deepest, darkest valleys, through raging torrents, over the highest mountain peaks, through rain and hail and snow, until they came to the edge of another cliff. The stranger dismounted. So did the seal killer. Then the stranger did an odd thing. He wrapped his arms around the seal killer, took a deep breath, put his lips to the seal killer's lips and breathed the air into the seal killer's lungs. Then he threw himself off the cliff with the seal killer still in his arms. The two of them went down like stooping hawks until they hit the surface of the sea, then carried on down to the ocean's bed.

When they reached the sea floor there was a door. They went through it and they were in a hall full of brown-eyed, pale-faced, weeping people. The stranger led the seal killer into a smaller room. There, on a bed, lay a beautiful woman. She was so still and pale that it was impossible to tell whether she was alive or whether she was dead. The seal killer saw that his knife was sticking out of her shoulder. Then the stranger spoke.

'This is our queen – the queen of the Selkie people. Yesterday morning you stabbed her in the back and now you are the only one who can save her. You must pull out the knife and kiss the wound.'

What could the seal killer do but obey? He leaned forward, pulled out the knife and kissed the wound, and the wound closed over as if by magic. The woman opened her eyes and looked into the eyes of the seal killer, but before either of them had time to speak, the stranger said, 'Right, that's it! That's your job over! Come with me.'

He led the seal killer back through the room full of brown-eyed, weeping people till they came to the sea door.

'Now,' said the stranger, 'before I let you go, promise me one thing.'

'What's that?'

'You will never, ever kill another seal.'

'No, I never will kill another seal.'

'Right,' said the stranger. 'Take this and, whatever you do, don't open it until you get home.'

The stranger reached under his cloak and pulled out a bundle. He pressed the bundle into the seal killer's hands, opened the sea door and pushed him out into the darkness. The seal killer rose through the black waters until he thought his lungs would burst. Then his head broke the surface of the sea. It was dawn and he was in the bay below the cliff where his cottage stood. He swam to the shore and dragged himself up the cliff path. He opened the door of the cottage and threw the bundle down onto the kitchen table. The bundle split open and the kitchen was filled with pieces of gold.

The seal killer never did kill another seal. He lived out his life in that little cottage above the bay. He never married and he never had children. But the people who live in that part of the world say that, whenever the moon was full, he went down to the beach and stood at the edge of the sea. Then he took out a silver whistle and played a tune. After a while a great seal pulled itself up out of the sea onto the shingle. Then a strange thing happened. The seal took off its skin and out stepped a beautiful woman. All night long she and the seal killer danced together on the beach. Then when the sun rose, the queen of the Selkies slipped back into her skin and flopped away into the waves.

21. A return to the Cambridge Folk Festival

After Billie died, Edward vowed he would never go to the Cambridge Festival again.

Between 1998, when the twins were two and we saw the blues singer Taj Mahal perform a blistering set, and 2005 when, with Billie on my shoulders, we were hypnotized by the Touareg musicians Tinariwan, we never missed a year. Billie and Edward loved the Cambridge Festival. It became a camping expedition to look forward to, and the kids were never satisfied on the day the tickets went up for sale until they knew we had managed to get some.

In 2006, in the weeks before the festival I asked Edward if he wanted to change his mind. He said, 'No, it wouldn't be the same without Billie.' We didn't go. We did go to Whitby, the kids' other favourite festival, but Edward was subdued for most of the weekend. He didn't want to go to the Black Horse, our favourite singing tap room; in fact, he started to say that he didn't even like the Black Horse. He wouldn't go into shops we knew and liked, and for the first time in years he refused to go into the Shepherd's Purse to smell the various homemade soaps, something Billie and he had done almost as a ritual. He didn't even want to walk down the same streets where he could have placed his feet in last year's footsteps. He wouldn't eat his fish and chips in the Magpie restaurant and was only placated when we ate in another place that we hadn't been to before.

In 2007, as the time to buy Cambridge tickets drew close, some friends suggested that we should all go to Cambridge, that it would be good for us. Jan, one of Edward's favourite surrogate aunties, soft-soaped him one afternoon in the Shoulder of Mutton. 'Edward, I've been thinking I'd like to go to the Cambridge Folk Festival, but I've never been before, so I'd like someone who knows the ropes to go with me.'

Edward looked at me, then to Jan. He looked back at me and said, 'Will you come to the toilet with me, Dad?' We went to the toilet and stood at the trough like mates.

'Jan's asked me if I'll take her to Cambridge.'

'What do you think?'

'Well, I'll take her, but I won't go to the Magic Corner.'

The Magic Corner was the name Edward and Billie gave to the circus-skills area, where they both learned to spin plates on pointed sticks and twirl the diablo.

Nine of us ended up going in two cars. We had a lovely time, but we cried every day because Billie wasn't there. Heather took a lovely photo of her and pinned it to a tree trunk among the ivy. There it sat with all the notes advertising spare tickets and little mandolin-for-sale ads. A weird thing happened as we walked through the main gates. Someone had made a twelve-foot-tall wicker figure. It was playing a violin.

That year the Ukulele Orchestra of Great Britain played. They did mad versions of 'Shaft', 'Smells Like Teen Spirit' and a take on 'Leaning On A Lamp Post' that sounded like the Red Army Choir. Edward came and put his arms round Heather and me while they were playing. 'Billie would love this, wouldn't she?' When he skipped off for an ice cream Heather and I had a good cry.

On the first day he pretended not to look at the Magic Corner and I didn't say anything. By the second morning he nudged me as we were walking past. 'Magic Corner there, Dad.'

I smiled and said, 'I know.'

'Do you think Billie would mind if I went over and spun a few plates round?'

'Not as long as you don't keep dropping them.'

He grinned and pushed me with the heel of his hand. After he had gone I waited for ten minutes, then snuck round to peek at him. He was showing a little girl a bit younger than himself how to spin the diablo. I cried at the back of a tree. Then I remembered the time when Billie, about four years old, stole an orange tie-dyed dress. The first I knew of it was when I saw her sprinting barefoot across the grass with it fast round her shoulders. I stopped her and told her it was naughty to take people's things. Then, when she told me where she had got it, I went and paid the woman who didn't really see the funny side. She said she thought that there were too many feral children about. I gave her a tenner, my best smile and reminded her that it was a festival.

I closed my wet eyes behind that tree and saw Billie sprinting again. When I walked back past the Magic Corner I saw that Edward had been successful in showing the little girl how to carry on with a diablo.

In 2008 we went back to Cambridge on our own for the first time, just me, Heather and Edward. All the way from the entrance to the campsite to where we pitched the tent I looked over my shoulder and wanted to see Billie struggling with her little rucksack. Edward pumped up the camp beds and recited every place where we had camped over a ten-year period. He remembered every one in order.

Down at the festival we sit in our favourite spot near to the Lost Children stand. Joop is here from Amsterdam. He's been coming since the middle of the 1970s when he was a hippie in his twenties. He's nearly sixty now and his beard and hair are silver. Ian, his mate from Bishop Auckland, is here too, sitting on a fold-up stool. They met at the festival in 1974 and meet up again every year to buy each other rounds of festival bitter and watch each other's bags when they go to the lavs. A young photographer comes up to Joop. 'I'm making a photography project about men with interesting beards. Would you mind if I took your picture?'

He takes a close-up, and when he's gone, Joop says, 'I'm sure he asked me that last year'.

Near to us, by the side of the ice-cream van, there's a family of fatties, a mother, father, three young women and a baby. One of the young women, dressed as a purple angel with wings attached to her T-shirt, is breastfeeding the baby. Her sisters are tucking into huge cardboard platefuls of Yorkshire pudding filled with sausages, gravy and instant mash. When they finish their dinners, they try on various items of fancy dress and hats that look like big strawberries. The dad is wearing a green kilt and a tall top hat made to look like a pint of Guinness. He gives out plastic champagne flutes and pours sparkling plonk into them. They sing 'Happy Birthday To You' to one of the fat sisters, then touch their plastic flutes together in the middle. Another family walk past, all dressed in large pink T-shirts with slogans on them. One says, *This is definitely the last time I'm coming,* and on the back, *And I said that last year!* And another says on the front, *There are two types of jazz,* and on the back, *And they're both shit.*

Later, I see this family in the Guinness tent. They're all roaring drunk and singing a badly out-of-tune version of 'Sloop John B'.

In the morning Edward helps to build a wickerwork hare, while Heather joins in with a Buddhist chanting group. Edward records some footage of this on his mobile phone so that he can make fun of his mam later. He rolls his eyes when I give him a lovely blue tie-dyed shirt that I bought for fifty pence from some girls who were having a sale in their back garden. He puts it on under protest, but later in the day he persuades Heather to buy him another shirt that says on it, 'Half man . . . half pasty'. He tells us we have to stop trying to turn him into a flower child.

While I sit watching the world go by, Edward puts his arms

round me and whispers, 'I'm glad we're back here, Dad, but I'm not too keen on all this hippie stuff.'

I jump up, throw him over my shoulder, spin him round and tell him I'm going to chuck him into a muddy puddle. 'I'd rather have a piece of watermelon.' So I buy him one and he tells me, 'It's bloody lovely, this.'

It rains all afternoon and we stay inside an old fishing shelter that we bought when the kids were babies so that we could lay them down to sleep, change them and store our things.

Altan come on stage and announce, 'We brought the rain from Donegal again.'

Ian from Bishop Auckland swigs from his pint and tells me, 'I'm sure it's fuller than it was.'

A little girl is standing at Lost Children next to a policeman who is eating curry from a polystyrene tray. I keep looking at her and wanting her mam and dad to come. The little girl starts to cry and the policeman puts his half-eaten curry into a bin and starts to blow bubbles for her from a tube. She laughs now. After twenty minutes, her dad comes, carrying a pint pot half full of cider. He picks her up, strokes her braided hair, then puts her down again. She shows him a rainstick that one of the staff at Lost Children has given her. The steward writes down the dad's name on a clipboard, and they walk off together – holding hands. The little girl looks over her shoulder and catches my eye. She smiles, then swings her braids like Billie used to do.

When k.d. lang comes on stage two lesbian girls in pink cowboy hats start to dance. They whirl each other round and kiss each other, first on the forehead, then each eye, both cheeks, nose and lips, a ritual they repeat at the end of every song. They knock their hats off every time they do it, then dance some more.

On the Sunday, the last day of the festival, Edward and I get backstage passes to see Richard Hawley. Richard is a late addition to the bill this year because John Hiatt has dropped out. He's nervous because he's not sure how he'll go at a folk festival. He need not be: his good humour and beautiful songs will carry him through. He goes on stage. 'I've been to a lot of festivals where I've seen people out of their heads on drugs, but never to one where everyone is out of it on rugs.' And on it goes. After his set, Richard signs Edward's backstage pass. Then, on the way back to our rain shelter, Edward says, 'Is that really Richard Hawley?' I tell him of course it is. 'He doesn't look like a famous singer, does he?' I ask him what makes him think that. 'Well, he seems like a proper bloke to me!'

I take him on piggyback to Heather. All weekend I have seen Billie in the face of every little girl. Every folk tune reminds me of her, every licked ice cream, every bite of watermelon. Every time Heather stops to look at homemade jewellery on a stall or try on a skirt or top, I see Billie's footsteps in the muddy grass, her mucky fingernails as she's tucking into corn on the cob. I see her smile when Edward drops his juggling balls for the umpteenth time, and hear her giggle when Edward puts his foot down and shouts, 'No! I don't want to join in with the bloody t'ai chi!'

It's dark now, and the rain is falling faster. Heather sits in the fisherman's shelter and clutches her knees. She smiles Billie's smile at us as I drop Edward off my shoulder and plonk him down next to her.

'I wish I could find my hat.'

Heather had bought a beautiful Berber goat-herder's hat in Morocco earlier in the year. She'd promised herself she'd wear it to the Cambridge Folk Festival. On the first day she lost it. I searched between the legs of thousands of people to try to find it for her, but to no avail. I even went to the police bus where the local bobbies drink tea on their break. 'Has anybody here seen a Moroccan Berber goat-herder's hat in blue and beige?' Anywhere else, a statement like that would bring jeers of derision, but not at the Cambridge Folk Festival. They promised to keep an eye out for it.

Everybody is packing up their travel rugs and folding chairs. We do, too, until we're left with a broken umbrella and the fisherman's shelter. I say to Edward, 'I think we ought to leave something behind this year.'

'What?'

'I think we should leave this half-tent.'

'We can't leave that. That's mine and Billie's, and it's been coming to Cambridge as long as us.'

Heather joins in. 'I think your dad's had a good idea. Sometimes it's good to leave a little something behind.'

'But not mine and Billie's tent!'

'Yes, let's leave it. Then there'll be a little bit of a memory of Billie at Cambridge for ever.'

Edward looks at his mam, then at me. He isn't sure. Then he looks at Joop, and Ian from Bishop Auckland. 'We haven't forgotten that tent, we're just leaving it.'

The lads smile. 'We'll see you next year.'

As we trudge through the mud and the rain to the exit gates, we hear Eric Bibb playing the last song of the night, a raucous version of his spiritual 'Don't Let Nobody Drag Your Spirit Down'.

Heather takes the drawing pin out of Billie's photo on the tree trunk. She puts the photo back into her coat pocket.

Billie didn't come to Cambridge this year, but we felt as though she was there with us. I'm sure we'll come again. Those you loved are never lost, and while you remember them you carry them with you.

Twenty years ago I helped to write a book about how people acquire education. It was a community book, featuring lots of different voices from people in and around Barnsley. One day I sat on a bench by a bowling green and talked to a gnarled old miner who had worked at Houghton Main Colliery for more than fifty years. He told me he hadn't read much since leaving school, but had always assimilated well the things he'd picked up along the way. He paused for thought. Then his eyes lit up as he said, 'In standard five at the church school they had quotes up on the wall. My favourite one came from *Hamlet*, Polonius's advice.

> 'To thine ownself be true
> And it must follow, as night follows day,
> Thou canst not then be false to any man.'

The old miner paused again, then stood up and shouted for his dog, but before he left he said, 'And if tha follows that advice, cock, tha won't go far wrong.'

On the day we got back from Hay-on-Wye, the day after Billie drowned, I dropped our bags on to the kitchen floor. Jane put the kettle on. Heather put her arm round Edward and told him he could stop up for a bit if he wanted to. I went upstairs and walked into Billie's bedroom. I held her pillow to my face and smelled it. I noticed a piece of green notepaper on her desk. It was the story she had been writing the night before we went on our holiday. I picked it up and read the nine handwritten lines.

There was a man whose job was to let trains go through the station and when to stop at the station. One day no trains came so he looked through the tunnel and he just saw darkness. He ran quickly through the tunnel and he nearly fainted because he saw his father and his baby brother who had died. His father died twenty years ago when he was fifteen and his baby brother died twenty-six years ago when he was nine years of age. He was in shock, he looked around to see if a train was coming the other way but it wasn't. So he turned back again, but no one was there, they had disappeared. He thought about it all night.

I don't know what happens next in this story.

Acknowledgements

Thanks to Tony Lacey at Penguin, who sat at my kitchen table and helped me to see this book before I started writing it, and to Hazel Orme for copyediting it; to Peter Wilson, Ned Thacker, Tony Lumb, Roy Hampson, Colin Tetley, Jan Hinchcliffe, Christine Johnson, Christine Talbot, Jane Hickson, Ian Daley, Graham Wrench and, above all, to Heather Parkinson and Edward Clayton, who read a first draft and offered constructive comments; and to Pam Oxley who types better than anybody else I know.

Permissions